UNFINISHED

UnFINISHED

A MEMOIR

PRIYANKA CHOPRA JONAS

MICHAEL  JOSEPH

MICHAEL JOSEPH

UK | USA | Canada | Ireland | Australia
India | New Zealand | South Africa

Michael Joseph is part of the Penguin Random House group of companies
whose addresses can be found at global.penguinrandomhouse.com

Penguin
Random House
UK

First published in the United States of America by Ballantine Books, 2021
First published in Great Britain by Michael Joseph, 2021
001

Photo credits are located on page 235

Grateful acknowledgment is made to Songs of Universal, Inc., and SONY/ATV
Music Publishing for permission to reprint lyrics from "I Believe", words and
music by Nick Jonas, Greg Kurstin and Maureen McDonald, copyright © 2019
SONGS OF UNIVERSAL, INC., NICK JONAS PUBLISHING,
EMI APRIL MUSIC INC., KURSTIN MUSIC and MO ZELLA MO
MUSIC. All Rights for NICK JONAS PUBLISHING Administered by
SONGS OF UNIVERSAL, INC. All rights for EMI APRIL MUSIC INC.,
KURSTIN MUSIC and MO ZELLA MO MUSIC Administered by
SONY/ATV MUSIC PUBLISHING LLC, 424 Church Street, Suite 1200,
Nashville, TN 37219. All rights reserved. Used by permission.

Ornament by iStock/alne

Printed and bound in Great Britain by Clays Ltd, Elcograf S.p.A.

The authorized representative in the EEA is Penguin Random House Ireland,
Morrison Chambers, 32 Nassau Street, Dublin D02 YH68

A CIP catalogue record for this book is available from the British Library

HARDBACK ISBN: 978–0–241–51284–5
OPEN MARKET PAPERBACK ISBN: 978–0–241–51143–5

www.greenpenguin.co.uk

Dear Papa,

Much like the title of this book, your story was unfinished.

With that in mind, I dedicate the rest of mine to you.

I miss you, Dad.

CONTENTS

PREFACE

I'M SITTING IN a meditative pose. In Sanskrit it's called *Sukhasana,* or "Happy Pose." Spine straight, shins crossed, shoulders pulled back, and chest pulled upward, I'm taking slow, focused breaths to bring all my attention to my center. The slow breathing calms my mind so that I can now tackle life's challenges.

Kidding.

I am, in reality, likely sitting on the set of my latest film project, or on a plane, or slumped in a hair and makeup chair. My breathing is erratic from the four espresso shots I've inhaled in the past half hour while simultaneously wolfing down some form of comfort food that's probably not the healthiest of options. (Doritos, any-one?) My overbooked schedule glares at me with seventeen emails that are marked *Urgent! Requires Immediate Attention!* And my phone is buzzing like a bumblebee on ecstasy. I am running on IST (In-dian Stretchable Time)—I'm late—and I am in no frame of mind to make sense of my day, let alone my life.

How is this possible when I come from mystical India, the land of yoga, meditation, the Bhagavad Gita, and one of the most learned civilizations of the world? Why am I unable to invoke the infinite wisdom of my ancestors to calm my raging mind when so many people around the world have embraced the teachings of my great country and managed to incorporate its lessons of peace, love, and happiness quite effectively into their lives?

Well, I am a product of traditional India and its ancient wisdom, and modern India and its urban bustle. My upbringing was always an amalgamation of the two Indias, and, just as much, of East and West. My mom was a fan of Elvis and the Doors; my dad listened to Mohammed Rafi and Lata Mangeshkar. My mom loves London, theater, art, and nightlife; my dad loved taking road trips through our subcontinent and sampling the street food at every opportunity. I lived in small towns in northern India for much of my childhood, and I also lived in the United States for three years in my teens.

Traditional and modern. East and West. There wasn't necessarily a plan to raise me as a blend of those influences, but here I am, someone who calls both Mumbai and Los Angeles home, who works comfortably in India, America, and plenty of countries in between, and whose style and passion reflect that global mindset. The cultural mash-up invigorates me, is important to me, because I believe we can all learn from one another. That we all *need* to learn from one another.

Cue my husband, Nick. As I embark on this new chapter of life with him, it seems like a good time to take stock. It's probably the first time as an adult that I've felt the desire to look back and reflect on how I've gotten to this moment. The first time since my life took a huge, crazy turn more than twenty years ago and I became a public person. Part of this desire to be introspective comes with maturity, no doubt. And I think it's safe to say that part of it came along with Nick, a mature, introspective individual if ever there was one.

Looking back, I remember how I felt as my seventeen-year-old self, a small-town girl who exploded into India's awareness back in January of 2000 when I was crowned Miss India World. I had no idea what to do with this unexpected widespread attention or how to prepare for what was next—representing my country on the global stage in the Miss World pageant. My family had no idea, either, because we weren't a "pageant" family or an "entertainment" family. Far from it; my parents were both doctors. With their love, support, and encouragement, I decided that I would do my best to learn from each new situation I found myself in, to throw myself into it wholeheartedly and work as hard as I knew how. Sink or swim. And if there was a choice, I was always going to do my damnedest to swim. Admittedly, sometimes my strategy has been flawed or I've haven't learned fast enough, but whatever my failures, they haven't been for lack of effort.

I have always felt that life is a solitary journey, that we are each on a train, riding through our hours, our days, our years. We get on alone, we leave alone, and the decisions we make as we travel on the train are our responsibility alone. Along the way, different people—the family we are born to and the family we choose, the friends we meet, those we come to love and who come to love us—get on and off the cars of our train. We are travelers, always moving, always in flux, and so are our fellow passengers. Our time riding together is fleeting, but it's everything—because the time together is what brings us love, joy, connection.

Which is why I'm so grateful to be right here, right now, reflecting with you on my unfinished journey. I hope that whatever I have learned along the way, from fellow passengers, from my efforts and my own mistakes, can contribute to your journey, too. Because as I have discovered, if you're willing to be a student of life, the possibilities are endless.

Priyanka

UNFINISHED

1

MONACO BISCUITS AND LADAKHI TEA

Oh, look at the moon,
She is shining up there;
Oh! Mother, she looks
Like a lamp in the air. . . .
ELIZA LEE FOLLEN

A S A CHILD, I never dreamed I'd be in the movies. Or be a
beauty queen. Or a fashion meme. I never dreamed I'd be in
any sort of limelight. When I was little, no one ever looked at me
and predicted, "She's going to be famous, that one." (Well, my
completely nonobjective father might have said that.) No, the journey toward my life in the public eye began in 1999 when I was
seventeen and my ten-year-old brother had a brainstorm.

"Mom," he said, walking into our parents' spacious bedroom
one cool evening while I was in my room studying. "Is *Didi* seventeen?" He used the affectionate term for "older sister" as he always
did.

"Yes," our mother replied.

"Is she taller than five foot seven?"

"Well, she's five foot seven."

"Is she pretty?"

"Sure." I imagine my mother smiling as she wondered what Siddharth was getting at.

"Why don't you send this in for her?" Sid held out a copy of *Femina* magazine, opened to a page with a call for submissions to the Miss India competition.

Mom didn't immediately agree to the plan, but Sid insisted. As fate would have it, I'd just had professional photographs taken for a scholarship program I'd wanted to apply for—my first professional photos ever—and he handed them to her. Then when my mother pointed out that a full-length photo was also required, he found one of me all dressed up at a recent birthday party and cut the other people out of it. To quiet her persistent son and with no expectation that anything would come of it, Mom finally filled out the application and they sent it and the photographs off the next day without telling Dad—and without bothering to mention anything to me. And that was how my public journey, and my career, began.

Thanks, Sid.

Sid now says that he pushed Mom to send in the application because when I'd moved back home about a year earlier after living with relatives and going to school in the U.S., he'd gotten kicked out of his room. There were only two bedrooms upstairs, and since he was a ten-year-old boy and I was a seventeen-year-old girl, Dad decided the second bedroom should be mine. Naturally, I didn't argue. Mom made my brother a new "bedroom" in the upstairs hallway between my parents' room and mine. (Or *his,* as he would call it.) She put a bed there, and a little wardrobe closet, and a table. Then she tried to spin the move as a good thing for him, but he didn't fall for it.

"This is a hallway, it's not a room!" he pointed out, loudly.

And this, apparently, was why he'd told Mom to enter me into the Miss India pageant. He wanted his room back, and it was a way to get me out of the house. Perfectly logical, my brother, Siddharth.

Eventually, he got his room back.

PRIOR TO MY brother's pageantry subterfuge, I was planning on studying to become an aeronautical engineer. Medicine, academics, and military service were in our family's DNA, and excelling academically was expected. Both of my parents were doctors in the Indian Army. My mother's father was also a doctor, and her mother was a nursing student. My father was from a Punjabi Hindu family in Ambala, a city in northwestern India. His father, Kasturi Lal Chopra, was a *subedar* in the army—a junior commissioned officer— who fought in Burma, the Congo, and with the U.N. forces. My grandfather, or Pitaji, as we called him, was married to Champa Kali Chopra, and after leaving the service he started his own business providing supplies to the military. My father's older brother, Vijay, joined the army at seventeen, and his two younger brothers, Pawan and Pradeep, skipped the military and joined their father in the family business of providing supplies to it. My father's sisters, Saroj and Kamini, both younger, are women of uncommon graciousness and warmth.

My father chose a path slightly different from that of his father and brothers. He attended army medical school and upon graduation served, and practiced, in the military for twenty-seven years, eventually retiring as Lieutenant Colonel Ashok Chopra, MBBS, MS. (In India, a doctor specializing in surgery is awarded the MS degree—Master in Surgery—rather than the MD.)

While Dad was a dedicated army doctor, his actual life's dream was to be a musician. Given that music and entertainment weren't considered real career choices at that time, at least not in his very traditional middle-class family, he followed a more conventional course. Still, he remained a deeply creative person for all of his days. A singer with a magical voice, he was gregarious and loud, always laughing. If there was a crowd at a party, he was in the middle of it. If there was a show at the army club, he had no doubt been the one to organize, produce, host, and star in it.

My mother was more of an introvert. Born in Madras, now known as Chennai, and raised in the part of the eastern state of Bihar that is now called Jharkhand, she was also from a middle-class background. Her mother, my grandmother Madhu Jyotsna, was Christian (she was baptized Mary John) before she met and married my grandfather Manhar Krishna Akhouri, who was a Hindu. Her marriage outside her religion meant that she was shunned from the church she'd been raised in, and sadly, she remained an outsider even in death, when her final request to be buried with her family in the cemetery at her home church was denied. Both of my mother's parents were also involved in local governance: my grandmother was the first female in her division to become a member of the Legislative Assembly in Bihar, and my grandfather was a trade union leader and served as a member of congress in Bihar.

On any given night of my childhood, the doors and windows of whatever home we were living in at the time would be open, the curtains swaying in the early-evening breeze and the smell of rose and jasmine floating in from the garden. There would be music, candles, and possibly a cocktail hour outdoors, after which we would eat together as a family. Throughout my childhood, my parents loved to entertain, and I adored watching them get ready to welcome guests on party nights. They knew how much I loved to be a part of any festivity, so they always made sure to include me. My mother even made me my own special hors d'oeuvres: Monaco biscuits—delicious salted crackers—topped with a small cube of cheese and a dab of ketchup or hot sauce. Bite-sized bits of heaven.

My mother was a combination of intellect and allure. As she would get ready to meet guests I would study her carefully applying her makeup, creams, and perfumes and then getting dressed for the evening. Her wardrobe was all color—chiffon saris in floral prints and solid hot pinks, bright oranges, deep reds, golden yellows. Her long, dark hair hung to her waist, and she usually wore it down in a braid or in a bun at the nape of her neck. I loved watching her put on her makeup—*kajal* to line her eyes, lipstick, and always a red *bindi* in the center of her forehead. I longed to be like her someday: elegant, eloquent, impeccably dressed, impossibly glamorous. She exuded quiet confidence and total competence—which, together with her natural sense of style, made her magnetic. Whether she was dressed in a French chiffon sari for work or in a pair of white bell-bottoms and big sunglasses on vacation, she was the epitome of beauty in my eyes.

Perhaps this is why as a child I loved playing with her makeup. She used to have to lock her dressing room to keep me out, but on those fantastic occasions when she forgot to, I was ready and waiting to pounce. Multiple times I was caught with my fingers inside her lipstick tubes, the red and pink contents smeared all over my face, kohl on my eyes, one of her beautiful saris wrapped around me. How mad she would get! But perhaps what I remember most was her perfume: Dior's Poison. How she smelled of it, how her closet smelled of it, how whenever she walked she left a scent trail, invisible but unforgettable, in her wake.

On party nights, my father would dim the lights and put Kenny G on the stereo system—a double Akai cassette deck with big amplifiers, which my mother still has. Soon our house would be full of officers and their poshly dressed wives, eating, drinking, talking, laughing, singing. I would be dressed to the nines, too, sitting on everyone's lap with my orange juice and my special crackers until I fell asleep and was carried up to bed. Another perfect night.

MY PARENTS MET in early 1981 in Bareilly, a small town in the northern state of Uttar Pradesh, where my father, Major Dr. Ashok Chopra, was a general surgeon in the army, and my mother, Dr. Madhu Akhouri, was treating patients in Clara Swain Hospital. (This after leaving Jharkhand in order not to practice in the shadow of her physician father; the desire to be one's own person runs deep in my family.) When my father first saw my mother at a party, gorgeous in a sari with her long hair down her back, he knew he had to figure out a way to see her again and ask her out on a proper date.

The next evening, he showed up unannounced at the hostel where my mother was living with her mother, who was acting as a chaperone for her unmarried daughter. The three chatted a bit, and my father returned the following evening, again unannounced. It turned out that Mom was working a night shift.

What to do? My determined father paid a visit to Clara Swain Hospital and asked to see her—because what better way to engage the beautiful doctor than with an important medical puzzle to solve?

"I have a terrible stomachache. Very severe," he said gravely.

She ruled out several possibilities, then gave him an intravenous painkiller. A few hours later he said he was greatly improved and he left, promising to visit the army hospital for further imaging.

Dad continued his speedy and miraculous recovery, and the next day he asked Mom if she would go on a date with him. Her mother refused to grant permission, so Dad tried again, this time taking along a married friend, who said she and her husband were having a small house party and my mother would be well looked after. My grandmother finally agreed.

At the party, during their third dance, Dad asked Mom if she would marry him.

Dumbfounded, she said she wasn't ready to marry anyone yet.

"What will make you ready?" he asked.

"Some bell will ring somewhere that you're the guy for me," she said. For the next two dances he kept asking, "Did you hear the bells? Did you hear the bells?"

A couple of dates later, after they'd discussed the things they wanted in a marriage and the things they couldn't tolerate, she realized that he was the one for her.

Mom told Dad he'd now have to get her father's permission. After that was secured, Dad's father met Mom's father, and, in typical Indian-family fashion, the deal was done. What would become an amazing thirty-two-year marriage of equal partners began without the accepted traditions of an arranged marriage and a long engagement, as they married ten days later.

Clearly, Nick and I were slow starters.

Only after my mother and father were married did Dad admit to Mom that he'd never had a stomachache in the first place. And only after they were married did Mom admit that when she examined him, she couldn't help but notice his killer abs.

DURING A STRETCH of time in her teenage years, my mom, the oldest of five, was the only child kept at home while the rest of her siblings were sent away to live with aunts and uncles. This was during the 1970s, a volatile period of political unrest in Bihar, so it just seemed safer to my grandparents—both of whom were involved in state politics—to send the younger children away. It's quite normal in our family and in India in general to do this; children often live with extended family for periods of time because of work, educational opportunities, or for other reasons. Many of my cousins have lived with me and my parents for long durations, just as I did when I stayed with my grandparents when I was small, and then again with my aunts and uncles so that I could go to high school in the United States. I know this may seem strange to some, but it's simply a cultural thing. In India, taking care of one another's children as if they are our own is just part of who we are. It's seen as a duty and a responsibility, not an imposition. India is not alone in this practice and mindset, by the way; dedication to the family network can be seen in many other countries around the world, too.

During that period when her siblings were gone and her house was quiet, my mother was free to focus on her studies. Her parents treated her like a young adult instead of like a child—something she would follow in her own parenting style—and she was able to develop into the fiercely independent person she was meant to be. She drove to school in an open Jeep, a seventies flower child with her favorite music playing.

My mother has always been my role model and my inspiration: I think of how she came from a small town but left the expected path of practicing medicine there to forge her own way elsewhere, eventually earning multiple medical degrees, becoming a certified pilot, and speaking nine languages. She's the one who taught me that I could be anything and everything I want to be; she's the one who made overachieving seem cool. She is the woman I've always aspired to be.

WHEN MY PARENTS married, my mother joined the army, so now there were two army doctors in the family. By the time my mother was pregnant with me, they had been posted to Bareilly, although I was born in Jamshedpur, in Jharkhand. That's where my grandparents lived and my mother had traveled there to be with them at the time of my birth. Portions of my early childhood were spent living with my maternal grandparents while my parents were doing their postgraduate work in Pune and establishing themselves in their medical careers; my mother's younger sister Kiran also helped care for me. Back in Jharkhand, my grandparents showed me pictures of my parents every morning and then I would sit with my grandfather in his rocking chair while he drank his tea and I practiced my ABCs. Each day, he would point to the tree in the yard, an ashoka tree with a beehive in it, and because my father's name was Ashok and my mother's name means honey, my grandfather would tell me that my dad was carrying my mom in his arms right outside, and that they were always there with me. I saw my parents almost every weekend and during school and summer vacations. I was always surrounded by family, always loved.

Like most little girls, I was totally in love with my dad. My earliest memories of him are of how he always entered the room with a burst of energy and laughter—and also of how long his legs were (he was six foot one). I wanted to be like him so badly that I would trail behind him in our house, pretending that whatever he was doing, I was doing, too. I would try on his uniform with his pants puddled at my ankles and my feet inside his giant shoes. I would spend hours watching him iron his uniform and polish the brass on the shoulders. (Once I started school, where I wore a uniform, too, this would become our own private ritual; we ironed our uniforms together nightly and shined our shoes until they were glossy.) Studying him as he shaved before work mesmerized me. He'd dip the shaving brush into a plastic mug full of water, then put it on his dark, angular face, and the white shaving cream against his dark skin always struck me as a beautiful color block. I loved the smell of his Old Spice, which he wore for years. One time, after he left the bathroom to get dressed, I decided to try the whole shaving ritual myself. It didn't end well. I had to get eight stitches on my chin and I still have the scar to prove it.

There were other scars and other trips to the hospital after that: like when I got bit on the butt by my dog; when I swallowed beads; contracted typhoid; suffered bronchial asthma attacks. I was actually something of a sickly child and required an inhaler to help with my breathing problems, which could be triggered by pollen, dust, allergies, and sometimes just physical exertion. Still use one. There was also the time my father had to be rushed to the hospital and ultimately undergo surgery because I'd put a beetle in his ear while he was sleeping. I'm embarrassed and horrified to admit that I did this because I wanted him to wake up and pay attention to me. (*Note to self: There are limits to what you should do to get someone's attention.*)

Other childhood ploys for attention had less dire consequences. When I was quite young, before I went to sleep each night I would ask my father, *So ke uth ke, kahaan jaayenge?* which translates as "After sleeping and waking up, where will we go?" I wanted him to make a plan with me of *exactly* what we would do together when he came home from work the next day. And he did; there was an actual rule involving a promise that I would be paid attention to when he returned. When I knew it was getting time for his arrival, I'd plant myself at the window, gazing through the iron bars that were attached on the outside, and wait for the sound of his motorbike—that loud, tinny *pop pop pop pop pop* of the Jawa engine. As soon as I heard it I'd race outside, and when he arrived, I'd sit on the front of the bike and he'd take me for a ride around the neighborhood. Bliss! Once I had my time with him—even now the thought of being with him, my twin in so many ways, makes me smile—he'd head inside to see Mom so they could catch up on the events of the day.

As a child, I viewed my parents' relationship as fairy-tale perfect. They had their problems, of course, like every couple does, but they had one rule: they never fought or had a disagreement in front of the kids. I actually never saw them argue, much less yell at each other, not once, though clearly they had occasional disagreements behind closed doors. Tension would come in the form of things being quieter than usual, like the time my mom came out of her room, headed silently for the kitchen, and dropped a pan on the floor. (Mom almost never cooked, so the fact that she was in the kitchen and picking up a pan at all was already a dead giveaway that something wasn't quite right.) Or there would be no flirting, which otherwise happened all the time. Often at home and especially at parties, Dad would put on the charm—he would sing to Mom, recite poetry for her, completely and utterly embarrass her. He was creative and romantic and thoughtful, and I dreamed of having a relationship just like theirs, one of true partnership, and of romance, poetry, and music. Who could have known that all that childhood imprinting would actually manifest in reality, just like those self-help books say it will?

One of the most astounding things about my parents' marriage is that it was equal in all regards—from the way they made their home as newlyweds, picking everything out together, to the way they had mutual respect for each other's careers, to the way they worked together to do what they determined was best for our family, to the goals they shared in providing medical care and supplies to those who couldn't afford them. Both of them were also ambitious and they respected that in each other, which taught me that it was fine to have large goals and to work hard to achieve them, and that marriage or even parenthood doesn't mean you have to stop dreaming big for yourself.

I looked up to my parents as if they were superheroes, not only because they were my parents and I loved them but because I always felt that being a doctor was sacred work. Imagine a human hand delving into the miracle of the brain with a scalpel, or holding a fragile new life. That responsibility takes my breath away. I have tremendous respect for the medical profession but I don't personally have the lion's heart required for it.

During my dad's posting in Leh, in the northernmost state of Ladakh in a dangerous combat zone, a soldier was once brought in for emergency treatment with a bullet in his head. He was just barely alive. As he was prepped for surgery—in a tent, with temporary stretchers in a makeshift operating room—he was conscious enough to understand there was only a slim chance that he would survive the procedure, much less ever make it home. He said to my father, "Just tell my family that I was martyred for my country. That I did my job." My dad said, "You'll tell them yourself." And he did. Two decades later, after my father died, the soldier came to his *chautha*—the ceremony marking the fourth day after a funeral—to pay his respects. He had kept the bullet that Dad had removed all those years earlier.

My mom did extraordinary things in her practice, too. She would see patients at the clinic, come home to have dinner with us, then go back at night for rounds—all the while stylishly dressed. She'd sometimes work thirty consecutive hours between her night rounds and the unexpected labor and deliveries that were part and parcel of her medical life. I'll never forget the night that she went to the hospital in a driving rainstorm to deliver a baby. It was normal for her and Dad to get called away at night, but this time, when she came home sometime after midnight, there was an unusual amount of activity and excitement. My grandmother, who had come to live with us when Sid was born, was up and speaking in a low voice to my mother, who seemed to be racing around the house.

Groggy with sleep, I got up to see what was going on and found Mom in the kitchen cradling a newborn in her arms. She told me that after the delivery, when she'd returned to her car parked on the road outside the hospital, she'd heard the sound of a baby crying. To her complete shock, while the rain was coming down in torrents someone had abandoned a newborn girl under the vehicle.

That night, I desperately wanted for us to keep the baby, this impossibly tiny thing swaddled in my brother's clothes. Gently, my mother explained that we couldn't. Instead, she said, she knew of a couple, patients of hers who wanted a baby very badly but were unable to get pregnant. She allowed me to accompany her as she delivered the newborn to them—a different kind of delivery for her, but just as dramatic. There was plenty of legal paperwork that would have to be completed, but I was unaware of that at the time, focused as I was on holding the baby snug in my arms as we drove through the stormy night to the home of that waiting couple. I will never forget the looks on their faces, how the woman fell to her knees in gratitude, how they both cried at the miracle of a baby showing up out of the blue, in the driving rain, during the festival of Janmashtami, the birth of Lord Krishna, who was also born on a windy and stormy night and who was also carried through a flooding rain to reach safety.

That night, I couldn't grasp why anyone would ever abandon a newborn baby under a car. In the days that followed, it was explained to me that girls were not as highly valued by some people in our country as boys were, thus making them "easier" to abandon. This was, naturally, deeply strange and upsetting to me. I knew I was treasured, and I could see that my mother and father were equal partners in their marriage. How could it be that someone would abandon a baby under a car just because she was a *girl*?

My paternal grandmother, or Mataji, as we called her, used to tell me that when I was born and people were telephoning to congratulate her, the group of friends who were sitting with her would say, after listening to the callers' good wishes, *"But it's just a girl.*

Maybe next time." And while that story perfectly and sadly illustrates how the cultural message of devaluing females is so deeply rooted in some people's minds, thankfully, that was not how I was raised. And now that the destructive message that girls are not equal in value to boys is being called out with greater urgency and condemned around the world, maybe things will change.

MY PARENTS' CAREERS as army doctors meant that our family moved all over India. We were stationed in Pune, Lucknow (twice), Delhi, Leh (my father only), and Bareilly, though I missed some of those postings because I was living with relatives or away at school. We also traveled a ton, because my parents believed in travel as the ultimate education—a way to literally broaden your horizons in order to have an understanding of the world beyond your own front door. Travel wasn't just Mom's thing or Dad's thing. It was *our* thing. And when we traveled together, just as in our home together, they were completely inclusive of me. They never treated me as merely a child—they treated me always as a person.

My parents usually got two months of annual leave, and from the time I was very small we'd use the leave to spend a couple of weeks with each set of grandparents every summer and then head up to the hill stations of the Himalayas. Hill stations are towns in the hills or low mountains that were often established by the British in colonized India as places to escape the blistering summer heat of lower altitudes. There are hill stations all over the country, although most are in the north, and with their beautiful scenery they make fantastic vacation destinations.

When it was time for us to head out on holiday, my parents would pack our red Maruti minivan, license plate number DBB 743—the first car I ever remember us having after Dad's motorbike—

and we'd take off. We'd go to Ranikhet, Shimla, and Manali; to Nainital in the Kumaon foothills of the outer Himalayas; to Pahalgam, Gulmarg, and Srinagar in Kashmir. Dad would tie thin, rolled mattresses to the roof of the Maruti, pack the back with suitcases, bags of clothes, and coolers loaded with sandwiches, *parathas,* and my favorite spicy *aachars,* and off we'd go.

Every trip was an adventure. The minivan would always be full of family and friends, with at least eight of us jammed into it. We traveled in packs. Still do. My favorite place to sit was in the very back. Dad had convinced me that a cramped, crowded storage space with cushions and blankets thrown over our suitcases and bags was a special place, created just for me. That it was "my room." I fell for it, as I always fell for Dad's charm. My cousins knew better—"You're in the boot!" they'd cry—but one of my cousins, Kunal, the son of my dad's sister Saroj Bhogal, used to join me there. We were similar in age and that became our territory. The best part of being back there was that when we were on smaller roads with little traffic, we'd keep the boot open and dangle our feet out the back. (Clearly this was a different time, when safety laws there were still somewhat lax.) We'd nibble at our snacks and wave at the occasional car going by as we made our way through the terrain.

Most of the games we played during these long car trips were music-related. One game was *antakshari,* where the last letter of the song one person has sung is the letter the next person has to start their song with. When we weren't playing a group game, we'd all be singing, usually to one of the mixtapes that Dad had recorded and brought along. We'd stop to buy guavas, cucumbers, and mangoes, Dad's favorite, from the vendors on the side of the road, then take a break for lunch near whatever stream we'd seen from the car. The fruit and the adults' beer were cooled in the ice-cold clear Himalayan springwater that flowed down from the mountains. A few more hours of driving, and we'd stop at a restaurant. Later, when I was a teenager living with my mother's family in the U.S., I took summer road trips with cousins, other relatives, and friends that reminded me of these carefree early childhood ones. We drove through the states of Idaho, North and South Dakota, and Wyoming, one happy extended family.

The summer I was nine, we spent two months in Leh when my father was posted there. On a trip through the higher reaches of the Himalayas on the way to Pangong Lake, which extends from India to Tibet, I saw my first yak, sampled yak jerky, and tried Ladakhi tea, made of yak milk and salt. Not a fan. During those months in Leh, I made two or three friends who were my age and who were also in Leh visiting their parents in the military. We'd run around the barracks, which were warmed in the daylight hours by coal-burning *bukhari* heaters, and search the hills for little dome-shaped Buddhist stupas. I was always out exploring, looking for adventure, trying to uncover something new. My urge was to do something that hadn't been done before, to discover something that no one had found yet. I always wanted to be first.

Maybe I remember that particular summer so well because that's when India's former prime minister, Rajiv Gandhi, was assassinated by a suicide bomber. On May 21, 1991, I was playing cards with some kids in the mess of the army barracks while a group of adults were watching television. Suddenly, several of them rose to their feet. It was eerily quiet, and then one of the adults started crying. The former prime minister's assassination and its aftermath marked one of the first times I understood that what happens somewhere far away—he had been in Tamil Nadu, more than two thousand miles away in the southernmost part of our country—can affect everyone, that the impact of certain events can't be contained. I remember the silence, the sobbing, and the crackling of coal as the small heaters tried to warm the large mess hall, which would never feel as completely safe and cozy to me as it had just moments before.

Years later, when I returned to Leh to film the movie *Waqt* in 2004, I discovered that the hills that had felt so massive at the time now seemed small, and that the barracks we had stayed in during my ninth summer had burned down. Nothing remained of them but ash. Another set of barracks had been built next to where the old ones had been, but they weren't the same, of course. The new barracks were neither the home of my memories nor of my childhood footprints. But they were the future. They looked sturdier, more comfortable, and they probably all had electric heaters.

THE SUMMER I turned eleven or twelve, I was really looking forward to our usual holiday break. A few days before it began, as I sat at the dinner table discussing my wish list of activities with great animation, my mother gently put her hand on mine and informed me that she had other plans. She wanted me to join her and my dad for a medical camp they were going to run in a nearby rural village that didn't get regular healthcare. It would mean starting our holiday a bit later, and needless to say, I was angry and upset.

Many tantrums and bouts of sulking ensued, but my mother was adamant. At 6 A.M. on a Saturday we set off, and when we arrived at our destination several hours later, I took my role of assistant pharmacist very seriously, helping the actual pharmacist distribute the medications and explain how to use them. We worked in a makeshift setup beneath a canopy strung from an ambulance borrowed from my mother's hospital. The first couple of hours were a blur because I was still sulking, unaware of the societal pressures my parents were navigating in an effort to provide care to all who needed it. But as the day progressed, I grew more involved.

A lot of girls in the village who needed medical attention were not being treated. Mothers fussed over their sons but were afraid to discuss their daughters' problems. My mother tried to persuade the women to allow their daughters to be examined; my father tried to persuade their husbands. Sometimes it worked, sometimes it didn't. I couldn't follow a lot of what was being said and what was happening.

During the ride home at the end of a very long day, I started to cry. Were the girls being punished? I asked my parents. What had they done wrong? Why couldn't they get help for their problems like everyone else? My parents tried to explain as best they could that in many parts of the country, and in a lot of developing economies around the world, parents didn't want their daughters to be seen by doctors because finding a medical issue would jeopardize their chances for marriage. But I was a daughter of the same country those girls lived in, and I was allowed to have medical care. I simply didn't understand the disparity. I couldn't grasp the distinction between girls who received medical care and girls who didn't; girls who had opportunities and girls who didn't; girls who were free to make their own choices and girls who had their choices made for them.

I don't recall now whether or not I made the connection then between what I had observed firsthand that day—that some of the girls of this village were not receiving medical treatment—and what I had observed firsthand two or three years earlier—that a newborn daughter had been left under my mother's car. In any case, that trip changed me. My parents' humanitarian values, already planted in me, took firm root. What I witnessed and learned became an unshakable part of my foundation, informing a myriad of future choices and an unwavering dedication to being an advocate for children—especially girls—who weren't afforded the choices and opportunities that I have been. Privilege and responsibility go hand in hand.

2

LIKE WATER

Be like water making its way through cracks. Do not be asser-
tive, but adjust to the object, and you shall find a way around
or through it. . . . If you put water into a cup, it becomes the cup.
You put water into a bottle and it becomes the bottle. You put it
in a teapot, it becomes the teapot. Now, water can flow or it
can crash. Be water, my friend.

BRUCE LEE

MY KINDERGARTEN YEAR was spent at a Catholic school in
Delhi, where my parents were stationed at the time. I adored
my teacher, Mrs. Bhasker; my best friend, Denise; and everything
about my little school. When Dad told me I had to bid farewell to
my happy life at St. Paul's because it was time to transfer again—
with my parents in the military, we moved every two and a half to
three years—I burst into tears.

In an attempt to calm me down and convince me of what he
believed was an opportunity, Dad sat me on his lap and flipped the

whole prospect of moving on its head. "You don't want to leave because you think you have your whole life set here," he said. "But in fact, you're one of the lucky few who can leave your mistakes behind. If there's a class you don't like, or if you're not doing so well in math, or if some teacher has a bad impression of you, the next school you go to will be like a clean slate. No one will ever know any of that. You can become whoever you want to be. That's your superpower." His clever approach swayed me. I began to get excited about the prospect of moving to a new place.

"Be like water," he said. "Find the best situation wherever you are and make it work."

Dad's wisdom set me up to succeed and helped establish a sense of adventure and wanderlust in me early on. As a young girl and then a teenager, it was freeing to know that I wouldn't be defined forever by who I'd been or what phase I was going through at any given moment. Bad hair? Made a social faux pas? Failed a class? As Aaliyah said, "Dust yourself off and try again." Nothing lasts forever, and I could always start fresh somewhere else.

Even now, every time I move to a new place or go on location for work, I look forward to packing my bags. I get excited thinking about what the next adventure will bring. Reinvention, adjusting and acclimatizing to new environments, overcoming fear of new places by opening up to possibility—these are some of the principles by which I have lived my life.

Of course, I didn't embody the "like water" principle all that consistently early on. In fact, after my brother, Siddharth, was born, I was less known for being fluid and more known for being a brat. I had been an only child for close to seven years, and the first girl-child on my father's side of the family. Suddenly there was this crying, attention-stealing *thing* that had come along. Sid was a much-wanted and much-awaited baby who'd been born prematurely. He'd had to stay in an incubator in the hospital for a period of time, and when he came home he was still so tiny that we had to feed him with a dropper. As the months went by, I came to adore his perfect curls, his giant brown eyes, and his baby babble. But as cute a baby as Sid was, I couldn't get past my jealousy over all the attention he was now getting. As a result, I acted out. A lot.

One evening, my parents and I were watching television together in their bedroom. I was lying on my tummy and snacking on some chips, and Dad asked me to pass them. "No," I responded, without taking my eyes off the screen. Dad asked again, and I said, "No," this time more firmly. And then, as if "no" wasn't bad enough, I added:

"Can't you see that I'm busy!" Which was a variation of what Mom used to say:

Give me time. Can't you see that I'm busy? I'll get back to you.

Mom looked at my father, then at me, and then at my father again. "Mimi needs to learn discipline," she said, using the nickname I was affectionately known by within the family. Then she announced that perhaps I would benefit from going to boarding school.

I can only imagine that when Mom heard me talk back to my father that evening, echoing her very own words, she panicked, wondering where this disrespectful, spoiled child had come from. Dad wasn't concerned, but for Mom it must have been the last straw after many months of enduring my tantrums and attention-seeking behavior. An idea that had perhaps already been percolating in her mind began to take clearer shape: In the northern part of the country where we lived, there were several boarding schools known for providing a fine academic education combined with a comportment component—sort of like Ivy League boarding schools with a touch of posh finishing school thrown in for good measure. I'd known some kids who'd gone to these schools; army families some-times sent their children to boarding school and in my own school in Bareilly it was considered a cool thing to go off to attend one.

My parents argued back and forth that evening about my school-ing, a huge disagreement that lasted all night. It was the only perhaps-exception to the rule of "no arguing in front of the chil-dren" that I can remember, though they did try to keep it in the realm of discussion rather than fight. Dad tried every line of reason-ing he could with Mom, but she wouldn't budge. Mom wanted to do what she thought was best for me, and what she thought was best for me was La Martiniere Girls' College (which started with the elementary grades and went through high school), a four-hour train ride south in Lucknow, the capital of Uttar Pradesh.

La Martiniere, well over a century and a half old, was British in its architecture and palatial in size. The Girls' College—there was an older and larger Boys' College, too, though the two were kept entirely separate—offered top-notch academics. The school also taught its pupils how to be ladies: how to dress, how to speak, and how to develop good, healthy habits. We were expected to obey a strict lights-out rule, keep our closets neat, and be well groomed at all times.

After their "discussion" that night, my parents started having conversations with me about attending a new and bigger school, but in none of these conversations was it mentioned that I was going to *live* in this new school. Without my family. I remember taking and passing an admissions test, and not long after, my mother dressed me up one morning and she and my father and I traveled to the school for a tour. I figured this would be a getting-to-know-you tour, to be followed, if we all liked the place, by a start date weeks or months away. The tour wore on and eventually we came to a dormitory, where I was shown a bed and a closet where I could put my things.

What things?

I turned to my mother and asked, "Am I going to sleep in this bed?"

"This is where the students come to rest when they're tired" is what she remembers telling me. While she had been adamant about sending me to boarding school, when it came right down to leaving me there at the age of seven, she faltered. She didn't tell me that I was staying that day. She didn't have the heart to.

I'm not sure exactly what happened next or how much time passed, but at some point I looked up and my parents were gone. The matron had told them, and all the other parents of new students, that the hour of departure had arrived. There was to be no lingering, no looking back. It was time for their children to adjust and they would do so under the school's care. Someone must have told me that my mother and father had left and that I was now going to live at the school, yet I have no memory of that moment. What I do remember vividly is the feeling of being abandoned, a feeling that lasted for a long, long time. I remember sitting on the little merry-go-round in the school's playground gripping the cold rusty bars and staring at the gate for hours that first week, and in subsequent weeks, too, as I waited for my mother to swoop in and take me back home where I belonged.

The first time Mom was allowed to visit was the following weekend. Because I was in my playground waiting spot staring at the gate, I saw her immediately as she entered the grounds. It was a bit of an unreal moment: the one person I had been longing for suddenly appeared, just like I'd dreamed she would. I jumped off the merry-go-round, ran to her, and fell to the ground. "Why, Mama? Why did you leave me here?" I cried as I grabbed her knees. "I'm sorry if I made a mistake! Please take me back! I won't do it again!"

She tried to explain to me that boarding school was for my own good, that La Martiniere was a wonderful place and I'd make new friends and learn all sorts of exciting and useful things. In an attempt, I think, to distract me, she asked to see my dormitory, even though she'd seen it the weekend before. I responded, "Promise me you won't leave me here. If you promise me, then I'll take you." She wouldn't promise, but I showed her where I slept anyway, guiding her through the large doors into a huge room with high French windows and a sea of iron single beds.

For the first month or two, Mom came every weekend, taking the train four hours each way. She'd bring me goodies to replenish my tuck box, the multicompartment box of food and trinkets that students in India and Great Britain take with them if they go to boarding school. My tuck box was everything to me—familiarity, family, home—and Mom kept it filled with my favorite treats: Uncle Chipps, the brand of potato chips I liked best; *aampapad,* a tangy mango fruit leather; *churan,* sweet tamarind balls mixed with spices; and an instant ramen-like snack called Maggi noodles. She put in plenty of other goodies, too, and once I started to feel a little more social I figured out that to make friends, I could share what I considered nonpriority items. The priority items, the stuff that I loved and that comforted me, I hid.

Having Mom visit was heaven, but her departures were agony for both of us. I'd be in tears, traumatized all over again by the separation, and as much as Mom must have tried to control her own tears as she was leaving, she would end up crying, too. For days afterward, I wouldn't be able to sleep or do my homework. It was obvious that I wasn't adjusting. Which was why Principal Keller (we called her "Mrs. Killer," God rest her soul) instructed my mother to reduce her visits to no more than once a month. When even that reduced visitation schedule didn't help matters, Principal Keller took the difficult step of instructing her to stop visiting completely for the next six months.

"If you are serious about your daughter continuing her education here," she told my mother, "you should not make it more difficult for her. You must give her the opportunity to become more independent. Please don't make the gateman's job any harder by arriving and asking to be let in."

I felt like whatever tenuous safety net had been supporting me had just been ripped away.

I still didn't understand why I had been sent away, why my mom had thought this was the right move for me, why the school would be "good for me." I didn't understand why she couldn't visit me anymore when it was the only thing that made me feel better. Some days I blamed the arrival of my brother; other days I blamed my own bad behavior. My confusion remained because Mom didn't explain her reasons to me—maybe she didn't fully understand them herself. All I understood was that I was alone, and that everything was different now.

First there was getting used to sleeping in the huge dormitory—getting used to how the coils under the mattresses creaked whenever we moved; getting used to the sound of the other girls' breathing as they slept; how they hung their washed socks and underwear on the head rails to dry during the day; how the temperature dropped the instant you walked into the room because it was so cavernous. Mealtimes were no longer family time with interesting dinner table conversations about my parents' medical cases and my school. Now I ate in a big dining room with long tables and benches, surrounded by people I hardly knew. At home, I adamantly refused to eat any vegetables, but in boarding school, you had to finish what was on your plate or receive detention. It was a very stereotypical English boarding school, with huge arches and vaulted ceilings, just like Hogwarts in the Harry Potter books. Only at the time there was no Harry Potter, so I didn't even have the comfort of feeling that maybe this experience, like Harry's, would eventually give me magical powers. I suppose the only slightly magical thing that happened is that I learned to enjoy the food I used to hate, like *baingan,* for instance. Even now, eggplant is one of my favorite foods. Out of torture came a new love.

One night soon after I arrived, I threw up in my bed after the lights were turned out. I'm not sure if I'd eaten something bad or if my sickness was due to the anxiety and fear that sometimes gripped my stomach. Not wanting to get in trouble for making a fuss, I went to sleep with a puddle of vomit in my bed and didn't tell a soul. In the middle of the night, I got up, washed my sheets, hung them up, and then returned to my bed to sleep on a bare mattress. Early the next morning, I rose before everyone else and remade my bed with the still-damp sheets—the solution of a third grader terrified of what would happen if she made another mistake, considering that the last mistake she'd made had been bad enough to get her banished from her family. None of my dorm mates ever noticed—or if they did, they didn't acknowledge it—and the only person who ever knew about it was another new girl whom I'd become a little friendly with; I told her two days later.

Sometime after this episode I did a complete turnabout regarding sickness. Instead of pretending that I wasn't sick, I'd pretend that I was. I didn't want to be in class; at that point I didn't like most people and most people didn't like me. But in the infirmary, there was a lovely nurse who used to make all the kids in her care laugh. It was the only bit of attention I could find, so I did whatever I could do to get it. There was a rumor going around that if you put cut onions under your armpits you'd get fever, so I used to steal onions from the food hall and put them under my armpits, desperately hoping it would send my temperature soaring so I'd be sent to the infirmary, where the nice nurse would take care of me. But the only thing that happened was that I smelled like onions.

Eventually I stopped questioning why I'd been sent away and

slowly began to settle in. It had finally sunk in that I didn't have a choice. One teacher, Miss Rose, took me under her wing, occasionally inviting me in the evenings to her quarters on the property. Those nights, we'd eat something together and then she'd help me with my homework. The one-on-one time was a balm, and I started to feel a little less alone.

And I think the orderliness of all the rules at the school started to comfort me in some way, too. From the very first day, we were taught how important it was to make a good impression. We had to iron our navy cotton uniforms every night because our pleats were checked every morning by monitors, as were the height of our socks and the shine of our shoes. It *mattered* how pressed and ironed your pleats were, how clean your hair was. I bought into this fully, making sure I always looked neat and clean and well put together. Even now my clothes have to be ironed, my shoes need to be scuff-free, and my closet needs to be orderly.

Eventually Principal Keller's tough-love approach worked, because after those six months of Mom not visiting, the whole thing kind of turned around for me. I made friends, did well academically, and felt more and more at ease. I loved returning home during school breaks and showing off to people how independent I was. And I think that was exactly what my mom had wanted.

Dad was posted out at the border in Leh, near China, during much of my time at La Martiniere. Mom chose to take early retirement from the military in order to stay back in Bareilly since my brother, having been born prematurely, was still too small and vulnerable for the high altitude of Leh. Now that I was more settled and adjusted, the principal allowed her to see me more often; unfortunately, it was too far away for my father to visit. Once I felt more settled, Mom's trips had only positive effects. In the early days, seeing her reminded me of being pushed away, of feeling rejected and banished, but seeing her now reminded me of how far

I'd come, how much I'd grown and changed. I loved showing her where I slept, my cubby, my classrooms. I loved introducing her to my friends and teachers. This was no longer just the place where she'd once left me. It was *my* place now, and I was proud to show her everything about it.

By my second and third years at La Martiniere, in fourth and fifth grades, I started to thrive. I'd made some close friends, and as eight- and nine-year-olds we used to spend recesses running around on the large playground or sitting on the little merry-go-round and talking—the school gave us a delicious couple of hours of outdoor play every day. It was a gorgeous setting, with plenty of bright green grass, flowering shrubs, and ashoka, mango, and guava trees, in which monkeys loved to perch.

One afternoon I was sitting on the merry-go-round talking with a friend when I noticed a monkey in one of the tall ashoka trees; usually the monkeys hung out in the shorter trees—they loved the guavas—but on that day the monkey overhead was watching us from the ashoka's higher vantage point. For some reason this fellow was having trouble peeling a banana. I noticed and started laughing loudly, maybe even pointing at him. At which point the monkey made eye contact with me, scampered down the tree, slapped my face, and clambered back up. I sat too shocked for words while my friend laughed hysterically, as did everyone else on the playground who'd seen the comic bit. Meanwhile, the monkey ate his banana calmly, having succeeded in peeling it upon his return to the high branch.

I take it as an indication of my feeling comfortable enough at school that I wasn't totally humiliated by this scene. A little humiliated, yes. But even then I could see the humor in the situation once my cheek stopped smarting. I mean really—having a monkey call me out for my poor manners in making fun of him? As much as I hated to, I had to admit that it was funny—and that I deserved it.

During fourth and fifth grades, I was finding things that I enjoyed and had some aptitude for. I was encouraged to get involved
in public speaking, debates, and swimming. Most Indian schools
focus largely on academics, but La Martiniere had an arts focus as
well, which suited me perfectly. I remember very clearly the first
time I was asked by a teacher to come up in front of the class and
sing for everyone. I danced for family and other people at any opportunity, but I'd never really sung for anyone other than my family
or the very encouraging audiences at my parents' dinner parties.
When I finished my song—"My Favorite Things" from *The Sound
of Music*—the entire class got to their feet and clapped vigorously.
And I loved it. I loved the warm, happy feeling that their applause
gave me. I loved being in a spotlight of any sort, whether it was for
singing, dancing, acting, public speaking, or sports.

La Martiniere provided a liberal education and all religions were
welcome there. It was a perfect school for me because it aligned
with the family values of peace, harmony, and secularism that I had
been raised with. My mother's mother was a Catholic before she
married my grandfather. My aunt Sophia converted to Islam after
marriage. My father sang in temples, mosques, Sikh *gurdwaras,* and
churches. It was no surprise, then, that when my parents discovered
the teachings of Haidakhan Baba in the 1980s, his wisdom reso-
nated with them. Babaji stressed respect for all religions, saying that
although he followed Hindu customs, following any religion would
ultimately help you reach God. My parents had long wanted a second child, and after encountering Babaji's teachings on a chance
visit to his ashram, their years of difficulty finally ended and Sid
came into this world. Since I can remember, Babaji has been a part
of my life and the face of my faith. Part of that faith is knowing that
every individual on this planet who believes in a faith has their own
face for it.

This acceptance of everybody is exactly what I saw at La Martiniere. We celebrated one another's faiths and holidays—Diwali, Eid, Gurpurab, and Christmas were all recognized—and we always got them off. We'd usually have celebrations the day before, giving one another gifts where appropriate. Religion wasn't used to define anyone; it was just another part of who we were. And no religion was considered more important or less important. We didn't need to be instructed to have mutual respect for all; it was the air we breathed.

My years in boarding school ended up helping me to be both adaptable and fiercely independent, so I look at them as a gift, a priority item in the tuck box of my life. Being on my own at such a young age taught me how to find my own solutions. If I needed something, I'd figure out a way to get it somehow rather than waiting around for someone else to get it for me. I'm still that way, absolutely. I developed a skill set that's served me well in my career and my life so far.

But I know that being sent away at such a young age affected me in other ways, too. I learned to compartmentalize difficult moments and events in my life—to focus on the next amazing thing I wanted to do and move on without always fully processing whatever had just happened to me. Keeping the sections of my tuck box neatly organized and separated, and moving forward, always moving forward, without looking back. My version of being like water.

GIVEN THAT I was so happy at La Martiniere, I might have stayed on there through middle school and high school. But the summer before sixth grade I contracted typhoid fever when I was home in Bareilly. I was treated there and returned to school in Lucknow as planned but had attended classes for only a few weeks when I had a relapse, which was severe; I ended up staying in the hospital for two weeks. I had gotten sick frequently during my years away at school (actually sick, as opposed to looking-for-attention-from-the-nice-nurse-in-the-infirmary sick), and this final, dangerous illness convinced my parents that it was time to bring me home. Dad had been transferred back to Bareilly and so our family lived together for the first time in years on Barrack Road, Bareilly Cantt. (Cantonment). This airy double-storied house—we were on the first floor, another family lived upstairs—was located in a neighborhood where all the officers and their families lived, one that offered multiple activities for a curious preteen. I rode bikes, played badminton, and built castles in the sand traps of the neighborhood golf course with other officers' kids. As much as I'd eventually liked boarding school, I was happy to be back with Mom, Dad, and even Sid, who was now a rambunctious three-year-old. The independence I'd discovered in boarding school allowed me to continue my nascent steps into a broadening social world even as I was safe in the arms of my family.

At La Martiniere, the teachers had been serious about our academics, comportment, and presentation, but they also knew how to laugh. Though the faculty and students of my new school were of all religions, the school itself was run by nuns. I'm not saying that all nuns are humorless, but this group certainly was. At St. Maria Goretti Inter College we learned that girls should be soft-spoken and boys shouldn't cry. We studied a subject called Moral Science and learned about the seven deadly sins; not a lot of room for humor there. Even at the age of ten, I couldn't help but have a bit of skepticism about classes like that.

Those years we wore blue tunics with white shirts, black shoes, and white socks. The ritual of ironing my clothes and shining my shoes had been drilled into me at La Martiniere, and now it was actually fun because as I attended to my uniform, Dad attended to his, too. It was a thing we did together.

As careful as I was to follow the rules regarding my uniform, however, there were plenty of other rules I wasn't so careful about. I quickly became the girl who always got sent to the principal's office for being too loud and for passing notes—there was *so* much to say to my best friend and unfortunately I just happened to feel the most communicative during class, especially when the teacher was speaking. I was at an age when I felt clever enough to get away with anything, the way all kids do—I'd been clever enough to survive boarding school, hadn't I? But of course I was destined to be caught more often than not. Upon being sent to the principal, I would be made to stand outside her office on one leg in an effort to cure me of my predilection for back talk. I didn't understand why talking or being spirited was considered to be so awful—the principal regularly told me that I was the naughtiest one in the class—or how standing on one leg was going to change anything, but the more I was told how naughty I was, the more I rebelled. I have often thought that the behavior that got me into trouble regularly then, all that boundary pushing, eventually helped me in my career, as boundary pushing is an advantage rather than a problem in most creative fields.

Despite the school's attempts to control my behavior, I was still able to find ways to assert my independence. This was the first time I traveled from home to school alone. Before boarding school, my parents had driven me to and from school every day. Now I took a rickshaw with six other kids, which made me feel grown up. In seventh grade, I got my first scooter and traveled back and forth that way. And I got my own dog, Brutus, a greyhound, when I was twelve, and was responsible for walking and feeding him. One afternoon I thought he might prefer a good run to a boring old walk, so I tied him to my bicycle and started to pedal; I found out the hard way that he was a lot faster than I was. (*Note to self: Never tie a greyhound to your bicycle.*)

My attitude in those preteen years can be pretty much summed up as *Nothing's gonna kill my vibe*. Not the principal making me stand outside her office on one leg; not the ridiculously awkward, gawky age; not all the bad hairstyles I sported. Ridhima, Saloni, Neelakshi, and I were a posse, a crew, gravitating to one another as we were the ones always getting sent to the principal's office. (Except Ridhima, who was the "good girl" in the group. She and I really clicked anyway and we're still friends today.) Most afternoons we would hang out at the Bareilly Club, a private club with both military and civilian members—the equivalent, more or less, of a country club in the U.S.—where we mostly just sat around and talked.

It was during my second year at St. Maria Goretti that I started to notice the older girls at school being met at the gate by their boyfriends after classes had ended for the day, and I began, ever so slightly, to look at the male of the species with different eyes. From the time I was little, I'd had plenty of friends who were boys because I was an active child, always climbing trees or on my bike. I loved the rough-and-tumble stuff that boys seemed to gravitate toward and I didn't hesitate to compete with them. Now something was beginning to shift. Though I didn't have a boyfriend yet as an eleven- and then twelve-year-old, I was pretty sure I could get one if I wanted to. I just didn't want to. Yet.

LOL.

3

NOMAD

I am no bird; and no net ensnares me; I am a free human being, with an independent will, which I now exert to leave you.

CHARLOTTE BRONTË, *JANE EYRE*

AMERICA. LAND OF the rich, gorgeous, and spotlessly clean. Mom had always tuned in to *The Bold and the Beautiful, Dynasty, Baywatch,* and *Remington Steele,* so naturally the America of those shows was the America of my fantasy. Then, in May of 1995, shortly before I turned thirteen, I arrived for a vacation with Mom in Cedar Rapids, Iowa. It was my first trip abroad. I didn't see any mansions and I had to search hard for perfectly blown-out hair and haute couture fashion. It wasn't like the glamorous television shows at all. The people in this midsize American city were just normal people, living in normal houses, doing normal things.

Still, it felt a universe away from India. The population of India is more than four times the population of America, yet America has almost three times the physical space. Which meant that as seen through my teenage eyes, American space was *mind-blowing*. There was so much *distance* between things. And with organized systems to everything—the neighborhoods, the traffic, the way people stood in line—where was the poetic chaos? The energetic commotion of a crowded country that's always in motion, always alive?

Mom and I had traveled to Cedar Rapids to visit her youngest sister, Kiran Mathur, a computer engineer who lived there with her husband, Amitabh, and their daughters, Priyam, age ten, and Pooja, age three. My disappointment in the real America as opposed to the TV version of it changed a few days after we arrived. My aunt Kiran, or Kiran Masi—*Masi* translates as "like mother"—asked if I wanted to check out an American high school and I jumped at the offer. I couldn't get over how huge the buildings were at John F. Kennedy High School—the vastness of the gymnasium, cafeteria, auditorium, and playing fields seemed absolutely luxurious to me, accustomed as I was to generally smaller spaces and fifty or sixty students in a classroom. The theater and music programs sounded amazing. And kids actually changed classrooms for their different classes! At my school and many others in India, our teachers came to us; given the number of students, it was easier to have the instructors go from room to room than to have kids flooding the halls between classes. Overall, it seemed to me that the kids here were trusted with more responsibility and allowed more independence, and I'd already gotten a taste of that at La Martiniere and loved it. So when my aunt asked me if I might like to go to high school in Cedar Rapids, I considered the question against the backdrop of students bustling through the hallways to and from their classes. The lockers were painted in cheerful blocks of color. The school mascot—the Kennedy Cougar—roared at me from the walls of the hallway. Sports trophies glistened in their glass cases. No one was wearing uniforms. I blinked. *Seriously? No uniforms? Kids can dress however they want? Girls can wear makeup and their hair down?*

Are you kidding? YES. Decision made.

I couldn't wait to get back to talk to Mom about staying in America. Boarding school had made me feel ready to take on the world, so the prospect of being far from home didn't scare me. My life had always been a little nomadic anyway—living with my grandparents early on, moving from city to city due to my parents' army postings, going to boarding school—so attending high school in America felt like it was just the next step in my peripatetic education. My cousin Priyam had stayed with my mom for two years when Kiran Masi was moving to America while I was in boarding school. Wouldn't it be nice if I now stayed with my aunt, who had helped care for me when I was a baby living with my grandparents?

Mom said she thought it would be a great opportunity for me and called Dad to see if he'd go for it. After a rational, logical Chopra Family Conversation, Dad agreed: "Let her give it a shot." If I liked it, I could stay. If I didn't adapt, I could come home. Nothing ventured, nothing gained. And so it was decided that I would stay with my aunt and her family and give the U.S. a try.

At least that's how I thought my move to the U.S. came about; only recently did I discover that wasn't the full story. When I was living in Bareilly, my cousins who had already moved to the States—Sana, Irfan, and Priyam (Pooja was too young, and so was my cousin Parisa)—were writing and telling me how great America was, and sending me pictures of themselves dressed in cool American clothes. In my persistent preteen way, I took to telling Mom how much I wanted to live in America, too. Of course, I knew that was impossible; my cousins all lived with their parents, but my parents had careers in India that they weren't about to leave. My mother's mother, Nani, told me that if I got good enough grades, maybe my parents would take me on a trip to America. So that's what I thought this trip was—a special vacation as a reward for my hard work in school.

Unbeknownst to me, before we arrived in the U.S., Mom had already reached out to her sister Kiran about the possibility of me living with her and attending school in the States. Knowing my independent streak and my love of adventure, Mom thought that I might relish the chance to live and study in the States; it would also give my parents time to settle into a new living situation after Dad's recent retirement from the army, and to establish their new joint private practice. But Mom wanted to make sure that going to school in America was what I truly wanted, and that I made the decision with open eyes and without feeling any pressure about it. She chose not to include my father in her thought process until she knew whether it was something I was actually drawn to.

"I would love to have Mimi live with us!" Kiran Masi responded when Mom asked her. "What's three kids instead of two?" Then she contacted the local high school to see about getting a student visa for me.

So that visit to the high school? It had all been planned in advance. There had even been a conversation with a guidance counselor. When it was clear that the possibility of going to school in the States excited me, Mom and Kiran Masi allowed me to think the situation had occurred spontaneously. And the conversation my mom then had with my father? Well, let's just say my mom got her way.

A note on family member designations for those unfamiliar with them. In Hindi-speaking culture there is a specific term for everyone in the family so you immediately know who's who and exactly how they're related. For instance, in addition to *Masi,* we have *Mausa,* which means "mother's sister's husband." *Mamu* means "mother's brother" and *Mami* means "mother's brother's wife." *Chacha* means "father's brother" and *Chachi* means "father's brother's wife." *Dada* means "paternal grandfather" and *Dadi* means "paternal grandmother" (though we called our paternal grandparents *Pit-*

aji and *Mataji,* because that's what my parents called them). *Nana* means "maternal grandfather" and *Nani* means "maternal grandmother," and so on and so forth. For someone new entering a large extended family, as many Indian families tend to be, these designations are incredibly helpful in making sense of all the relationships.

Although the setup had been engineered, the actual decision to stay in the States to attend school had not, and it was the first time I was given primary responsibility for a major decision about my life. Right before my mother left to head back to India, she said, "Now that you're going to live away from me, remember what we discussed about the pros and cons. Remember that this was your decision. And if you change your mind, Dad and I will always be there to come back home to. You can call us for anything. And whatever happens, try your hardest so that you'll always know you gave it your best shot."

Short version: Own your choices. Or, as my mother must have told me hundreds of times growing up, "have courage of conviction."

IOWA—DEEP IN THE American Midwest and known to be conservative both politically and socially—was incredibly welcoming and accepting for a girl like me: immigrant, brown, different. Different hair, different skin, different accent, different clothes, different food—the ways I was different seemed endless. I was acutely aware of my status as Other. But it wasn't so much that other students considered me Other. It was that *I* did; I had never been more aware of my ethnicity than when I left my own country and moved to America. The most obvious way I was Other was my skin, and even in India there were issues having to do with skin color. Girls like me, who were darker, were often referred to pejoratively as "dusky." But I wasn't *different* at home. Here, I was, even though there was no unkindness associated with that status—yet.

I acclimated to John F. Kennedy High School with a minimum of difficulty and spent the eighth grade falling in love with hot dogs, Hot Pockets, and a hot boy named Seth (though I'm sure he and his green hair didn't know that I existed). Part of what may have made it relatively easy to acclimate was that I didn't have to worry about keeping up academically. Whereas the American school year generally goes from August or September to May or June, the Indian school year generally goes from April to March, with summer and winter breaks. I had entered eighth grade back in Bareilly earlier that spring, and I would now be reentering it in Cedar Rapids. The more important reason, though, is that when I was in school in the U.S. in the nineties, many Indian schools were far more rigorous than their American counterparts (or at least that was my impression). On day one of Advanced Math class in Cedar Rapids, for example, I discovered we were to be studying quadratic equations—which was going to make the class awfully easy for me, since I'd learned them the year before. When I was handed a scientific calculator for an exam in that class, I didn't understand what I was being tested for if I could use a calculator. I was a good student in India, but I was never one of the best in my class. Here I earned that distinction quickly.

Unlike math and other subjects that I was comparatively advanced in, the social aspects of this huge new school were harder for me. One of the most difficult adjustments I had to make, believe it or not, was figuring out the food that was being served in the big, noisy cafeteria. At my previous school I'd always brought my lunch from home, as is the norm in India. Knowing that I had been sheltered and protected at home, as most middle-class Indian children are, Kiran Masi wanted me to learn the independence that kids in the United States have. So, like many parents in America, she gave us money to buy our lunches at school. For the first few days, I simply watched what the other kids did—how they each got a tray, went through the line, pointed at what they wanted, and took their food to a table to sit with friends. Negotiating the lunch lines and trying to quickly figure out the unrecognizable foods that were being offered by the cafeteria staff was overwhelming at a time when looking cool and unfazed was very important to my teenage self. Afraid of looking stupid, or worse, of calling further attention to the fact that I was an outsider, I decided I'd just buy chips from the vending machine and eat them in the girls' bathroom. After about a week, I got the courage to venture back into the cafeteria. I'd made one friend by then, who, like me, existed without status— not popular, not invisible—so I went through the line, got food on my tray, and sat down at a table with her and a few other kids. So far, so good. As I was finishing my meal, I started to eat what I'd thought was my dessert—a white mound of vanilla ice cream that, oddly, hadn't started to melt. I gagged when what I put into my mouth was not cold, sweet, and delicious, but warm and gloppy. *Mashed potatoes,* I was told as I choked down the first bite. Moments later, when the creamy, buttery mouthful actually registered on my taste buds, mashed potatoes had a new fan. From then on, they were on my plate every time they were offered. Still are.

Food confusion was a frequent occurrence at the time, whether it was because something new looked like something familiar or because the name made no sense to me. (Imagine my bewilderment when it came time to try buffalo wings.) There were other things to get used to, too. When I was living with my parents, I'd been driven to school for the most part. It would have been hard for Kiran Masi to drive me; she had a job and three children to look after and mornings were busy. While the school district provided bussing to Priyam's school, my new school was within a mile of our house and so bussing wasn't available. Still, it was too far to walk.

Masi thought it would be smart for me to be able to handle myself on public transportation here, so now I was taking a city bus the short distance to the school. Every morning, I was given $2.00—50 cents for the bus and $1.50 for lunch. On the first day of school, Masi rode with me on the bus.

"This is how you put in the coins, and this is how you find a seat. When you sit down, don't engage, just keep your head down. And then you get off when you arrive at school."

Chores were another big change for me. "This is America," Kiran Masi said. "You will make your own bed. You will pick up after yourself. You will help to do laundry. We cannot afford to pay people to do these things for us here."

My mother had always tried to impress upon me the importance of tidying up after myself in spite of us having help a large part of my life. I'd belligerently ignored her because I knew there was someone to do it for me if I didn't. Here that wasn't an option, and I have Kiran Masi to thank for keeping after me until I finally learned how to do the chores of everyday life, and then turned those life skills into habits.

I HAD AN amazing school year at John F. Kennedy High School. It wasn't *Beverly Hills, 90210* or *Saved by the Bell*—my only previous references to what high school in America was like—but sometimes it felt close. I loved the hubbub in the halls between classes, the cool fashions, and the general feeling of freedom. And I adored participating in the school choir. The director, a soft-spoken, encouraging, and at the same time energetic man named Storm Ziegler—who as of the writing of this book is still the director of choral activities at the school—nominated me as one of two singers to represent our school in the state Opus Honor Choir festival in

Des Moines. It was indeed an honor, and a treat, and I practiced so diligently that I think my family knew the alto part of Monteverdi's "Cantate Domino" as well as I did. Mr. Ziegler also introduced me to the concept of musical theater, something I'd never heard of before. I knew music, and I knew theater, but I'd never seen them combined. I auditioned for a role in a nearby production of *Fiddler on the Roof,* and when I didn't get the part, Mr. Ziegler knew just what to say.

"It doesn't matter that you didn't get the part this time, Priyanka. You're good at this. We'll try for a part in a show again next year, and you'll get it next year." His faith in me caused me to realize that *one* failure doesn't mean *failure*. It means you didn't get the part this time, but you can prepare hard for your next opportunity and maybe you'll get that one. Or the one after. All these years later, I'm happy to know that Mr. Ziegler is still offering musical students at John F. Kennedy High School the same kind of encouragement and wise counsel that he offered to me.

The year I spent in Iowa gave me my first experience of a whole winter living with snow. Until then, snow meant throwing snowballs at my dad when we vacationed in Kashmir. Snow for months on end in Iowa was not nearly as glamorous. It meant waking up at 5 A.M. to help Masi shovel the driveway so she could back the car out and get us to our bus stops in time to catch the bus for school. #GetsOldFast.

At some point during the year, Amitabh Mausa had found a new job in Lincoln, Nebraska, more than three hundred miles to the west. He'd return to Cedar Rapids on weekends, but during the week it was Masi and the three of us girls. Then, in the summer of 1996, Kiran Masi changed jobs. Her new one was in Indianapolis, Indiana, almost four hundred miles to the east. It was decided that she would take a few months to find the right apartment, pack up, and move. In order to not uproot us so quickly after the start of the school year, Priyam, Pooja, and I were sent to New York City to live with my mother's brother and his family while Masi settled into the new apartment and her new job. This was not just an example of the commitment to extended family that is seen in most Indian families; it was part of the pattern in our specific family encouraged by Nani, who was adamant about her daughters having every possible opportunity to further themselves in their careers. "If you need time to focus on your studies or establish yourself in a new job, take that time," she impressed upon them. "The family will always tend to your children." And the family always had. It's part of the reason I was in America in the first place.

My cousins and I arrived in time to start the school year in New York, joining Vimal Mamu, Vimla Mami, and their children, Divya and Rohan, who had just moved from New Delhi to Flushing, Queens. Though taking us in meant there would now be five kids and two adults sharing their one-bedroom, one-bathroom apartment, they welcomed us with big smiles and open arms.

It turned out to be a great move. Queens, the largest borough of New York City and the second most densely populated, is one of the most ethnically diverse places in the world, with almost every country and language represented on its streets and in its shops and restaurants. Robert F. Kennedy Community High School, where I spent much of ninth grade, was completely multilingual and multicultural. Everyone in Flushing was from somewhere else, so blending into the crowd was effortless. Because of that, I felt a sense of ease, of belonging, that I hadn't realized I'd been missing so much.

Vanessa Smarth, born in Haiti and raised in New York, quickly became my best friend, and we're still in touch. She taught me all sorts of things about New York, and style, including how to do my hair in tiny braids, a project she enthusiastically embarked on one day after school. She'd never tried braiding hair as thick as mine, though, so it took her far longer than she'd imagined. After two hours-long sessions of watching the painfully slow progress, my clever cousin Divya rolled her eyes and said, "Just make the braids thicker. It will go quicker." So that's what we did. I ended up with a headful of braids that were a mix of super-skinny and thick, but it was the first time I'd ever had braids and I loved it.

And I loved New York. The music, the fashion, the massive laundromats with so many machines, the pizzerias on every corner. I'd never seen so many washing machines in one place and I'd never seen pizzas so big! Everything was new. Everything was exciting. New York was almost poetic in its frenzy—almost like a global India. I could meet people from China, Australia, Guatemala, Haiti, France, Russia, Greece, the Philippines, and more in this one borough. All I had to do was walk out the front door of my apartment building and the world was there to greet me. Queens was where I discovered hip-hop. Not only did I love Tupac and Biggie but also the fashion that accompanied the music—hoop earrings and puffer jackets, Rollerblades. It was in Queens that I realized I could be cool if I chose to be. I could be cute if I chose to be. *I could be whatever I wanted to be.* What a sense of power for a fourteen-year-old girl.

New York was also bursting with culture, history, and fun things to do, and Mamu and Mami wanted to make sure we took full advantage of those offerings. They took us all over the city, to places like the Statue of Liberty, the New York Hall of Science, and the Children's Museum. One day Mamu decided to take Divya, Priyam, Rohan, and me to visit the world-famous Museum of Modern Art, or the MoMA as it's known to New Yorkers. Living in Queens as we did, we had to take a bus and two subways to reach the museum, which is located in midtown Manhattan. I'm sure we viewed all sorts of great works of modern and contemporary art that day, but I only remember one of them: *The Starry Night,* by Vincent van Gogh. I must have been utterly fascinated by the deep swirls of color and texture, because apparently I stepped right up to this masterpiece of Impressionism—and touched it. A nearby security guard swooped in and immediately escorted me, my cousins, and my uncle down the escalator, into the huge lobby, and out of the building. With all the people staring at us, poor Divya was super-embarrassed on that long escalator ride down to the first floor, and I was mortified that I was the reason all of us had gotten kicked out. Somewhere inside, though, I was also silently exhilarated. I'd touched *The Starry Night*! What a story to be able to tell someday!

Queens shaped my understanding of America. I'd arrived in Cedar Rapids thinking that all Americans looked like the polished, perfect characters on television and in the movies, and that all Americans—or almost all of them—were one skin tone: white. Now I was coming to understand that America doesn't look like any one person, and it definitely doesn't look like any one character in a made-up story on TV. New York taught me that you don't have to have the same hair, eyes, skin tone, or language to be an American. It taught me that unless you're one of the Native peoples, everyone in this country has come from someplace else, and together, all of those people from someplace else have built this country.

NEXT STOP: Indianapolis, Indiana.

Having moved around so much already, it didn't seem like a big deal when Priyam, Pooja, and I packed up to rejoin Kiran Masi in March of my ninth-grade year. Like Iowa, Indiana is in the Midwest and is socially and politically conservative. In other words, it's a world away from diverse, liberal New York. Politics and diversity were the last things on my mind there, though, because Indianapolis is where I met my first boyfriend. His name was Bob (not really; I'm protecting his privacy here) and we both attended North Central High School, where he was in tenth grade. Dating him was definitely a hard flex and I fell for him in a big way. The guy played varsity football, had a really high GPA, and was everything high school dreams were made of.

Our great romance consisted mainly of Bob standing outside the door of whatever classroom I was in, out of the teacher's view but in mine. He'd wave at me and make funny faces as we both waited for the class to be over. Then he'd walk me to my next class, completely willing, it seemed, to be tardy on my behalf. We got to the point where we'd even hold hands in the hallway. He wrote me notes in his careful, beautiful handwriting. One day he took off the gold chain around his neck and put it around mine. *OMG,* I thought. *We're getting married!*

The whole romance took place inside the school, because Kiran Masi was not only a brilliant engineer, she was also a brilliant sleuth. She was somehow always magically aware of everything her kids and I were doing, making sure we weren't getting ourselves into any trouble or breaking any of her strictly enforced rules. One of those rules was that dating was absolutely not allowed. The same rule applied to my cousins, but since I was the oldest, fourteen to Priyam's eleven (and Pooja's four), it didn't apply to them yet. It was all on me.

For a while, I tried to outsmart Agent Kiran. In order to talk to Bob on the phone, I used subterfuge techniques, ones that would make my future *Quantico* character, Alex Parrish, proud: Bob would get his sister to call my house so that Masi would give the phone to me, thinking the girl on the phone was my friend. (Such tactics were possible in the late nineties, before cellphones.) Then his sister would hand the phone to Bob. But Masi was too smart for such tricks. I don't know what made her suspicious, but one evening she picked up the other landline extension—I could hear her lift the receiver even though she tried to be super-stealth when she did it—and that was the end of our phone calls.

I wasn't giving up that easily, though. In order to spend more time with Bob, I came up with a plan to enroll in summer school classes.

"I need more credits," I told my aunt. Which was actually the truth. Sex Education was a requirement to graduate, but because of all the moving and changing of schools I'd done, I still hadn't gotten around to taking it. She agreed, so, ironically, Sex Ed was the class I attended in the mornings and after which my boyfriend picked me up. Then he'd drive me to the bus stop near our apartment, where I'd pretend to have exited the bus. Then I'd walk home.

Again, Agent Kiran realized something was up. One morning she waited in the school parking lot until my class was over, and then she followed Bob's car from the school. When I got out at the bus stop and saw her pull in behind Bob, it was clear that the jig was up. Again.

We made yet another plan: I would take the bus home, and Bob would come to the house while my aunt was still at work.

One day Bob and I were sitting on the couch watching television, innocently holding hands and switching channels back and forth between BET and MTV because they had the coolest music. While Boyz II Men was playing "I'll Make Love to You," Bob inched toward me. I turned to look at him, wondering if it would be that moment—my first kiss—when suddenly, outside the window on the sidewalk below, I saw my aunt making her way up the stairs. She was glancing around furtively as if she didn't want to be seen.

I panicked. It was two in the afternoon, not her usual four o'clock arrival time, and I realized in a flash that there was no way to get him out, as we lived on the third floor of the apartment building and there was only one door. There was also no place to hide him in the two-bedroom unit. Bob and I ran to my room and I shoved him into my closet.

"Stay there until I can send her to the grocery store!" I said breathlessly. "I'll tell her we're out of something! Then you can leave!"

Kiran Masi entered the apartment and walked through it ever so slowly, finding a reason to go into every room. Into the living room. Into the kitchen. Into her bedroom. Despite the air-conditioning, a bead of sweat dropped from my brow as I waited for her next move. I sat on my bed with my biology book open, pretending to be studying, pretending that everything was fine, even though it wasn't fine *because my boyfriend was hiding in my closet.*

She was taking her time, making me wait. Finally, she stood in my doorway. "Open it," she said. She'd sniffed us out. Was it Bob's teenage cologne that gave us away?

"Open what?" I said, in my most innocent, I-didn't-do-anything-wrong voice.

"Open your closet!"

"I can't!" I stalled. "You'll be mad at me because it's such a big mess!"

"Open it now!"

I was shaking so badly I could hardly stand and walk to the closet. I'd never seen my aunt this angry. I opened the closet door, and it *was* a big mess: a boy came out.

Pandemonium ensued. Kiran Masi called my mother. It was the middle of the night in India, but she was too upset to care. "I cannot believe that she lied to my face," Masi said. "There was a boy in her closet!"

When Masi finally handed the phone to me, Mom, half-asleep and not as strict as her younger sister, simply asked, "Why did you have to get caught?" From half a world away, I could tell she was rolling her eyes.

If I'd been living with my more easygoing parents back home in India, I would have had far fewer rules to follow. But because Kiran Masi had been entrusted with my care, she felt the need to be extremely cautious and strict with me, something I now understand and respect, but back then, not so much. And I think there was another layer, too. Kiran Masi and Amitabh Mausa were first-generation immigrants, so America was a completely new country and culture for them. They were working seven hundred miles away from each other in different states so that their kids could have a great education and the prospect of a bright future. I understand now that Masi must have felt enormous pressures, but at the time, all I knew was that she was too strict. I've often wondered what my life would have been like if my aunt hadn't so generously welcomed me into her home just before I turned thirteen. Her bighearted offer changed my life and put me on the course I'm following today. Thank you forever, Masi.

BECAUSE KIRAN MASI was concerned about where my relationship with my older boyfriend was headed and firmly believed we needed to be kept apart, after the Bob-in-the-closet incident I was sent back to Vimal Mamu and Vimla Mami just before the start of tenth grade, about five months after I'd arrived in Indianapolis. I didn't mind leaving Masi's strict rules behind, but I was sad to leave my Indiana family, especially lively, funny Priyam, my companion in the small adventures of everyday life, and the perfect audience for all my romantic stories about Bob.

Vimal Mamu and Vimla Mami had left Queens and were now

living in Newton, Massachusetts, a suburb of Boston, so that Mamu could start his medical residency at Beth Israel Hospital in that city. But being exiled from Indianapolis didn't change my feelings for Bob. I was still completely in love with him and we corresponded by snail mail and email that summer. This was the late nineties, the relatively early days of personal computers and email, and unfortunately, I didn't yet know about clearing my history.

"You're not supposed to be in touch with this boy. He's bad for you," Mamu said sternly, pointing to his computer screen and the emails to and from Bob he'd discovered. (*Note to self: Technology can come back to bite you in the butt if you don't actually know how to use it.*) But once Mamu had made his disapproval known, he didn't belabor the point. In spite of the distance between my true love and me, I was committed to making the relationship work. Bob and I still wrote letters and postcards to each other, and I continued to email him, too, but now from the computer in the school library. Until I discovered that he'd started dating my best friend not long after I'd left. So much for true love.

Bye-bye, Bob.

I ENTERED NEWTON North High School at the beginning of tenth grade. There was definitely more of an ethnic and socioeconomic mix in Newton than there had been in Cedar Rapids or Indianapolis, though far less than in Queens—I don't think any school anywhere could top Queens on the diversity scale. Navigating a big new high school was always an intimidating prospect, but my teenage self was way more confident than I'd ever been before. I'd been an honor roll student since I'd arrived in the U.S., and I'd become more and more independent. And I'd had a *boyfriend,* so I was surely a woman of the world. Forget the fact that we'd hardly kissed.

Again, I spent the first few weeks eating vending-machine chips for lunch; I just couldn't bear the thought of descending the stairs into the mammoth cafeteria and seeing all the tables filled with pairs and cliques. The fact that I was entering the school in tenth grade rather than ninth, when my classmates and I would have been equally new to the school, meant that people had already found their friend groups. I noticed something I hadn't noticed in my three previous American schools: kids of the same ethnicity definitely stuck together. There was very little mixing and overlap. There were so few Indian kids in my school that I felt as if I were the only one, although that may not have been true; Divya *was* the only Indian in her grade of 550 students. Eventually I settled in and made friends—Luba, Forough, Camiele—and we hung out together during the week and sometimes went into Boston on the weekends. Our crew was one of the few integrated ones: Luba is from Azerbaijan, Forough is from Afghanistan, Camiele is American, and I am Indian. I got involved in the theater and with singing programs offered at school. I went ice-skating at what was formerly known as the MDC rink and went for runs along the Charles River, to and from the IHOP on Soldiers Field Road.

Vimla Mami was like a Pied Piper of children. She and Vimal Mamu cared for so many of us over the years—not just me, but my friends, her kids' friends, and her friends' kids, too. Even though there were five of us living in their two-bedroom, one-bathroom apartment, she had an incredible knack for making everything—chores, shopping, the routines of everyday life—fun.

Like Kiran Masi, though, Vimla Mami took her responsibility for my safety and well-being seriously, and at fifteen, I was getting a lot of attention. Too much for my family's liking. Puberty had hit hard since I'd arrived in America: flowing hair, expanding chest, swaying hips. The idea of me with my dark hair flying loose around me as I ran along the river or walked down the street worried her, because in her mind, *beautiful long hair* + *teenage girl* + *out alone* = *attracts too much attention* = *trouble!* When a simple request to tie back my hair didn't work, she tried to scare me into it by reminding me of a folkloric belief widely held in some parts of India.

"Priyanka!" she would plead. "If you walk around with loose hair, especially at night, you will be possessed by a *churail!* Please, *please* tie back your hair!"

I'd heard of *churails,* demonic ghosts said to enter a living being through its most vulnerable spot—loose hair—but I wasn't really worried about evil Indian ghosts chasing me all the way to America. If Mami had known how I was dressing at school, she wouldn't have been nearly so worried about my hair. Divya and I were all about the fashion in those days, and we'd figured out that we could go to the Salvation Army and Wal-Mart and The Limited/Express with money from Diwali or Christmas or that we'd saved by skipping lunch, and we could buy what we needed to assemble the wardrobes we wanted. (This seems somehow prophetic: artistic, independent Divya eventually did have a career in fashion, and later when I traveled to the U.S. for music, she styled me for many years.) For me, that meant a lot of tight clothes and high heels. So each morning I left the house in normal jeans and a T-shirt with my hair in a ponytail. (I granted Mami's wish at the start of the school day just to make life easier.) Once I got to school, I'd head straight to the girls' bathroom, open the backpack I brought with me every day, and pull out something much more stylish. Off came the jeans, on went the tighter, shorter skirts and the heels, the thick coats of lipstick and mascara. The queen of understatement and subtlety I was not.

Some things don't change. My locker was my new closet.

I SPENT MOST of my sophomore year in Newton hanging out with my friends and involved in school music, theater, and choir, all the while making sure to keep my grades high. The academic component of life wasn't my favorite part, but my ambition was to become either an aeronautical engineer or a criminal psychologist—Vimal Mamu steered me away from the "weird" field of psychology and toward engineering, saying, "Science is a good thing. All Indians do it." Fine advice, since I've always been fascinated by science and innovation—and so I needed good grades. Everything was great except for one thing: I was getting bullied.

Each morning after I'd pulled my quick-change trick in the girls' bathroom, I'd have to walk down "Main Street"—a hallway that ran right through the middle of the school where all the lockers were, and where the stairs to the cafeteria were located. Everyone sat and hung out on those stairs between classes, and whenever I had to pass by on my way to class, my bullies—Jenny (name changed to protect the not-so-innocent), a ninth grader, and a devoted group of her friends—would yell out to me:

"Brownie, go back to your country!"

"Do you smell curry coming?"

"Go back on the elephant you came on."

When the taunts first started, I tried to ignore them. I put my head down and made my way through that section of the hallway as quickly as I could. Then I tried avoiding Jenny and the other hecklers: I stopped taking the school bus because I knew they'd be on it; I took different routes to classes even though they were longer; I stayed away from where they congregated near the lockers. Sometimes I was alone; sometimes I was with my friends Camiele, Luba, and Forough, fellow outsiders who were treated by Jenny and her clique exactly the same way I was. The four of us clung together, an exclusive club unto ourselves, trying to create a sense of being cool and superior in order to combat the battering our egos were taking. We dressed well, and in school, we talked to almost no one except one another. It just felt safer that way.

As much as I tried to manage the bullying situation and avoid direct conflict with Jenny and her friends, things eventually escalated. I was tired of being called names, having vile things written about me in the bathroom stalls, and getting shoved against lockers and buses. I'd spoken to my guidance counselor, and although she spent quite a lot of time talking to me about it—trying to be sympathetic, I guess—I'm not sure how much time she spent talking to Jenny. Nothing much changed. I would hope the situation would be different now, as the dangers of bullying are far better understood, but back then, there didn't seem to be any school policy or any repercussions for the offenders.

I was hugely relieved when my sophomore year came to an end. I needed some time to recover my equilibrium, and maybe Jenny and her crew needed some time to grow up. And summer meant that it was time to pile in the car and take a family road trip, just like I'd done with my parents when I was a child. All of my mom's siblings and their families were included. Kiran Masi and her family and Vimal Mamu and his family were joined by my mom's other two sisters—Sophia (Leela) Masi and Neela (Munnu) Masi—and Parwez Mausa, and my cousins Sana, Irfan, and Parisa, and we'd take two or three cars and hit the road. During the years I was in America, we traveled all over: to Yellowstone National Park in Wyoming; to the Carolinas or to Maine on the East Coast; to the windy city of Chicago on Lake Michigan or Kansas in the Great Plains. Mom and her four siblings were so close to one another and raised us nine cousins as siblings, taking the time and energy to make sure all of us got together regularly and really knew one another. It clearly made a lasting impression on me, as I do that now with my cousins and their kids.

Unfortunately, the start of my junior year meant the start of bullying again. I'd essentially been on my own with the problem for almost a whole year. Divya knew about it in a very vague way, and of course Camiele, Luba, and Forough at school, and my guidance counselor. But I hadn't told my uncle and aunt. Nor had I told my parents in our weekly or biweekly phone calls. I hadn't wanted to involve them in something I thought I should be able to handle myself. My parents had raised me to be someone who finds solutions, and since I hadn't been able to find a way to stop the bullying, I was starting to think that my solution was to go back home.

The hostility coming at me from out of nowhere, for no apparent reason, was getting just too hard to process. While I had been happy and self-confident when I arrived in Newton, my self-esteem was now suffering. My parents had taught me that confidence is not a permanent state of being, a piece of wisdom I still believe. It's something you can work to develop and something you have to work to maintain. Well, the taunts and the graffiti and the physical aggression had done their jobs, and no matter how hard I worked, I couldn't maintain my sense of self-worth. I started to believe that I was somehow less than those around me. I couldn't sleep. My grades dropped.

I've thought a lot about this whole painful period over the years, and long ago I came to the conclusion that I will never know exactly why Jenny and her friends, both black and white, targeted me and my friends. Because we looked and sounded different? I imagine this was a large part of it. What's ironic here is that Newton was so much more diverse than Cedar Rapids and Indianapolis, where my schools were largely homogenous and predominantly white. So why were my friends and I harassed for being different here, where difference hypothetically should have been better understood? Were there other factors contributing to the bullying in Newton? Perhaps there were, perhaps there weren't. I will never know for sure.

ONE CALL HOME was all it took. My parents heard my pain, confusion, and complete emotional exhaustion, and my mom was on the next plane with my brother.

Living in the U.S. for high school was a decision I'll always be glad I made. It brought me closer to my aunts, uncles, and cousins, and it opened up a new universe of people from different countries and cultures. The exposure to such an array of distinctly different people broadened my thinking and helped me to interpret the world more independently. It allowed me to see that I didn't have to be just one way, or from just one place. It helped me grow up, and it absolutely influenced my global outlook today. But at that moment, I couldn't appreciate any of those things. My heart hurt. My spirit hurt. I just wanted to be home, protected by my parents in a cocoon of comfort and safety.

Mom accompanied me to school to help me clean out my locker, which was really only a formality at that point, since there were no books inside it, just makeup and various wardrobe items.

"Where are your school things?" she asked.

I shrugged. "I don't need them, Mom. I'm smart here in America." (*Note to self: Pride goeth before a fall.*)

Mom shook her head and we had a big laugh. She was always cool about things like that and she deserves props for it. In times of strife, rather than being judgmental she's totally supportive of me. Instead of reprimanding me or telling me how something should be done or should have been done, she's always let me find my own way. At the same time, she makes sure I know I can fall back into her protective arms.

My dad was like that, too. I never heard a "because I said so" in my life. Each of my parents is an example of the kind of parent I want to be someday: one who sees their child as an individual, someone to be raised to live their own life thoughtfully, intelligently, independently, and empathetically.

That day, as Mom and I stuffed into a backpack what was inside the metal locker—all the bits and pieces of my thirteen months in Newton, who I'd been and who I was still becoming—it was hard not to feel like I'd failed. But slowly, over time, Mom and Dad each helped me to rebuild the confidence I'd lost. It was only fitting that Mom was with me again on that final day in Newton North High School. She'd been with me when I first made the decision to stay in the U.S. just over three years earlier in Cedar Rapids, and now she was there on my last day as I left a place and an experience that had helped form me. The symmetry felt right to me, as if there were bookends to a chapter of my life I was now closing.

Five days later we were on a plane heading home.

4

TEEN TO QUEEN

I'm not a girl,
Not yet a woman.
PERFORMED BY BRITNEY SPEARS

THE JOURNEY FROM America to India takes more than twenty hours and used to require a layover somewhere. Mom chose Paris and built in a couple of extra days there—partly because she has a travel bug, which is why I call her "heels on wheels," but also to help me out of the funk I was in after I'd made the decision to come home. She understood that I needed something to revive my spirits and help me to dream big again, and where better to feel life's sparkle than in the City of Light?

Mom was right. Paris, with its sophistication and elegance, its fashion and food and culture, was the perfect transition for me before returning home. The boat ride we took on the Seine is my most visceral memory of that city—the sounds of the water and the birds, the feeling of the sun on my face as we glided past famous landmarks like the Eiffel Tower and Notre-Dame. There were other amazing things to gaze at, too—like all those French boys. I must admit they did divert a large portion of my sixteen-year-old attention from the advertised sights.

Our trip to the Louvre was also memorable. We decided to go straight to the *Mona Lisa* upon our arrival, to start with the biggest attraction and work our way down from there. There was a crowd behind a barricade in front of the painting, watchful guards hovering nearby. When we got near the front, I told Mom I wanted a picture of Mona and me, but with the people and the barricade, I couldn't get close enough for a good one.

"Well then, go closer," Mom prodded.

"But there's a barricade."

She raised her camera and lowered her voice. "Just do it fast. It's only a photo. Go on."

I quickly stepped over the barricade, trying to be surreptitious and nonchalant at the same time, and Mom snapped the photo. *Flash.* Which was *Interdit! Forbidden! Nishedh!* And so was stepping over the barrier. It will come as no surprise to anyone that Mom, Sid, and I were immediately escorted out of the museum. According to my mom, as the security guards brusquely showed us the exit, Sid kept asking, "Why are they being so mean to us?"

And now the *Starry Night* episode makes so much more sense. #AppleDoesntFallFarFromTree.

WE LEFT THE warm air of Paris and landed in hot, humid New Delhi. Home. I was finally home. I hadn't realized how much I'd missed the sights and sounds and smells of my native country until we emerged from the terminal to look for Dad. And there he was! Looking from Mom to Sid and back to Mom again, puzzled.

"Where's Mimi?" he asked. He was standing literally two feet away from me.

I looked at him and gave a little wave. "Right here, Dad."

He cleared his throat and nodded. "Yes. Yes, of course," he said, offering me a slightly awkward hug.

I'd left India a gawky, almost thirteen-year-old tomboy and was returning a womanly sixteen-year-old. My parents hadn't visited me in the States because they were just starting their own hospital in Bareilly following my father's early retirement from the army; a trip to the U.S. would require far more time than they could take off. I hadn't been home to India because I'd been traveling back and forth between living situations so much that I couldn't take the long trip home without further disrupting my studies. Just over three years had passed. My hair was long and full and I'd grown several inches; with my big wedge heels, I was almost five foot ten. My body had filled out with curves and I was wearing the clothes to show it. In fact, my mom had repeated the trick that Vimla Mami had played on her when she and Sid had arrived to pick me up. Mami had encouraged me to wear very short shorts and my highest wedge heels when we'd gone to meet them at the airport in Boston. On the strictness scale, she was about halfway between Kiran Masi and my mom. She didn't necessarily approve of my shortest shorts for general wear, but she thought it would be fun to give Mom a little jolt upon her arrival. She didn't let me in on her thinking, though.

"*These* short shorts?" I kept asking her. "*These* shoes?"

"Yes, yes. You look lovely," Vimla Mami assured me, smiling sweetly.

Mom was jolted all right, and she decided it would be fun to play the same trick on Dad, so she encouraged me to wear a sleeveless white Tommy Hilfiger dress that was short and tight. Super-high platform shoes and big earrings completed the look. This time

I understood what was happening, and I wasn't surprised when Dad didn't recognize me. My mom had a big laugh. My dad not so much.

Returning home to Bareilly revived me. Like a withering plant that is finally given water and sunlight, I came back to life. My confidence had suffered a terrible blow from the bullying, but as my father had taught me, with each new experience comes a new opportunity to reinvent yourself. I recognized that as long as I could find the confidence I'd lost, I could then *choose* who I wanted to be.

The school year had already started at the Army Public School in Bareilly, where I was to be entering eleventh grade. There's a formality to schools in India that largely doesn't exist in America, at least not from what I've seen. Students in most Indian schools wear uniforms, and the relationship between teachers and pupils is much more formal. The whole atmosphere is generally a little quieter. It was into this environment that I chose to wear tight jeans, a long T-shirt, huge hoop earrings, and some serious swag to the meeting Dad and I had with the principal of the school prior to my starting classes. People noticed. Luckily, Principal Kandpal had been posted with my father in their army days, so he forgave the inappropriate dress.

The more that kids came out of their classrooms into the courtyard to stare at me that day, the more I loved it. I became an instant mini-celebrity. As a result, I walked straighter, taller, bigger. This was how I wanted to feel. This was the New Me. There was empowerment in reinvention. I started to leave behind the narrative that the mean girls in Newton had written for me and began writing one for myself.

It was more than just the clothes that day that gave me my new status, though. Kids in small towns all over India dreamed of making it to the Big City one day, whether that was Mumbai or Bangalore or Kolkata or Jaipur. I hadn't just left my hometown, I'd left the country. I'd left the *continent,* and at a time when long-distance travel like that was not nearly as common. I'd made it to the land depicted in all of those bright, shiny TV shows we loved watching. For all my fellow students knew, the high schools I'd attended in America were just like West Beverly Hills High School, the fictional school in *Beverly Hills, 90210.* After my years in the States, I not only dressed differently but I walked differently, I talked differently, I thought differently. And this time I enjoyed being different.

When I saw how people were looking at me—as if I were a fantastical, brightly colored unicorn—I realized that I wanted to see myself that way, too. I wanted to feel interesting and unusual and amazing, to feel that I was deserving of people's gaze. I wanted to leave behind my fear of being different, the quality that seemed to cause trouble for me in America. From now on, if I was going to be an anomaly, I was going to be the shiniest damn anomaly around. I had no idea if I could pull off that sort of attitude or not, but I was sure as hell going to try.

I had to wear a uniform at my new school, there was no way around that, but I tried to do it on my own terms. Skirts were supposed to be below the knee, which I thought didn't look cool enough, so I kept my skirt above the knee. If I could just make it through the morning assembly and into my classroom, I was usually safe; as is true in most schools in India, kids stayed in one classroom for all their academics. Since I was always a back-bencher, staying as far away from the teachers as possible, there was little chance that I'd get in trouble for my skirt length or the fact that I was wearing makeup—very subtly applied—which was not allowed.

Unless I got called upon to answer a question, which meant standing up. There were a couple of teachers who had no patience with my rule-bending. "Are you wearing makeup?" one of them would ask slowly, drawing out the words as she scrutinized my face. Maybe I should be thankful to her, since her attention to my appearance definitely motivated me to perfect my makeup application techniques. My chemistry teacher seemed to love to bust me on my skirt length. One day when she called on me she was in a particularly exasperated mood. She took one look at my skirt, strode to the back of the room, and tore out the hem. "There," she said. "That's the length for a good skirt." I lost the battle on that particular day, but it didn't matter. I was always going to find a way to get around the fashion rules.

I'm sure the pressure of having switched school systems in the middle of high school contributed to my pushing-the-boundaries behavior. When I'd started high school in Cedar Rapids, I'd quickly become one of the best students in my grade because the Indian schools I'd attended were so far ahead of my new high school in terms of content covered. The flip side of this was that when I returned to India three years later, I was seriously behind.

On top of that, my board exams were looming. In most of the Indian education system, the board exams taken during the tenth and twelfth grades are crucial to your academic career, the boards taken in twelfth grade especially so. Not *too* much pressure. As a future engineering student, I had to study physics, chemistry, math, and computer science. I felt like I was falling further and further behind every day, and in order to close the gap, I got tutored in chemistry before school, and math and physics after school.

At the close of each school day, I would travel to my tutor's house in an open rickshaw with a few other girls, and sometimes boys would follow on their bikes. I didn't engage in conversation with these boys—you weren't supposed to if boys followed you or talked to you, so I dutifully kept my head down and tried to ignore them. But my father was concerned by the attention, especially after the day that a guy who'd followed me home after tutoring jumped our gate and climbed up to the balcony of my room, terrifying us all. Dad immediately had wrought iron bars installed on all the windows of the house. Now my bedroom felt like a cage, but at least it was a safe one.

One day my worried father sat me down for a heart-to-heart talk. "You can't wear tight jeans," he said, afraid of the attention I was getting and how out of control it all felt. "Boys are following you, and it's dangerous." His solution was to try to convince me to wear Indian clothes.

At first I agreed to the plan, and twelve stylish *salwar kurtas* were made for me. When I later pushed back against the pant and tunic sets, my parents and I compromised: I would be allowed to wear jeans, but only if I wore loose shirts with them. So I went into my dad's closet and took out a bunch of his favorite shirts, which I would then tie at my waist. To complete the look, I pulled off a few of the top buttons so the shirts couldn't be fastened up all the way. Basically, I destroyed his shirts. He was, of course, not happy about that, but somehow—I'm not actually sure how—I escaped serious consequences. Mom ended up buying him a few new shirts, and they kept those purchases locked in his closet. I'm surprised they trusted that solution, given my history of getting into Mom's closet, but I guess they realized that at this point I was busy getting into other kinds of mischief.

My one true regret about that time was my relationship with Sid. When I moved back home, the age difference between us was great enough to keep us in different worlds, especially since we'd already spent so many years apart. I was busy being a teenager, having friends and going to parties, starting yet another new school and preparing for my pre-boards, which were practice exams for the actual boards; my eight-year-old brother wasn't really on my radar. My parents' attention, too, was focused more on me than it was on him, as they dealt with helping me readjust culturally and catch up academically on top of all their responsibilities with the new hospital. Because of that, Sid depended a lot on my mom's mom, Nani, who had been living with us since his birth. It would be years before he and I would live close enough to each other and spend enough time together to develop the relationship we have now.

While academics were causing me a lot of stress in my junior year, I was having a blast in other areas. I was participating in things I'd excelled at and gotten positive attention for ever since my days at La Martiniere—dancing and singing especially. I had my own tight-knit group of friends at the Army School—Gullu, Karan, Vikas, Avinash, Moniesha, Rajat, and Andrea to name a few—and we did typical teenage things, which I hadn't done in the U.S. We'd get together and go to friends' parties; we had crushes; we dated. I loved the fact that I didn't have to sneak around like I did in the States. I relished the freedom and the feeling of being treated more like an adult.

IN MIDDLE SCHOOL, the Bareilly Club is where I used to hang out with my friends after class, talking and ambling around the grounds. Now, in high school, I looked forward to spending time there in the evenings, accompanying Dad and Mom, who went there most Friday and Saturday nights. We always dressed up a little, which I loved. Dad had to be in a shirt and a tie or a casual suit, Mom would usually wear a sari, and I'd wear a dressy shirt and nice jeans or a skirt. And my platform shoes, of course. And big earrings. Inside the club's large, heavy gate was a massive garden on one side where you could eat outdoor dinners and have bonfires; on the other side was another garden for strolling through. The air always smelled so fresh, so sweet. The main building of the club itself was an old brick building, and inside was the dining room and a large space that was used for a variety of functions: Sometimes people played cards there, sometimes an indoor/outdoor bar was set up there, and on important holidays like Diwali and Holi, there would be big parties with a DJ and a dance floor. From time to time Dad would host a night of Tambola, a bingo-like game, but racier when he was running it.

One such festive night at the club in May 1999, after the end of my junior year and two months before my seventeenth birthday, we ran into the local district commissioner at the time, Deepak Shingal, and his wife, Anita, who were friends of my parents. It just happened to be the night of the annual May Queen Ball, and Mrs. Shingal encouraged me to enter the competition, saying I was pretty and smart and that's just what May Queens were supposed to be. I had never once considered the idea of competing for a beauty title. Sure, some boys followed me on my way to tutoring, presumably because they thought I was pretty, but I didn't really think of myself as someone who could legitimately enter a *beauty* contest.

When I voiced my doubts, Mrs. Shingal, who was on the judges' panel for the ball, responded, "I've done this for a few years, and I can tell you from experience that if you sign up for this, Priyanka, there's a good chance you can win. And tell me," she added, knowing the answer already, "what's the worst thing that could happen if you enter and *don't* win?" I saw her point.

I told my parents about the contest, and since it was a small event taking place at the club that he knew, and within the community that he knew, Dad was totally comfortable with it and actually excited about the idea. I think he understood how much joy I got from winning, and perhaps, like Mrs. Shingal, he thought I had a chance at it. I really did love getting trophies and medals in debates and elocutions, as well as in dance and singing competitions.

When I was crowned May Queen later that night, the "fake it till you make it" brand of confidence I'd been projecting was somehow transformed into the real thing. The win reinforced the belief that my dad had tried to impress upon me when I was much younger: that if I wanted to, I could reinvent myself when I moved to a new place. When I moved back home from the U.S., I chose to be a new person, and my reinvention looked like it was working. Part of that reinvention, I was realizing, meant continually digging deep for courage, establishing and reestablishing my confidence. Just three hours earlier, when I'd been reluctant to enter the May Queen Ball, I hadn't had any. Now I did. The idea that confidence is not a permanent state was crystallizing in me, and I was beginning to sense that the harder I worked at being able to access it when I needed it, the better it would serve me.

ALL OF THIS was well and good, but I still had to take my boards. In a country where so many people are struggling for survival, a lot of emphasis is put on formal education. This pays off because kids in India who attend high school—not all have that privilege—are set up to be so academically advanced that they are able to excel at the college and university level whether in India, the U.S., or anywhere else.

Given the academic struggles I'd had since returning from the United States, I sometimes berated myself for not having stayed there to graduate. It would have made everything so much easier because I wouldn't have had to take the boards—but then again, I'd been miserable in Newton at the end. Here I was thriving. When I wasn't stressed out about academics, I was having a great time with my friends and enjoying extracurriculars.

The Army Public School was divided into four "houses," or sections, and throughout the year we had intra-school competitions in academics, debates, sporting events, and performing arts. In my senior year I was chosen by the students in my house, Nilgiri, to be

Girls' House Captain. Every fall the school celebrated something called Annual Day, a competition between the four houses in the form of a full day devoted to races, relays, plays, concerts, and dance performances. At the end of the day, the house that had been awarded the most points would get the Winner's Cup, and as the Girls' House Captain for Nilgiri—there was also a Boys' House Captain for each of the houses—I *really* wanted that cup. I made sure my team was super well prepared for every aspect of the show, and I also inserted myself into just about every performance we did that day—group dance, solo dance, theater, choral. Afterward, I was asked for my autograph by a young girl who said, "I want to grow up and be like you." And if that wasn't weird enough, I was soon asked to judge a local dance competition in the city. I felt like I was being treated as more important than I actually was and it was a strange new feeling.

There are always going to be two ends of any particular spectrum, though, and at the other end of this one, there were kids who thought I was being opportunistic, or that I was just showing off. I suppose I can see why some might think that, but for me and my male co-captain, the goal was to win, and that's what our house-mates wanted, too. I might have lagged in my studies because of falling so far behind during those years in the U.S., but I could hold my own with anyone when it came to performing. Occasionally I had the thought that the positive attention I got from all my extra-curriculars was a gift from some divine presence who had witnessed the difficulties I'd had in Massachusetts, a way of saying, "You sure had to put up with a lot of crap. Here's a little something to help make up for all that." But mostly, I didn't overthink it. Who knew that within a few years performing would become my way of life?

And yes, Nilgiri won the cup.

As the autumn wore on, I tried to motivate myself academically by concentrating on a new goal: going to Australia to study. Of the career paths that were normal for my family to consider—doctor, engineer, businessperson—with my affinity for numbers and my love of math and physics (well, my love of them until returning to India), engineering appealed to me most. I'd always been fascinated by the physics of modern technology—ships, trains, computers, televisions, and planes. Planes, perhaps, especially, since the time I'd flown alone on a military transport to Leh when I was nine and my father was transferred there. It was my first time flying and I don't think I ever quite got over my disbelief that something so huge and so heavy could actually stay in the air, and eventually I began to refine the idea of "engineering" into "aeronautical engineering."

It was an aeronautical engineering program at a college in Melbourne, Australia, that had piqued my interest, and in order to complete the scholarship application for it, I needed to include a passport-type photo. There happened to be a small photo studio at Butler Plaza, an outdoor mall near our house, the sort of place where a beauty salon was next to a fast-food shop that was next to a music store. Everyone in Bareilly hung out at Butler Plaza in the evenings: the cool kids would be by the music store; newlyweds and couples would be near the restaurants. My parents would go almost every night after dinner to get *paan,* a preparation combining betel leaf, areca nut, and optional other ingredients that's a bit like chewing tobacco without the tobacco.

The photographer at Suri Photo Studio took a batch of photos of me, and after reviewing the proofs, he asked if he could take some modeling shots. "Of course!" I said, offering to go home and get more clothes immediately. When I called Mom, super-excited about the opportunity, her cooler head prevailed. Like any good parent, she injected a dose of reality into the situation, warning me that it could be a shady situation. We compromised: I could get the additional shots on a later date as long as she accompanied me. And those additional photos were the ones that Sid had Mom send off to the Miss India contest not long afterward. Those shots still adorn the Suri Photo Studio walls in Bareilly.

Even though Sid was the one pushing for it, I think one of the reasons Mom agreed to send my pictures to Miss India was because she could see how anxious I was about my boards and felt that some kind of break in the action and pressure was needed. At this point, I was certain I would fail the boards. I took extra classes and worked really hard. My cousin Kunal, who we call Sunny, even flew down and stayed with us for two months to help me with science and math. But still I was struggling. I told my parents that I might want to take a gap year so that I could devote more time to catching up academically.

In November of twelfth grade, about a month and a half after Mom and Sid submitted the photos, I was sitting at home eating lunch on a quick break between school and tutoring when I received the call that would change my life. Engrossed in the old Bollywood movie *Mera Naam Joker,* I picked up the ringing phone, eyes still glued to the television screen.

"Hi, this is Ela from *Femina* magazine," I heard the businesslike voice on the other end of the line say. "You've qualified on the short list for the Miss India pageant representing North India, and the preliminary round is the day after tomorrow in Delhi. This is the address." I scribbled down what she said. "Be there at eight A.M. sharp, and make sure you bring a swimsuit and heels." She hung up. Clearly she had about a million of these phone calls to make.

I was stunned. Having no idea that Mom and Sid had submitted an application, in my ridiculously innocent mind I thought that the pageant people had somehow heard about my local May Queen win. "Oh my God, Mom! I'm so popular in Bareilly that even the Miss India pageant knows who I am!"

Once Mom explained the situation, I realized what an opportunity I had been given. The question was: Who was going to tell

Dad that I would be participating in a *beauty pageant* in *New Delhi* right before my pre-board exams? The pre-boards were in January and the actual boards were in March. I needed to do well at them to get a good job and secure my future, because people in my family were respected professionals with conventional, sensible careers. They did not parade around in swimsuits and high heels.

Ever the brilliant strategist, Mom came up with a plan. "When he comes home today, just be really nice," she said. "No attitude. I'll put some music on, we'll all have dinner together, and then you'll go up to your room and I'll deal with it. I'll talk to him over champagne." Champagne was always involved whenever Mom had to convince Dad to agree to something, and this night was no exception. Dad's only stipulation was that I not go alone. Which meant that Mom would go with me to the preliminary competition. But first we needed to pack and get ourselves to New Delhi, India's capital, which was fortunately reachable by train in about five hours.

Oddly, what I felt first and foremost was not excitement but relief: relief from the pressure of studying and the pressure of the looming exams. While I was happy, of course, about making the preliminaries, I didn't take my chances for advancement seriously; there was simply no world in which I would make it beyond this preliminary round to the next round of the Miss India pageant. There was no real reason to be nervous, nor did the opportunity spark my inherent sense of competitiveness—yet.

While beauty pageants are often viewed as superficial in the U.S., in a lot of other countries they are generally more highly respected. From what I've observed, pageants around the world tend to emphasize not only looks, as some American pageants seem to do, but also personality and eloquence. You need to be able to be confident and command attention when you speak, to know what you're talking about and be well versed in the subjects you're addressing. For sure, you have to be a certain height and a certain weight (their standards), but if you impress the judges with intelligence, confidence, and compassion, that's what they'll focus on.

When I was growing up, women who became Miss India were honored and respected. I remember how much I admired the first Indian to be crowned Miss Universe—Sushmita Sen—who won in 1994 when she was eighteen and I was twelve. She was a self-made girl who ended up winning the Miss India and Miss Universe pageants in no small part because of her incredible ability to form thoughts in commanding English, which wasn't even her first language. The year she won, I made a collage for my room of her newspaper clippings because it was such a big deal that an Indian girl had won the Miss Universe crown. The icing on the cake for my country that year was that Aishwarya Rai, another Indian, was crowned Miss World. A harbinger of things to come, perhaps?

Mom and I reached Delhi the day before the preliminary rounds, and Mom took me to a salon to get me *zhuzhed*. It was like a makeover montage in a romantic comedy: I got my unruly hair blown out, my thick eyebrows threaded, and a rare and luxurious mani-pedi. After more than a year of largely being an academic cockroach, I could feel the weight of my stress lifting to the point where I was almost lighthearted.

On the Big Day, I woke up at the crack of dawn, did my makeup—which at that point consisted only of mascara, lots of eyeliner, lipstick, and a dab of powder—put on an outfit that Mom and I had spent hours of deliberation on (can't remember what it was now), and walked into the lobby of the Ashoka Hotel with Mom at my side. I felt super-relaxed and confident about my new look. But that feeling lasted only until the hotel doors flew open and a bevy of impossibly tall, gorgeous girls entered the lobby and floated toward the elevators, leaving me in a cloud of their perfume and my own insecurity.

I turned to Mom. "Let's go home."

"Let's go *shopping*," my mom responded, addressing a fixable problem we'd both just become acutely aware of upon seeing those fashionably attired beauties I'd be competing against. We made a quick dash to a nearby store, upgraded my outfit to something more appropriately sophisticated and glamorous, and returned to the hotel lobby to wait for my name to be called. When it was, I went upstairs to a hotel suite where the preliminary session was taking place. There was a large living room that had been cleared out to hold the panel of judges. Pradeep Guha, who at that time was the national director of the *Femina* Miss India pageant and the president of Bennett, Coleman and Company, publisher of *The Times of India* and *Femina* magazine, which runs the Miss India pageant, was there. So was Sathya Saran, the editor of *Femina;* two other people from *The Times of India*—the biggest newspaper in the country and the main sponsor and owner of the Miss India franchise; and a popular Delhi model. They sat behind a long table chatting to one another as I was shown into a bedroom.

The room was overflowing with beautiful girls. They were lounging on the bed, perched on the windowsill, busy in the bathroom shaving their legs and jockeying for position in front of one single mirror. Ela and another woman from the pageant were calmly taking height and weight measurements. I could make out snippets of conversation in the cacophony. Savvy was talking about her new Parachute hair commercial, Mona described her latest *Gujarati* magazine cover, Lakshmi gave the details of her new sari campaign. Many of the girls seemed to know one another. I knew no one, and at seventeen, I was the youngest of the candidates. The last thing I'd done was go to chemistry class. My only real qualification was having won the May Queen Ball, where there were roughly sixty people in the audience. Millions would be watching the television broadcast of the Miss India contest.

After our measurements were taken, we were walked out, one by one, in front of the judges in the clothes we'd arrived in. First we stated our names, then our aspirations. When I answered, I was quickly asked if I was American; since I'd just come back from the U.S., I still had a full-blown American accent. I was certain that I'd be voted out after that round because everybody else was speaking Indian English, which is British sounding and in my mind far more chic than American English.

When another group of girls was brought up to the hotel suite, my group was dismissed. We all took the elevator to the lobby and went looking for our respective families as soon as the doors opened. As Mom listened to every detail that spilled forth from my mouth about the preceding hour or so, I could practically hear the gears in her brain turning.

Preparation. Logical thought. Strategy. This was always the Chopra Family Plan. Whenever I had a decision to make or was worried about something, we would talk about every possible scenario and outcome and then strategize a plan around it. That day was no different. Mom and I sat for a few hours talking through every possibility as if we were solving a math equation with multiple variables and unknowns. "What's the worst that can happen?" she asked me. "That you don't make it to the next round? If so, we get some ice cream, take a train, and go home. At least you got your eyebrows done and your hair will still look great. But if you *do* make it to the next round, then we need to think about what makes you better than everyone else in the room."

I thought about the incredibly gorgeous girls upstairs, girls who were far more beautiful and sophisticated and experienced than I was. "Nothing about me is better than these girls."

"You can articulate your thoughts in English better than most people, and that could be a strength," she said. I thought about that a moment. For the most part, the pageant was being conducted in

English, so maybe I did have an advantage there, since I'd grown up speaking Hindi and English in equal measure. (If a girl wasn't comfortable speaking English, she could speak in Hindi, though that was an option few contestants chose.) "And you probably know more about current events and what's going on in the world." I was suddenly grateful for the rule in our family that every night around the dinner table we'd talk not only about my parents' work and Sid's and my school but, as we got older, about global events, too. It was my parents' way of giving us a broader sense of the world.

A few minutes later, I learned I'd made it into the second round. Once I was back upstairs with the girls who had also made the cut, the boost I'd experienced from advancing to round two dissolved instantly. No matter how good my English was or how well versed I was in world events, it wouldn't help me now: we were told to put on our swimsuits and heels.

This made no sense to me. Who does this? Who struts around in a swimsuit and heels in a hotel room? It's not natural! I'd seen girls do it onstage in pageants before, but man, it did not feel good. I'd always been a tomboy and so I had scars on my legs from tree climbing and falls and bike crashes. I had stretch marks and dry skin. I was self-conscious about my behind and my back. (Naturally, if I couldn't see a particular part of my body, I didn't want anyone else seeing it, either.) I was so nervous during this round that instead of sticking my butt out and sucking my stomach in the way I would now, my butt was clenched tight, like a dog with its tail tucked in. Somehow I managed to walk in front of the judges without betraying my discomfort, and even managed to have a semi-normal conversation with them about my life's aspirations.

Judge: "So, Priyanka Chopra: What do you want to be?"

Me: "I want to be an aeronautical engineer."

Judge: "That's great! Now turn around and walk back toward the door."

I did as requested, thinking, *I hate this! Smile!*

That short walk felt like it would never end. I made it back to my starting point, then spun around as quickly as possible so I could untuck my tail and end my torture. Convinced I wouldn't make it to the third round, I relaxed enough to be a little more myself.

"I hope I get the opportunity to compete further!" I blurted. At least that's what I think I said. There were smiles, maybe even some laughter. Whatever I lacked in the perfect skin and perfect butt department may have been salvaged by my burst of spontaneous enthusiasm.

When I was back downstairs again with Mom, I told her about the swimsuit and the heels and my clenched butt and how much I'd hated that round. It hadn't seemed to be an issue for the models among us (almost everyone else); they were comfortable in their own skins, not just in bathing suits, but in anything they wore. They made gliding across a room in a slightly unreal situation look so natural, but clearly it wasn't natural to me at that point.

Mom was confused. "What are you talking about? You wear a bathing suit all the time on the beach, in the pool, at the club," she pointed out. "You were on your swim team at school. It didn't matter then, so why does it matter now?"

That made me think. She was right, sort of. Not completely, but sort of. I decided to let my discomfort go, at least for the time being.

I looked around the hotel lobby at the girls sitting with their families and friends and saw Miss Chandigarh, who was from a city in the northern state of Punjab. She was a beautiful, light-skinned girl, so that was another thing that was playing in my head: *I'm dark, I'm dusky, and that's not beautiful.* When I was growing up, my father's brother used to call me *Kaali*, which means "black." "Kaali's here!" he'd say when the whole family got together. (With the exception of my father, my brother, and me, most of my family is lighter-skinned.) It was intended as a joke, but given the premium put on light skin in Indian society and in many others around the world, it didn't feel like one to me. At thirteen, I started making homemade "fairness" concoctions, mixing talcum powder with various creams to try to change my skin tone. In fact, I continued to use skin-lightening products, whether homemade or store-bought, until a realization I had some years into the future. But we're getting ahead of ourselves.

Finally, someone from *The Times of India* came down with a list of the ten girls who had made it to the next and final round of the day. I was shocked when Miss Chandigarh's name did not get called. *Let me repeat: Miss Chandigarh's name did not get called.* But my name did.

At nine o'clock that night, the ten finalists of the day went back upstairs to wait for the last Q&A session. We were all exhausted, having been there for thirteen hours at that point. One by one we were called in. I was one of the last to go before the judges, and when it was all over and I was packing up to leave for good, I asked one of them, with what I now recognize as astounding naïveté, if I could have his number. Just in case I needed to get in touch.

"I have my board exams coming up, and if this is not going to happen, I'd just like to know," I said. "I don't think I can wait for the official letter. I'd rather you just text me."

I know, exceptionally millennial. (Which, by the way, I am. By the skin of my teeth.)

It turns out that I'd asked Pradeep Guha himself, the publisher of *Femina* and the director of the pageant, for his number. He laughed at my audacity. Apparently, he found my confidence so amusing that he wrote his actual name and number down on a card and gave it to me. "Text me if you need anything."

When I met up with Mom downstairs and showed her the card, she looked at the name, picked up a copy of *Femina,* and pointed to the masthead. Oops.

BACK IN BAREILLY, I returned to my normal life, or tried to, anyway. None of my friends and no one at school knew that I had entered this pageant. Life appeared to go on as usual. I continued prepping for my exams—this was November and my pre-boards were in two months; my board exams were two months after that—but I was on pins and needles, dying to know what was going to happen, how the rest of my life (or at least the next few weeks and months) would unfold. If I didn't make it to the pageant, I'd have to take the boards and I was terrified, knowing I would fail. So after four or five unbearable days without any word, I took matters into my own hands and I texted Pradeep Guha. After all, he'd given me his number and told me to text him if I needed anything.

I want to be able to plan my life, so it would be great to know if I'm going to be part of the pageant. Impatience and impudence clearly went hand in hand in me.

After a few interminable hours, he texted back: *Have you not received a letter?*

And sure enough, official notification arrived the next day. I'd made the cut. I was to travel to Mumbai for a month of pageant preparation and training.

Fortunately, some important preliminary planning had already taken place. In New Delhi, Mom and I had stayed with my father's older brother, Brigadier Vijay Chopra, and his wife, Dr. Savita Chopra. In Indian culture, elders have traditionally been given a strong voice in a family's decision-making process. Parents will generally have the final say in decisions regarding their children—

not always, as the balance of authority varies from family to family and generation to generation—but the opinions of older siblings and parents matter. Sometimes that's a blessing; sometimes it's a curse. My father was one of six children, four boys and two girls, and my dad and his older brother, or *Badepapa,* always had a say in their siblings' lives. While we'd been in New Delhi, the family was divided between whether I should go to Mumbai or continue my schooling if I made it to the next round. While at first Badepapa didn't want me going, after considering the reasoning of his wife, *Badimama,* he came to see the pageant as an opportunity for me. And so it was agreed that if I made it into the next round I could go to Mumbai, but not alone: no matter what, either Mom or Dad needed to be with me there. Since both of my parents had medical practices at the hospital that they jointly ran, they knew that whoever didn't accompany me would be covering two practices. Nani was there to help with Sid, but no matter how you looked at it, there would be a lot of responsibility on the shoulders of the parent who remained home. Eventually it was decided that it would be Mom who would go with me, since we had traveled the pageant journey together so far, and Dad who'd stay behind. It would only be for four weeks, after all.

With that decision already made, once we knew I was moving on in the pageant, Mom quickly arranged for us to stay with her cousin Neelam Verma. Neelam Masi and her husband, Manoj, lived in the suburbs of Mumbai in a town called Kandivali, almost two hours from Juhu—an hour-and-a-half train ride to Vile Parle followed by a twenty-minute rickshaw trip—where most of the Miss India training would start each day at seven in the morning. Neelam Masi's offer to take us in was incredibly generous, since she and her husband had two small children, Soumaya and Chinmay, and lived in a two-bedroom apartment. Mom and I slept in the children's bedroom, and Manoj Mausa and Neelam Masi took the kids into their bed, where all four of them slept together. Each night, Neelam Masi made dinner for all of us and the next day's lunch for Mom and me. The next morning she rose at 4 A.M. to pack up our provisions before we headed into Juhu, and before she prepared for her day of tutoring local students and looking after her children.

My mother's cousin, God rest her soul, did not need to do this for me, and us. Whenever I've needed something, members of my extended family have always stepped in to provide it. I've seen their love and generosity in action my whole life: from my youngest days when I lived with Nana, Nani, and Kiran Masi, to my years living with Kiran Masi and Vimal Mamu in the U.S., to my cousin Sunny moving to Bareilly for months to give me extra help with science and math. Now Manoj Mausa and Neelam Masi were doing it again: giving me the chance to chase this crazy and unexpected dream.

THE ACTUAL MISS INDIA competition was held on January 15, 2000, at the Poona Club in Pune. Every year there are three winners of the pageant, and each goes on to represent our country in a different international contest. The first winner is crowned Miss India Universe and goes on to compete in the Miss Universe pageant; the second winner is crowned Miss India World and goes on to compete in the Miss World pageant; for many years, including the year 2000, the third winner was crowned Miss India Asia Pacific and went on to compete in the Miss Asia Pacific pageant. The third winner now goes on to compete in the Miss International pageant.

The year 2000 was the millennium year, and there was an especially good panel of judges: Pradeep Guha, of course, whom we all called PG by that point; media baron Subhash Chandra; legendary actor Waheeda Rehman; fashion designer Carolina Herrera; Mar-

cus Swarovski of Swarovski crystals; cricketer Mohammad Azha-
ruddin; painter Anjolie Ela Menon; and several others. During the
competition, there were smaller pre-competitions, like Miss Perfect
10, Miss Congeniality, Swimsuit, and Talent. I didn't win any of
them.

As the day wore on, I became convinced that compared with
the other girls, especially the ones I expected to win—any combination of Lara Dutta, Dia Mirza, Waluscha De Sousa, and Lakshmi
Rana, all gorgeous, compassionate, eloquent contestants and everything a Miss India should be—I fell far short. Lara in particular
stood out. She'd already won another pageant and had started a
modeling career. Not only was she one of the most beautiful
women I'd ever seen but she carried herself with grace and compo-
sure, and everything she wore was perfect in my eyes.

During the full month of training, in all the yoga classes and
gym workouts, at all the cocktail parties and dinners, I never considered myself among the most beautiful girls or in any way a perfect candidate. Not by far. I'd known the whole time that the one
thing I wore best was my confidence—as long as I wasn't comparing myself with the other girls, which I sometimes struggled not to
do. I could speak in front of people; I could strike up conversations
with strangers; whatever I did, I almost always did with conviction,
even when I was bad at it. But that night as the competition wore
on, I felt my limitations especially intensely. I knew I was a long
shot. It's not that I was lacking confidence in myself, exactly. I felt
I was being realistic.

Somehow I made it into the final round, the round of five.
Mine had been the last name called, which had meant a nerve-
racking several minutes. And now I stood onstage with the other
four finalists—Lara, Dia, Lakshmi, and Gayatri Jayaraman—under
the gaze of the millions of Indians watching the pageant on live
television. I'd made peace with the fact that I was not going to be

one of the winners. Despite having no modeling or pageant experience, I was still in the top five of the Miss India competition. It was an incredible achievement, I told myself. One I could be proud of. This was what was going through my head when my name was called announcing that I had been crowned Miss India World.

Wait, *what*? I was in shock. My parents were in shock. None of us had a clue what to do next, because we hadn't planned that far ahead. We'd assumed there was no need to. Our heads were spinning that night and they continued to spin in the days to come. I was seventeen. My parents had to quickly start making plans for a career path we knew nothing about and had no experience or connections in. We were a medical family; we had no idea how to tackle entertainment. I smile as I write that now.

That evening, Lara Dutta was crowned Miss India Universe and Dia Mirza was crowned Miss India Asia Pacific. All three of us would go on to win our international pageants that year, the only time it has ever happened in India's history.

So yes, Queen Bey. You're always right.

Who run the world?

Girls.

Whether heading to work in a chiffon sari or gliding through the house in a cloud of Dior perfume, my mother was always impossibly glamorous.

Upon her marriage to Dad, a major, Mom enlisted in the army as a captain.

With my maternal grandfather, Manhar Krishna Akhouri. Nana, as I called him, taught me my ABCs under an ashoka tree.

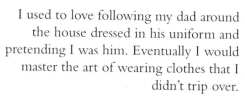

I used to love following my dad around the house dressed in his uniform and pretending I was him. Eventually I would master the art of wearing clothes that I didn't trip over.

From my earliest years, my dad and I had an understanding: Whenever he was performing at the army club he would look me in the eye during the first song. The New Year's Eve I was five he forgot, so I started to leave in a huff. Dad jumped off the stage and pulled me up onto it with him, coaxing me into a duet—a nursery rhyme—and winning my forgiveness.

My kindergarten class at St. Paul's in Delhi with my teacher Mrs. Bhasker, whom I adored and did my best to please. That's me in the top row, second from the left. I hadn't yet learned that Less is More.

Queens, New York, 1996.
Vanessa Smarth had no idea
what she was getting into
when she volunteered to
braid my hair!

With Kiran Masi and cousins Priyam and
Pooja during a visit to Purdue University in
Indiana, where Neela Masi, Kiran and Mom's
sister, was getting her PhD in agronomy. Our
cheeks are painted with butterflies and bugs in
honor of the Purdue Bug Bowl, one of the
largest insect festivals in the U.S.

Summer vacation on Cape Cod
with Vimla Mami and cousins
Divya and Rohan, 1997.

Vimal Mamu, my mother, and
me in 1998, when she traveled
to Newton, Massachusetts, to
bring me home.

Taking in the sights of Paris from the Seine with Sid before the infamous Louvre visit. For me, the "sights" included all the cute French boys on the boat.

The House Captains at the Army Public School in Bareilly my senior year, the year Nilgiri House snagged the Winner's Cup on Annual Day. Notice anything about my skirt length compared to the other skirts?

My first professional modeling job, age seventeen. Before I knew I'd be competing in the Miss India pageant, someone in Bareilly saw my photographs in Suri Photo Studio, where the owner had posted them, and offered me five thousand rupees (about a hundred and ten dollars) to model their dresses. You can tell I did my own hair and makeup.

No one was more surprised than I when I was crowned the new Miss India World on January 15, 2000!

In my classroom at the Army Public School during my Miss India homecoming. These were the classmates I'd been studying with six weeks earlier and with whom I would have been sitting for my boards had things not turned out the way they did.

On November 30, 2000, I was crowned the millennium Miss World! Notice my left hand pressed against my strapless gown in an effort to keep it from sliding off my body.

India hit the trifecta in 2000 when all three Miss India winners won our respective international pageants that year: Lara Dutta was crowned Miss Universe, I was crowned Miss World, and Dia Mirza was crowned Miss Asia Pacific. It's a feat no country has duplicated since.

With President K. R. Narayanan of India during my Miss World reign. Meeting heads of state was one of the honors that went along with the title and would become a privilege that accompanied me on my career trajectory.

I was so happy to share my win with not only my parents but my maternal grandparents, Nana and Nani, who helped raise me.

Although we completed the *mahurat* shot—the first shot of a film, which marks the beginning of principal photography and is preceded by blessings and accompanied by press—on *Asar*, the movie was one of those shelved after the debacle with my nose. Here I am with the legendary Dilip Kumar and our co-actor Ajay Devgan.

President Pratibha Patil presenting me with a National Film Award—the country's most prominent film award, administered by the Indian government's Directorate of Film Festivals—for the 2008 film *Fashion*.

My flashy gold bathing suit in the 2008 feel-good movie *Dostana* was my ode to Bo Derek's star turn in the 1979 film *10*.

While I was filming *Dostana* in Miami, Tamanna Sharma came to visit me. From sharing a tiny one-room apartment in Mumbai to being my maid of honor, she's been my sister from another mister for almost twenty years.

In 2013 my father insisted I continue training for the based-on-real-life *Mary Kom* even as his health declined. Shooting on the film commenced days after his death, and the sheer physicality of the role was in some ways therapeutic.

Shooting the final scene of *Dil Dhadakne Do,* one of the last few Hindi movies I did before my life pivoted to the U.S. in a serious way. With Anil Kapoor, Shefali Shah, and Ranveer Singh.

5

TOP OF THE WORLD

Uneasy lies the head that wears a crown.

WILLIAM SHAKESPEARE, *HENRY IV, PART 2*

I HAD TO KEEP pinching myself. I'd actually been crowned Miss India World! Less than two months earlier I'd been studying overtime, getting tutored in chemistry, physics, and math, and generally stressing out over my academic future. I'd kept my eyes on the prize of Passing the Boards with little awareness of anything beyond that. Now I was to be living in Mumbai for the next ten months fulfilling my Miss India commitments, and then representing my country on an international stage in the Miss World pageant. It was a lot to wrap my mind around.

While my family had planned in advance for how we'd handle the logistics of spending a month in Mumbai in the unlikely event that I made it beyond the preliminary competition in New Delhi, no plans had been made beyond that. Why put any energy into it? There was no chance that I'd win! But now that I had, my family had to kick it into gear instantly, as my Miss India commitments would begin immediately. I was seventeen, so Mom and Dad divided up the tasks of their lives and mine and worked the equation. As usual, they approached the whole thing as if it were a giant mathematical logic problem.

The first and most pressing problem was to find me a safe place to stay in Mumbai. Once that was accomplished, Mom would temporarily return to Bareilly. My father had taken over most of her patients for the month we'd already been in Mumbai, but that was always understood to be a short-term arrangement. The new plan needed to be something everyone could live with for the long haul, as I would be in Mumbai until November, when I would go to London for the Miss World competition. That meant I'd be away for almost a year, and Mom would be with me for months at a time. Among other things, my parents would have to hire a new doctor to assume my mother's duties at their hospital. Thank goodness Nani still lived with us so she could take care of Sid, who was eleven. What would we have done without her as a steady presence in our household for more than a decade, helping raise us, supervising homework, helping to shape the adults we would grow into?

Mom quickly found accommodations for me—a single room in the Santacruz neighborhood of the city. I was supposed to have the room to myself, but then a girl named Tamanna Sharma arrived and she was supposed to have the room to *herself*. When we figured out that the landlord had lied to both of us so that he could get double the rent, we foiled his evil plan by sharing the room and splitting the rent between us. There was one bed, one closet, two shelves, a little dressing table, and a window. That's it. But we made it work, and Tamanna and I became best friends. Eighteen years later, she would be the maid of honor at my wedding.

In spite of all my travels, I was still only seventeen, and I'd almost always had some kind of adult supervision. When I was in school, my teachers and principal were responsible for me. When I was at home, family members were responsible for me. In both places, there were rules to follow and people to be accountable to at different points during the day. Once Mom returned to Bareilly, all that changed, and, well, you can guess what this boundary-pushing teenage girl did.

Here I was in Mumbai, one of the most populous cities in the world, and the energy of the never-sleeping metropolis was calling out to me. I was practically giddy to be living in a place with so much vitality, excitement, and nightlife. Various family members had done their best to rein me in over the past few years, and I was ready to make up for lost time, going through a crazy phase with Tamanna where we partied several nights a week. Tamanna was working as a flight attendant for Sahara Airlines then, and all her flights were short daytime hops. If I didn't have any responsibilities on a given day, I might stay in bed until after noon. When Tamanna got back from work, she and I would figure out which party we were going to that night and spend hours getting ready. There were always fashion industry parties that were eager to have the presence of the new Miss India, and boy, did we take advantage of that. We'd leave the apartment at around 10 P.M., ready to take on the world in our tiny skirts and extremely high heels—not the safest thing to do, even though Mumbai is generally a safe city. To make things even riskier, we didn't have a car, which meant that we arrived at every party assuming we'd meet someone we knew who would be able to drop us back home. Well, that's not exactly true. I'd been gifted a Daewoo Matiz after winning Miss India, but neither Tamanna nor I knew how to drive, so for the longest time it just sat on the street. Finally we figured out that we could hire a driver to get us to and from parties safely. The three of us made quite a sight zipping around late-night Mumbai in the tiny Matiz: our massive driver took up most of the front of the car—it was two sizes too small for him—as Tamanna and I squeezed together in the back. Freedom was a whole new concept to me, something I clearly hadn't yet learned how to handle. Somehow, we made it through unscathed and came out the other side armed with a ton of stories. We made a best-friends pact never to share them, ever, except maybe with our kids someday.

These months while Mom was gone, I wasn't only partying. In my Miss India capacity, I appeared at inaugurations and charity events, visited schools, and met heads of local government. I was also free to work, so I was able to model and get runway experience in fashion shows, as well as do cover and editorial shoots for magazines.

When Mom returned to Mumbai after a few months of taking care of business in Bareilly, I happily gave up the late-night revelry. I'd gotten it out of my system—permanently, it seems. I moved with her into accommodations arranged by Badepapa, and Tamanna moved to a rented apartment of her own. We saw each other occasionally, but now I had to sharpen my focus on the task at hand: training for the Miss World competition.

Training for this international competition was far more advanced and intense than the training for the Miss India competition had been. There were about thirty girls competing for the Miss India title, and we'd received a month of group training, with classes and demonstrations. All of that had been valuable to me and I'd eagerly soaked it up. This training was to be one-on-one, though, and was preparing me to compete against ninety-four contestants from around the globe. One of the many professionals I trained with was Sabira Merchant, a world-class public-speaking and diction coach. She was responsible in large part for my polished presentation skills, having taught me how to formulate my thoughts and articulate them in complete sentences on the spot and under pressure. She trained me to pause and think, foregoing unconscious stalling mechanisms like "um," "uh," and "well" so that my speech was clear, direct, and unself-conscious. In the process of all this, she helped rid me of my nasal twang, which she said made me come across as a "Yankee-sounding person," and worked relentlessly with me on enunciating my vowels and speaking with a global English accent, which meant no more rolling of my *r*'s. I worked hard and faithfully and still use some of the skills she taught me today.

I got plenty of exercise preparing for the talent round through my training with Shiamak Davar's dance troupe, members of which helped train me for the Bollywood-meets-contemporary-Indian-dance piece I'd decided to perform. Then there was the gym, Talwalkars, where I showed up reliably each morning. I could have skipped it, but I didn't want to be considered a slacker. In this one regard, though, I kind of was: I'd show up there and sign in, then go outside to the juice counter and talk to friends. I didn't have an athletic body, but I was slender and blessed with a metabolism that kept me that way. #NowYouKnow.

Dr. Jamuna Pai, a well-known dermatologist, taught me about skin care. I consulted with Dr. Anjali Mukerjee, a dietician who advised me on healthy eating and sent me to London with a supply of nourishing snacks. I saw Dr. Sandesh Mayekar, a cosmetic dentist who made sure my smile sparkled; I still see him today. The husband-and-wife hair and makeup team of Bharat and Doris worked with me to make sure I knew how to look my best at all times.

Perhaps the most fun part of the prep was meeting with top fashion designers who consulted with me on what to wear and how to wear it. Since I'd always loved making a statement with my clothing, I relished these sessions. I ended up wearing a lot of Ritu Kumar's designs during the month that the Miss World contestants spent in London before the pageant itself. On the final night of the televised show, I wore a gorgeous soft peach strapless gown custom designed by Hemant Trivedi. There was one slight challenge with it, though, that only became apparent on the actual night of the pageant. More on that later.

Lara, Dia, and I were responsible only for our accommodations and travel while we were training; the Miss India pageant organization generously took care of everything else, and I will be forever grateful for everything I learned in my months of prep. We were trained and groomed until we were the absolute best versions of ourselves that we could possibly be. We knew we weren't in our pageants as mere individuals at this point. We all felt both the responsibility and the honor of representing India in the eyes of the world.

BY EARLY NOVEMBER it was time to go to London. Arriving at the airport in that city was a replay of arriving at the Ashoka Hotel for the Miss India preliminaries almost a year earlier. I watched as a stream of tall, gorgeous women from all around the world strode and sashayed and glided toward the baggage carousels, each arriving from her own point on the globe. I watched as they retrieved their bags ever so gracefully and floated through the throngs of other travelers to the exit doors and then disappeared outside to find the vehicles that would take us to our hotel. I was just giving myself a stern talking-to in order to prevent my insecurity from taking over, when wait! There was Lionel Richie! Having my very first European celebrity sighting be one of my absolute favorite singers was enough to lift my spirits and send me out to join the other girls happy and reenergized.

The Hilton in central London was to be our home for the next few weeks, and I settled in quickly with my roommate, Ganga Gunasekera, Miss Sri Lanka. Each day was packed full. At 8 A.M. or so, all ninety-five of us, plus chaperones, would pile onto the buses that awaited us outside the hotel and head out for a day of press conferences, photo shoots, media appearances, charity events, and sightseeing. Every morning, Mom would take a train into London from Hounslow, where she and Dad and Sid were staying with family friends, the Upadhyas, to offer me a cheerful wave and a bit of encouragement from afar before I climbed onto the bus. Even though there was no opportunity to speak on those mornings, she wanted to be sure I felt her support. When we returned to the hotel in the evenings, there was about an hour when we were free to visit with any family who may have traveled to London. Mom was always there—sometimes with Dad and Sid, sometimes on her own—and she was always the last to leave. She was my anchor, there for me morning and night. Even now, when I pass that London hotel, I can picture the buses parked there and the girls coming in and out, and the spot in the lobby where we used to meet our families. Even now I can remember seesawing between the anxiety and the total excitement I felt every day. Rarely did I find a midpoint of calm equilibrium.

After seeing me off in the morning, Mom would sometimes be joined by the rest of my family. They'd spend the day sightseeing and shopping for things for the pageant—a certain shade of makeup or a particular item of clothing, perhaps. (That had to have been lots of fun for Sid.) Or Mom would frantically contact Vimla Mami back in Newton, Massachusetts, with requests for random but essential items. Mami would immediately send multiples of whatever my mother said I needed—little black dresses or strappy sandals—so that I could choose whatever fit and looked best.

A year earlier, prior to the Miss India competition, my mother had prepped me every night for the question-and-answer rounds I'd be facing in the pageant. Back then, she'd gone to the street market by the majestic Flora Fountain in the Fort business district in south Mumbai to look through the tons of books for sale on the sidewalk. She'd bought an assortment of general knowledge volumes and then combed through them to come up with her own questions. She'd also compiled a master list of Miss India questions from the past ten years. Then she'd quiz me using the lists and help me craft relevant, thoughtful, and articulate answers to political and societal questions. But now we had just sixty short minutes each evening to prepare in whatever way we could.

"I was thinking about . . . ," she might begin, or "Maybe you could say something like . . ." And then she'd build on whatever we'd talked about the prior night, or do her best to help me think through a new scenario she'd been mulling over in the twenty-four hours since I'd last talked to her. She knew that we were being introduced to the press and to the world at large through a variety of events around London—at dinners, fundraisers, sporting events, meet-and-greets—and she was certain that being well informed and well-spoken would make a defining difference.

All of us felt that we were being graded at every moment by the chaperones, who accompanied us everywhere. We were convinced that they were reporting back to the esteemed Julia Morley—businesswoman, former model, and chair of the Miss World Organization, which her husband had founded in 1951 and had run until his death earlier that year. Mrs. Morley, as we were instructed to call her, was perfect: her manners were perfect, her voice was perfect, and she walked with such effortless grace that she seemed to float an inch above the ground. We all desperately wanted to be like her. The Miss World 2000 pageant was the first one that she was running on her own, and every time she spoke to us I was awestruck and intimidated. I'm pretty sure we all were. When she or any of the chaperones were anywhere near, we wouldn't gossip, complain, slouch, talk with our mouths full, or do anything else that wasn't 100 percent Mrs. Morley–worthy.

By now I had access to the most stylish clothes, but that doesn't mean I always put all my wardrobe components together in the most artful way. I may have occasionally over-accessorized with the bangles and the dangly earrings, or sported too many sparkly items, or worn more makeup than necessary. I hadn't yet learned what I know now: Less Is More. But I was able to speak and carry myself with confidence—or, in those moments where my confidence failed me, with a conviction that seemed like confidence. I was not the same person that I'd been when I'd participated in the Miss India pageant eleven months earlier. Then, I didn't have a lot of tools in my toolbox—or brushes in my makeup kit. I hadn't really understood what would be required of me; I was just a high school girl busy with high school things who, with plenty of determination and family help, pulled out a miraculous win. Once I'd garnered the Miss India World crown, I'd had to learn fast and under pressure. My toolbox was as full as it was ever going to get, and that knowledge gave me a sense of self-assurance. I knew what was required of me, and I knew, theoretically at least, that I should be able to do well.

When asked by the press at a dinner or charity gala, "How does it feel representing India?" or "India's had so many amazing winners; do you feel pressure to win your pageant?" I tried for two things in my answers: (1) to sound confident, and (2) to embody "beauty with a purpose," the phrase used to distinguish the Miss World pageant from other international pageants. I didn't go in as a favorite to win, but by the end of the month, I'd heard and read that I'd gained considerable momentum with the bookmakers in England, especially after the final week of interacting with the media and others at all our events. The ten months of preparation and growth had paid off. And yes, there is betting on the Miss World pageant in England and elsewhere!

In order to make myself stand out in the crowded international field, I had been encouraged by my Miss India team to represent my culture to the fullest. I took the counsel to heart when it came to dressing and accessorizing myself for the pageant—especially for one particular event before the ceremony. I was grateful for Mrs. Morley's choice to not have an onstage swimwear round for Miss World that year; instead, prior to the actual pageant, all the contestants were flown to a resort in the Maldives where we shot videos on the beach that would be used in lieu of the live event. For me, who had *so* hated the swimsuit and heels part of the Miss India preliminaries, wearing a bathing suit in a natural environment *on an actual beach* rather than on a stage or in a hotel suite was a gift. This was something I could easily do without being self-conscious.

The international press was brought to the Maldives to cover our day in the sun and sand. We frolicked in the water, wearing our country sashes, as a huge group of photographers snapped photo after photo. Because I'd been advised by my various trainers to bring Indian culture and ethnicity to the fore, I decided to wear a *bandhani* sarong, and then added bangles and a bindi to the mix. In my sarong-covered one-piece, with my bangles and my bindi and a large flower tucked behind my ear, I thought I was both fashionable and true to my country. In retrospect, the outfit was overkill. But it worked: though I was being encouraged by the photographers to take off my sarong, I took a stand that I wouldn't—and in spite of the fact that I was the most covered-up body out there, I still ended up being one of the most photographed contestants that day. I guess my culture had my back.

MISS WORLD 2000, the fiftieth Miss World pageant, was held on November 30, 2000. That morning, Ganga and I and our fellow contestants descended on London's Millennium Dome to get dressed and coiffed and made up for the television cameras in an explosion of sound and motion and color. Imagine the scene: close to one hundred young women laughing and calling out to one another and practically bursting with nervous excitement. There must have been fifty glam stations throughout the massive ballroom that was our staging area, and with the voices of all the hair and makeup artists and their assistants and the coordinators, the cacophony was almost dizzying. I felt like I was part of a huge, chaotic ballet with an overactive sound system and an unruly corps de ballet. The energy in the room was contagious and building on itself by the minute.

After I'd made it through my own hair styling, I decided I could use a quick touch-up and asked to borrow a stylist's curling iron. With all the congestion, I got jostled and accidentally burned my forehead with the hot metal. The skin scabbed, which meant I had to apply a ton of foundation to try to cover it up. That didn't fully work, so I added another form of camouflage—and now I can finally explain why I had that crazy tendril of hair swirling down over my left eye!

Before I went onstage for the first round, I pulled out the picture of Haidakhan Baba that I had tucked into my dress. In times of stress, it reminds me of who I am and where I come from. I took a moment to ask Babaji for his help and to express my thanks for all of the ways in which I had been so incredibly blessed, and then I tucked the picture back into my dress.

As we went through the various rounds of competition that evening, the tension in the Millennium Dome was palpable. When I was chosen as one of the five finalists, I was both stunned and thrilled. This was the question-and-answer round, and, thanks to Mom and her endless research and quizzing, I believed it was my strongest event. Each of the five final contestants—Miss Italy, Miss Turkey, Miss Uruguay, Miss Kazakhstan, and I—were to write a question that would be randomly assigned to one of the other four to respond to. With little time to prepare the question, my mind went blank. Everything Mom and I had discussed went out the window. Finally, in desperation, I wrote down the only question I could think of and hoped for the best. Then I said a few prayers for the next round.

When the five of us were called onstage together, I was more nervous than I had ever been in my life. Between being one of the youngest girls there and my sudden hyperawareness of the number of people watching—two billion people in one hundred and fifty countries—my palms were sweaty and my breathing was erratic. I had just enough brain power left to remind myself to focus not on my feelings but on what I needed to do and not do: *Take a moment to collect your thoughts. Breathe. Don't say "um." Don't trip on your dress.* You might think I would have found some reassurance by reminding myself that the bookies had me among the favorites to win, but I went in the opposite direction, taking pressure off myself by thinking about the two significant reasons why I was *unlikely* to win. First, the preceding year another Miss India, Yukta Mookhey, had won, so the chances that two Miss Indias would win consecutively were almost nonexistent. And second, Lara had won the Miss Universe 2000 pageant just six months earlier, in May, which seemed to make my odds even slimmer. How long could Indian women keep emerging victorious in these pageants? Wouldn't the judges want to spread the glory to some other countries? The pressure was on—I was representing my country on a global stage—and the pressure was also off—I almost certainly wouldn't win.

Miss Kazakhstan and Miss Italy were called to answer the questions that had been randomly picked for them, and then Miss Uruguay was called upon to answer the one I'd written: "If ignorance is bliss, then why do we seek knowledge?" When I heard it aloud, I realized what a tough question it was. The only reason I'd written it down was that it was a question I'd been asked during my Miss India pageant! I thought Miss Uruguay did a great job with it. Her response, given in English rather than her native Spanish, ended with the observation that "ignorance is the main cause of so many problems around the whole world."

Finally it was my turn. I was the second-to-last person to be called upon, and my question had been written by Miss Turkey: "Who do you think is the most successful woman living today and why?"

After a few seconds of nervous laughter that I desperately hoped would buy me more time, I launched into an answer that was no doubt influenced by my experience in convent schools—convent schools run by the very organization the woman I named had founded. In retrospect, my choice was a bit cliché. As much as I admire and respect the woman whom I singled out, I could have come up with a more original response. Instead I said:

"There are a lot of people I admire, but one of the most admirable people is Mother Teresa. I admire her from the bottom of my heart for being so considerate, compassionate, and kind, giving up her life for people in India."

(Spoiler alert: Mother Teresa had died in 1997.)

I don't know exactly how much time elapsed between that final Q&A round and the announcement of the winner. I was backstage with the other four finalists getting touched up—another spritz of hairspray, another layer of lip gloss—and trying to stay calm. Finally, the moment to reveal the next Miss World had arrived. This had always been an honor reserved for Mr. Morley, and now, in his stead, the new director of the Miss World pageant stepped to the microphone. Mrs. Morley first announced Miss Turkey, Yuksel Ak, as the second runner-up, and then Miss Italy, Giorgia Palmas, as the first runner-up. Then there was that hush, that anticipatory moment when everyone was holding their breath before the new wearer of the Miss World crown was announced—and then, incredibly, my name was called. Of course I had dreamed about winning over the months that I'd been so diligently training, but I'd never actually believed it could happen. Thank goodness Margarita Kravtsova, Miss Kazakhstan, and Katja Thomsen Grien, Miss Uruguay, immediately reached out to hug me, because my knees were weak and that moment of physical contact and support steadied me. Somehow I made it to center stage, where the outgoing Miss World, my fellow countrywoman Yukta Mookhey, hugged and kissed me as she placed the crown on my head. I cried. I smiled. I did the wave.

I was in shock.

I took my slow, teary victory lap around the stage as the new Miss World. I searched the audience for my family but couldn't see them in the blinding glare of the lights. In the footage I've seen of those minutes after being crowned, I look both ecstatic and dazed in equal measure. And it's true, I *was* ecstatic and dazed—and I was also desperately trying to keep my strapless gown from sliding down my body! Earlier in the evening, the gown had been strategically taped to my skin to secure it in place, but as the evening wore on and I got more and more nervous, my perspiration caused the tape to loosen. I pressed my hands together in a namaste and kept them close to my body as much of the time as I could in an effort to hold my gown up, and I hoped for the best. I now do a namaste at almost every red carpet—and you know the origin story.

Then celebratory pandemonium broke out onstage—glittering confetti descended from the rafters, music played, and the ninety contestants who hadn't made it to the final round now streamed onstage to dance, hug one another, and have their photographs taken. Those moments, like so many others that night, are almost a complete blur: I remember being surrounded by photographers and security, and I remember looking for my parents and Sid and finally finding them thanks to Diana Hayden, Miss World 1997, who—along with Lara and Sushmita Sen, Miss Universe 1994—had called to wish me good luck the night before. "Are you Priyanka's family?" Diana had asked, when she'd seen them looking lost in the throngs of people trying to get onstage. Then she'd shepherded them through all of the reporters, photographers, and others congregating around me to deliver them to my side. I remember hugging them all and crying tears of joy with my dad. But if so much of that night is a blur to me now, what Mom said to me in that moment is crystal clear in my memory:

"What will happen to your studies now?"

Seriously? *What will happen to your studies now?*

To this day, I tease my mom about that. Here I had just won Miss World, the goal we had been working toward together for almost a year and that she had completely upended her life for, and she was worrying about whether I would ever take my board exams and finish school! *Can we please talk about this tomorrow, Mom?* She was still in shock, of course. We all were. Everything about our lives—every single thing—was just about to change in a huge, totally unforeseen way.

Shortly thereafter I was whisked away to the official coronation ceremony, which was a huge celebratory banquet with all the contestants and judges and sponsors. Trophies were awarded to the winners of the other competitions of the pageant—in an embarrassment of riches I received one for being chosen Miss World Continental Queen of Asia and Oceana—and I was crowned Miss World once more and presented with that title's trophy in the form of a beautiful glass globe. I was so grateful to Pradeep Guha for his help and support and that of his *Times of India* team that when I returned to India, I gave him the shiny orb as a token of my appreciation. It's still on his mantel with Sushmita Sen's crown.

All the pageant contestants had been instructed to pack up the night before, and my bags had been moved for me from the very nice Hilton to the Presidential Suite at the luxurious Grosvenor House, in London's upscale Mayfair district. A chaperone was assigned to stay with me in a room attached to mine. When I went to my new hotel, I was hoping to spend some time with my family, since I'd still only seen them for a few chaotic minutes onstage. It would be the last chance I'd have to see them before heading out on tour to appear in my new official capacity. For their part, Mom, Dad, and Sid were flying to Boston the next day to visit Vimal Mamu, Vimla Mami, Divya, and Rohan, arrangements made months earlier for all of us when we'd assumed I wouldn't win; it would be a trip to cheer me up and distract me, my parents thought, much like the stopover in Paris that Mom, Sid, and I had made when returning from Newton, Massachusetts, after my years in the States. None of us could have imagined that my ticket would go unused. When my family arrived at the Grosvenor House that night, eager to hug me and congratulate me and talk about everything that had happened, they were told by security that they couldn't see me. "But I *must* see my daughter," my mother insisted when Mrs. Morley was finally reached by telephone. "She's leaving tomorrow and I haven't even talked to her and I *must* see her." Mrs. Morley gave the okay, and at last security let Mom, Dad, and Sid upstairs.

When they arrived at my suite, I was sitting on the huge bed wearing my crown and jabbering about my desperation to eat pizza. Since I wasn't allowed to go out without an official chaperone, Dad brought a large pepperoni back to the room. We ate and talked about the craziness of the night and eventually the three of them left so I could get some sleep before my press conference the next morning. When my parents hugged me goodbye, they thought they were losing their daughter for the next year; they'd nearly been prohibited from seeing me that night and they had no idea when they'd see me again. When I hugged Sid goodbye, I didn't realize it was to be our last hug for a very long time.

That night I slept clutching my new crown. It was pretty, it was shiny, and it was mine.

THE NEXT MORNING, moments before my first press conference as Miss World, I was told in a very matter-of-fact way, "Priyanka, there's something we need to discuss. Last night the question you were asked was who you thought was the most successful woman living today. You answered Mother Teresa. Since Mother Teresa died in 1997, the issue of how you've won in spite of your answer will come up. You're articulate, you deserve to be Miss World, but it will come up. You're just going to have to acknowledge it and move on. Whatever happens out there, don't let it shake you. *Go.*"

No one actually said *Go* and pushed me onstage, but that's how it felt. Miss Scotland, Michelle Watson, was hosting the press conference, but I barely heard a word she said because my mind was working overtime processing this new information, trying to think of a way to explain to the press how I could possibly have misheard the question. When it was my turn to speak, I stared at the reporters for a few moments, registering the staccato clicks of all their cameras before my survival instinct kicked in. Then kick in it did. I remember saying how grateful I was to have been chosen for this honor and how wonderful it was that we live in a world where mistakes can be forgiven. And then I added that most important of all was how Mother Teresa still lived on in my heart, so I hoped they'd accept my answer. There was some subsequent public criticism about my having answered the question incorrectly, but I tried not to pay attention to it. In any case, I didn't have much time to worry about negative remarks in the news, because I was immediately whisked away for a quick European tour.

A week or so later, my parents got a surprise call in Boston from someone on the Miss India team who wanted to tell them where to be the next day for my homecoming. *What?*

In India at that time it was the norm for the winner of an international pageant to be celebrated with a homecoming tour upon her return to her native soil. It was both an opportunity to honor the winner and a chance to express national pride and joy in the country's victory. The tour was invariably an exuberant affair, accompanied by a lot of press and fanfare. Nobody had imagined that my parents weren't going to be in the country.

"*What?* You're in *America?*" the Miss India staffer said.

"*What?* We need to come back to *India?*" my parents responded.

"Well, it's always better to have the support of your family on these occasions," the staffer said. "If possible."

Mom and Dad threw their clothes into their suitcases and raced to the airport.

But first they'd had to figure out what to do about Sid. The return trip to India would likely take almost twenty hours, and then they'd be traveling with me and the Miss World entourage for the next ten days or so. It seemed unfair to put eleven-year-old Sid through all of that, and so the decision was made to leave him in Vimal Mamu and Vimla Mami's care temporarily. "I'll come back for you soon, Sid," my mother told him. "As soon as I can."

Mom and Dad squeezed onto a flight to London, but then they were stuck. Absolutely no seats were available to New Delhi, so there was no possibility of meeting me in time—until a British Airways agent from Pakistan named Shahid Malik heard them speaking Punjabi, understood their predicament, and deftly arranged for two fellow airline employees on an immediately departing plane to exchange their seats for spots on another flight. Then he not only bumped Mom and Dad up to first class but had it announced that the parents of the new Miss World were on board, helping them to temporarily forget the arduousness of their sudden journey. I'd say it was a miracle, but in fact it was a very human gesture on the part of the compassionate Mr. Malik. I hope for the day when acts of simple kindness and shared humanity are as freely offered between our countries as they were offered that day by Mr. Malik and the two gentlemen who gave up their seats for my parents.

I was flying back from Europe at the same time my parents were in the air. My first time flying first class. Before we touched down in Delhi, I asked if we might make a stop on the way to the hotel so that I could visit the Mangal Mahadev Birla Kanan Temple in Shivaji Marg, Rangpuri. The temple itself is a simple one, but outside it stands a magnificent one-hundred-foot-tall statue of Lord Shiva; other grand deities stand and sit nearby. I wanted to take blessings in this temple before my India journey got under way, to express my immense gratitude for winning the pageant and for all the people who had helped me along the way—especially my parents, without whose constant encouragement in all my unusual endeavors since childhood this would not be happening. Mrs. Morley and the whole Miss World contingent accompanied me and we all took blessings. Then we got back into the cars and continued on to our hotel in the heart of India's capital. As we pulled up, I saw my name on a massive billboard-sized sign: THE MAURYA SHERATON WELCOMES MISS WORLD 2000, PRIYANKA CHOPRA. It took my breath away. My ambitions and goals changed and crystalized in that moment, and I remember thinking, *I want that. I want my name to be in big letters whenever it's written.* Twenty years later, I can look back and say to my younger self: "*You did it.* With a couple of decades of constant perseverance, you made your dreams come true."

My exhausted parents were waiting for me in my hotel room when I arrived, and in classic Punjabi fashion, so were at least twenty members of my extended family.

Next stop: my hometown of Bareilly. I was so proud to be going back home to share this moment with all of my friends. But there was a complication. Before I ever entered any pageant, there was a member of the state government in Uttar Pradesh who had criticized beauty pageants for participating in *nari shoshan,* or the exploitation of women; pageants went against the culture of the country, the minister said. Now, there were those in the state government who were opposed to having any kind of homecoming celebration for me in Bareilly, as being crowned Miss World made me a representative of the pageant system. It took *The Times of India* to negotiate an agreement. Rather than my hometown throwing me a day or two of massive celebratory events, I would be allowed to return to Bareilly for just a few hours to hold a press conference and visit an orphanage.

My parents and I, along with Mrs. Morley, a couple of people from the Miss India team, and security personnel, flew home in an eight-seater and proceeded to the Bareilly Club, the comfortingly familiar spot where I'd roamed the grounds with my middle school friends, hung out with my high school crew, and been winner of the May Queen Ball. All along the route, the road was lined with people smiling and waving at me. They clogged the sidewalk and they perched in trees. It was totally and utterly mind-blowing—these were the streets where I used to ride my bike with friends and travel in a rickshaw to tutoring. I suspect that part of the reason there was such a massive outpouring of support for me in the streets is because I was here for such a disappointingly quick visit; we weren't even spending the night. I wasn't going to be able to hug my friends or visit my old haunts or celebrate with those who'd known me since childhood.

I was sad about that, but the reality of my new world was kicking in. I was coming to understand that my life was not my own anymore. I had public responsibilities to live up to, and for the next year they would have to come first. I would need to be where I was told when I was told, fresh, alert, and ready to be in the limelight. Seeing the people of my hometown crowding into the streets to show me their love and support sent surges of adrenaline rushing through my system, and the excitement of it all appeased my sadness about the brevity of my visit to some extent. Looking back on it, though, I can see that in some ways I was operating on autopilot, as it was all so new and unlike anything I had ever experienced.

Once we left Uttar Pradesh, things didn't get any easier, in spite of the national government standing up for me. Rumors began to circulate about my family. My parents became increasingly concerned about bringing Sid back to Bareilly in this strange, unpredictable environment—too much harsh scrutiny, too much cruel gossip, and some threats that they had no idea how to evaluate—and so they made an emotionally wrenching decision. They asked Vimal Mamu, and ultimately Kiran Masi, too, to watch over Sid in America for an undetermined period of time until they figured out how to navigate this new reality. It would be more than a year and a half before they brought him back.

Being left in America was a blow to my brother. Unlike me at his age, he had never been separated from our parents. I'd lived with Nana and Nani as a baby and toddler. I'd gone off to boarding school at age seven. Also, I was a different person, much more extroverted than Sid. He was eleven when he was left in America with no say in the matter; I was just shy of thirteen, and it had been my choice. Our aunts and uncles were loving and generous, as always, but understandably, Sid felt abandoned by my parents and resentful of me. Which was a complete reversal of our earlier life, when I was sent away after his birth and had felt abandoned and resentful. The decision was hard for him to make peace with, be-cause he never really understood why he couldn't just be with us in India. I may not say it enough, but I'm so grateful to Sid for his kindness and support all these years. As an eighteen-year-old, I simply didn't understand until much later the degree to which my life's sudden change of direction had affected him.

THINGS EVENTUALLY SETTLED down a bit, if you can call traveling around the world meeting heads of state and attending constant photo shoots, press events, and fundraisers "settling down." Then, early in the summer of 2001, a lingering head cold developed into what I thought was a very bad sinus infection, and I was having trouble breathing. This is a problem someone with asthma can't ignore. I was in London for work when this happened, so Mom and I went to see a doctor who'd been recommended by family friends. He discovered a polyp in my nasal cavity that would need to be surgically removed. Fortunately, a polypectomy sounded like a pretty routine procedure. Unfortunately, it wasn't. While shaving off the polyp, the doctor also accidentally shaved the bridge of my nose and the bridge collapsed. When it was time to remove the bandages and the condition of my nose was revealed, Mom and I were horrified. My original nose was gone. My face looked com-pletely different. I wasn't me anymore.

I felt devastated and hopeless. Every time I looked in the mirror, a stranger looked back at me, and I didn't think my sense of self or my self-esteem would ever recover from the blow. The experience was very emotional for my whole family—my parents were doc-tors, after all; how could this have happened?—and to make matters worse, the experience was a public affair.

Plastic Chopra. Let's just call it out right now. Immediately the name started to show up in articles and newspaper items and it has followed me my entire professional life. I was dared to give an explanation for the obviously different nose, but I chose a course then that I've followed in all the years since. I decided that there was a line I was going to draw in my life. I am an entertainer. That's what I've signed on to do, and that's what I love doing. I will say my lines, dance my dance, hit my mark. I'll do my best to make you laugh, and I'll do my best to make you cry, but just because I'm a public person doesn't mean everything about my life has to be public knowledge. I get to choose what I share and when I share it.

I'm talking about this now because it was a long time ago and we're all over it at this point—we *are* all over it, right? Following the polypectomy I had several corrective surgeries, and over time, my nose normalized. While it took a few years of seeing a stranger gazing back at me every time I looked in the mirror, I've gotten accustomed to this face. Now when I look in the mirror, I am no longer surprised; I've made peace with this slightly different me. On the other side of thirty-five, with somewhere around sixty-five movies and a two-decades-long career in India and the U.S.—and with high-definition television, no less!—I'm just like everyone else: I look at myself in the mirror and think maybe I can lose a little weight; I think maybe I can work out a little more. But I'm also content. This is my face. This is my body. I might be flawed, but I am *me*.

IN THE WEEKS before the 2000 Miss World pageant, I remember feeling that being from India was my superpower, a quality that would distinguish me anywhere I was, in anything I did. That superpower fortified me throughout my roller coaster of a year, and though my official Miss World duties ended when I placed the crown on the head of Miss Nigeria, Agbani Darego, in November of 2001, that feeling, that awareness of India as my strength, has stayed with me. Representing my country and culture gave me confidence on an international stage and it would continue to give me confidence as I broke into an industry that can be brutal on those who haven't had their mettle tested in the glare of public scrutiny—the entertainment industry.

6

DESI GIRL

Not hammer-strokes, but dance of the water,
sings the pebbles into perfection.
RABINDRANATH TAGORE

EARLY IN MY Miss World tenure, I attended Jai Hind College in
Mumbai. I'd assumed there'd be time to attend classes between my various official Miss World duties—I think my mother's
question "What will happen to your studies now?" had lodged in
my brain somewhere—but offers for movies started coming in almost immediately. A few had come in after I won Miss India World,
but now that I was Miss *World,* there were a lot more. I soon realized that if I was going to do either academics or entertainment
well, a choice would have to be made.

One night my parents and I had a conversation about the di-
lemma. "Maybe you can look at this as an opportunity rather than
a choice, Mimi," my father suggested. "Try the acting for a year and
a half," he said. "That's the opportunity. If you're terrible at it or

you hate it, you can always go back to school." Then he added, "I don't want you to ever have a what-if in your life." I decided he was right: I didn't want any what-ifs in my life, either.

It might seem like a crazy career trajectory—going from winning pageants and having zero professional acting experience to being offered film roles—but at that time, when you won a major pageant you became very famous very quickly in India. Saying you had signed a Miss India for a movie, or better yet a Miss World, seemed to appeal to lots of producers.

The Miss India organization handled any requests that came in after I was crowned Miss India, and then, when I became Miss World, that organization handled them. After a time, my father helped out and managed my career for a while. He and Mom had switched places after the Miss World pageant. She had moved back to Bareilly to resume work in their hospital by then, and he was now living in Mumbai in order to help me navigate an industry I knew nothing about. I was so focused on what I needed to do to establish myself professionally that I didn't see how the momentous changes in my own life were affecting everyone else in my family. It didn't fully register that the previous year my mother had given up medicine—at least temporarily—to move to Mumbai with me. It didn't fully register that both of my parents were now giving up the hospital they'd founded together, Kasturi Hospital—named after my father's father—so that they could both live in Mumbai with me as I embarked on my new life. My brother had had to move to America and of course I understood that, but I didn't spend much time considering how he might feel about the move, or what it might have been like for him.

I may not have thought about it much then, but I have been aware for many years of the things that my family gave up on my behalf. Once, when I expressed my gratitude to my mother, she said, "Your father and I always took your career seriously, Mimi.

When we were considering closing the hospital and moving to Mumbai, he said to me, 'We can practice medicine wherever we are. The building of our careers is behind us. She is building hers now. So we have to support her.' Naturally," Mom added, "I agreed."

If my family hadn't shown me through their actions that my dreams and ambitions were important and to be taken seriously, I might never have believed in them or taken them so seriously myself. My gratitude to the guiding forces in my life knows no bounds.

Although I always consulted my parents before making big decisions, eventually I felt the need to hire professional management and representation, and during that time I started taking meetings with producers and directors. One of the first meetings was with a director/producer who was known as much for his purported sexual misconduct allegations as for the movies he made. I didn't know that when I walked into his office with my then-manager, of course. At the time, his experience and all the awards hanging on his walls were what impressed me. Clearly he was a man who knew what he was doing, who knew how to make successful films, who knew what audiences liked. After a few minutes of small talk, the director/producer told me to stand up and twirl for him. I did. He stared at me long and hard, assessing me, and then suggested that I get a boob job, fix my jaw, and add a little more cushioning to my butt. If I wanted to be an actress, he said, I'd need to have my proportions "fixed," and he knew a great doctor in L.A. he could send me to. My then-manager voiced his agreement with the assessment.

I left the director/producer's office feeling stunned and small. Was he right that I couldn't be successful unless I had so many body parts "fixed"? I thought of how individuals in the media and others in the industry had referred to me as "dusky" and "different-looking," and I wondered if I was cut out for this business after all.

All the talk of body parts and skin tone collectively made me feel devalued and unseen and uncertain about my future. Having experienced the aftermath of a supposedly simple polyp removal, I knew I wasn't willing to follow the course he'd laid out for me, even if he, as the highly successful expert, was right. And needless to say, I parted ways with my then-manager not long after.

Looking back, I see that this early feedback I was getting from some of the players in the industry taught me one of the first, and most important, lessons that I was to learn over the next few years, a lesson I had understood in another context when I'd returned home from the States and insisted on expressing myself through my style: *My difference is my strength.* If I looked like other "classically beautiful" girls, then I wouldn't stand out, and more important, I wouldn't be *me*. I'm grateful that some instinct back then told me not to fall prey to the insecurity of not fitting into the existing mold. I took a hard line with myself and made what some considered my weakness into my strength, and I believe that's part of what has given my career its trajectory.

THE INDIAN FILM industry releases close to two thousand films each year—almost double that of Hollywood. With estimates ranging from one to two *billion* movie tickets sold annually in India, it is the leading film market in the world. Then add on all the revenue generated by ticket sales to Indian movies outside India—estimated to be between $300 and $500 million a year for the past few years—and it's easy to understand how the country's film business thrives.

Indian cinema is composed of many smaller, local film industries. The Hindi-language industry based in Mumbai that's popularly known as Bollywood is by far the largest of these local industries. When many Western film viewers hear the term "Bol- lywood," they may think of the kind of big-budget production that mixes together several genres in one film—what used to be called a "masala" film. *Masala,* as anyone who appreciates a good Indian meal knows, refers to a mixture of ground spices. Similarly, in film, it means a mixture of different elements or genres. Action, ro- mance, drama, and comedy, punctuated by lavish musical numbers with dancing and lip-synced singing, may all coexist happily to- gether in one film. While the Hindi film industry is famous in the West largely for its masala movies—they're not actually called ma- sala movies anymore; they're just called commercial blockbusters— that's way too confining a box to contain the ebulliently robust industry. Hindi movies include every type of film you could pos- sibly imagine: dramas, biopics, historical sagas, thrillers, comedies, romances, documentaries, horror movies, quirky art-house films, and more. And given that most Hindi-language films are available with subtitles, I'm happy to say there's something for just about everyone in both of the countries I call home.

Within six months of winning the Miss World crown, I signed on for four movies. Three of them were Bollywood projects, and one was a Tamil film. I was full of energy and hope and I was ready to work. Then the bridge of my nose collapsed and I started under- going corrective surgery to normalize it. I was dropped from two big movies—my very first acting jobs, movies that were to have launched me—after the producers heard rumors that I looked dif- ferent post-surgery. One producer did me the courtesy of arranging a screen test, or a "look" test, to see what my face would look like blown up on 70mm film to movie-screen size. The second pro- ducer didn't even bother with a look test. As if the physical and emotional pain of the original and subsequent corrective surgeries weren't enough, this was a terrible blow. My career, a career based so much on physical appearance, seemed to be over before it had even really started. I felt as if a doorway to paradise had been opened and then slammed in my face. And it hurt.

Anil Sharma, the director of the third Hindi movie I'd signed on for, *The Hero,* decided to keep me on but changed my role to a supporting one. "No one will know until the movie comes out that you were originally supposed to do a different role," he told me. "At least you'll be part of one of the biggest movies of the year. And I promise you, you'll still be on the poster." A previous film of his, *Gadar,* had broken all records in India, so keeping me on was a very kind thing to do, especially given that I was literally just starting out. His compassion and consideration meant the world to me and turned out to be a preview of the kind of thoughtfulness I would encounter from a number of individuals in Hindi cinema.

The fourth movie I'd been signed to ended up being the very first movie I shot: *Thamizhan*. It was a Tamil film, and what a gift it was.

With twenty-two official languages spread out over the twenty-eight states and eight union territories that make up India, almost every state in the country has its own language. The language of Bollywood movies is Hindi, but not everyone in India speaks Hindi. The language spoken in Tamil Nadu, the southernmost state of our country, is Tamil, and that state has a huge film industry that speaks the language and culture of its own people. While my Hindi film plans had more or less imploded, there was never a question—as far as I'm aware, at least—that I wouldn't shoot *Thamizhan,* which starred the amazing actor Vijay in the role of a crusading lawyer. I played his girlfriend. I didn't speak Tamil, but I had a Tamil coach who helped me learn the lines phonetically, and I did my best from there.

Thamizhan was the perfect first film for me. In Tamil Nadu, more than eight hundred miles from Mumbai, I found myself surrounded by a supportive and talented cast and crew in a situation where I could do a good job and feel respected for it. The opportunity to do solid work without any discussion of how my looks had changed allowed me to regain some of the confidence that had been ebbing away. And working with the gifted and gracious actor Vijay on my first movie was tremendously inspiring and instructive. We shot outdoors, and there were fans who stood behind the barriers for hours and hours just to get a glimpse of him. After wrapping a fifteen-hour day, he would greet those who'd waited and take photographs with them for another hour and a half.

Vijay's humility and his generosity with fans made a lasting impression on me. Almost a decade and a half later, a portion of the pilot episode of *Quantico* was filmed in front of the imposing New York Public Library, and there was a line around the block of people watching. As I stood and took pictures with them through my lunch break, I thought about my very first co-actor ever and the example he'd set.

Reconstructive surgery and film work went pretty much hand in hand for the next two years. By the time I started my next movie, *Andaaz*—with Lara Dutta in the female lead and Akshay Kumar as the male lead—my face looked a bit closer to the one I used to see in the mirror before the polypectomy. The *Andaaz* opportunity seemed like the answer to my prayers, a second—or third—chance to have a major role in a major movie. Since I knew what it felt like to have big chances slip away, I was determined to make the most of this one. I was now filming *The Hero* and *Andaaz* together, and perhaps it should have been intimidating for me, a twenty-year-old, to be working on these film sets with major actors and directors. But I had already worked on the Tamil movie, been in two extremely high-profile pageants, and endured the public fallout from my nasal surgery. I'd spent plenty of time in the public gaze and gained a bit of moviemaking experience. With so much at stake, I refused to be daunted by these somewhat daunting circumstances. In my race not to fail, I would do whatever needed to be done, address whatever problems I needed to address. That was my mindset.

And so all was going well on set until one day my lack of experience caught up with me. We were filming a romantic song on a gorgeous afternoon in Cape Town, South Africa. The director wanted a shot that opened with my co-actor Akshay Kumar and me in a sunlit field of yellow flowers. I was to spin joyously with my arms spread wide, run through the flowers toward Akshay, do another spin with him, then propel myself into his arms and start lip-syncing the lyrics of "Allah Kare Dil Na Lage" to the melodious voice of Alka Yagnik. There was plenty of that wonderful slow-motion movement—running and hair flipping included—that I'd dreamed of doing in a big film. The air was soft, the sun was shining down on us, and everything was perfect. Except that I was completely blowing it.

Although the choreography didn't include any complicated steps, it did have just enough stylized movement to throw me off. Each time I tried the sequence, I'd mess up some piece of it and we'd have to start all over again. We needed a crane to get the scene, and the reset was relatively slow because it was a wide shot. It was the end of the day, we were losing light, and I was on take thirty. Or thirty-five. The pressure was on.

Finally, the choreographer Raju Khan threw the mic down and told me to pack up for the day. "Just because you're Miss World, don't presume you can dance. Learn to do your job before you report for work!"

Coincidence and timing were operating in my favor, though. The film had to break unexpectedly for ten days, and filming in Cape Town temporarily ceased. Dharmesh Darshan, the brother of the *Andaaz* producer Suneel Darshan, had seen me crying off set after the humiliating episode with Raju, and he gave me the name of the renowned classical dance teacher and actor Pandit Veeru Krishnan. "Call him as soon as you get back home," Dharmesh Sir suggested, as most of the cast and crew were returning to Mumbai. (Culturally, it's common in India to add a suffix to someone's name as a form of respect for seniority in age or authority. "Ji," for example is a common one. My father used "sir" and "ma'am" as part of military protocol. I adopted the habit of "sir" from him.) And so of course I did. Veeruji, or Guruji to his students, was known for his ability to transform nondancers into dancers, so he was the go-to guy for new actors. I started taking classes with him alongside a few other newcomers whom I'd already crossed paths with, like Lara, Harman Baweja, Sameera Reddy, and Katrina Kaif, as well as others I'd continue to be connected to in the future. And my mom. Yep. While she was in medical school, she also did postgraduate studies in Kathak dance, one of the eight forms of Indian classical dance. When I started studying Kathak with Guruji, Mom decided she wanted to refresh her skills and take classes with me. And maybe show off a little.

I worked for almost eight hours a day with Guruji while I was on break in Mumbai, and suddenly I found coordination. Guruji and Kathak infused it straight into me. My hands knew what to do. My feet knew what to do. My head knew what to do. When I returned to Cape Town a couple of weeks later to shoot the same shot with the same music and the same choreography, Raju Khan, happily surprised, said, "I don't know what you did, but now you're a dancer."

The episode was another critical piece in the foundation of my career. It taught me the difference between being an amateur and a professional, and how essential it is to be prepared. From that experience onward, I've always prepped assiduously before going onto any set. As best I could, I've developed whatever skills are necessary to portray my characters convincingly. That might mean a new martial art form for action sequences, or a new type of dance for dance sequences. Or I might learn a different accent, or even bits of a new language, as I did for *Bajirao Mastani* and *Kaminey,* when I learned enough Marathi to convincingly portray my characters, and season three of *Quantico* when I learned Italian well enough to speak the dialogue that required it. For the biopic *Mary Kom,* I learned how to box. For *Don,* I learned tai chi, and for *The Legend of Drona,* I learned Gatka, a Sikh martial art. I also learned to ride—which I absolutely hated, having had a bad fall from a horse when I was eight. In fact, I was so scared that we had to use a simulation horse for my close-ups, and here I was supposed to be a warrior. But I don't choose my characters based on the skills I'll need to acquire in order to play them. Once I've taken on a job, I give 100 percent to it, whether I like every aspect of it or not. For *Drona,* I persevered until I learned to ride well enough to do what was required for my role.

My experience in *Andaaz* was significant in other ways, too. The movie was hugely successful at the box office, which of course was good for the careers of anyone involved with it. It also netted me my first Filmfare Award, which was for Best Debut Female—an award I shared with Lara Dutta! Working with her was such a pleasure; we had traveled together on our millennium pageant journeys, and I'd been grateful to have someone familiar to me on set on one of my first big movies. And now we had both won recognition as we started our film careers together.

The choreographer Raju Khan went on to become a dear friend. I always told him that it was his tough love that day that forced me to learn not only the skills necessary to succeed in Hindi movies but the mindset required to succeed in any profession.

✳

I WAS ON a huge learning curve for the first few years of my career, and one of the things that I was learning was that the Hindi film industry was mostly patriarchal: male producers usually called the shots, and things centered on the male actor. I saw this play out on the set of one of my early movies. I would arrive as scheduled at 9:00 A.M. every day. My male co-actor, however, wouldn't arrive until 4:30 in the afternoon, keeping the crew and all the other actors waiting. That was his pattern and it was simply accepted by the director and the producer.

"This isn't fair. I don't want to do this," I told my mother over the phone after the first couple of times it happened. To which she responded, "You should be someone whose word is your bond. When you're finished with the commitments you've made and fulfilled the contracts you've signed, if you still don't like the way things are done, then don't sign any more contracts."

When I expressed my frustration to one of my other co-actors, he responded by saying, "It doesn't matter if you're sitting and waiting. Your producer has paid you for your participation. It's your commitment and your work, even if you have to play video games in your trailer while you're waiting. How they use your time is up to them." When he put it that way, it made sense and really stuck with me. I should focus on *my* commitment to the process, not on anyone else's, and that's what I've endeavored to do ever since.

My parents did their best to keep my confidence intact as we all tried to figure out the business, taking whatever steps made sense at the time. Perhaps in a nod to what a male-dominated industry the film business was, in the early days of my career, before I hired outside management, my father established one unbreakable rule. "No nighttime meetings, nothing after sundown." That was it. At the time, of course, I didn't understand it. Whenever I questioned the rule, he'd stand firm: "All meetings will be in the daytime, when you'll be in the presence of either Mom or me." Clearly my father was smart to fear the big bad world of entertainment, which his teenage daughter was so naïvely heading into. I'm convinced that because of his protectiveness and this one absolute, nonnegotiable line in the sand, I was spared from having some of the terrible experiences that so many young people have when they are breaking into the entertainment industry. While I did feel saddened and frustrated by the patriarchy and favoritism of the Bollywood system, I never felt physically threatened during my rise in it, and I attribute that to a combination of luck—bad things can and do happen in broad daylight, all the time, with people close by in the next room—and my father's wisdom.

That's not to say that I didn't have my share of uncomfortable and unpleasant moments. Like the time my character in a big film was to perform a seduction song during which I would take my clothes off slowly, one piece at a time. Since it was a long song, maybe four minutes, I asked the director if it would be smart for me to have lots of layers to take off so that I wouldn't be down to skin way too fast.

"Maybe I could have stockings, and a jacket, and maybe a hair ribbon I could do something with." I was picturing all sorts of creative ways to make the number really tantalizing. "You know, various things I could remove before my actual clothes."

The director suggested I speak to my stylist, so I called him and briefly explained the situation, then passed the phone to the director. Standing right in front of me, the director said: *"Jo bhi ho, chaddiyan dikhni chahiyen. Nahi toh log picture kyon dekne aayenge?"*

Which translates as: "Whatever happens, panties should be seen. Otherwise, why would people come to watch the movie?"

I quit the next day. When I'd signed on for the job, of course I'd known there was to be a seduction song with the removal of clothes; that was not the problem. The song made sense as part of the story and as something the character would do, being someone who wore her sexuality unself-consciously and for all to see. I was ready to go full-out as a temptress in the number. The director's words and tone, though, conveyed that he regarded me in a way that I found unacceptable: as a mere commodity for titillation. What I thought I'd been hired as—a professional who brought her talent, hard work, and willingness to embody a character with all her strengths and flaws—and what he apparently thought I'd been hired as—a sexual object—were two irreconcilably different things. The character may have sometimes put herself in the position of being seen as a purely sexual object, but I am not whatever character I am playing, and I wasn't willing to be directed by someone who saw me that way. Instead, I trusted my intuition and exited.

When the producer found out I'd quit, he was livid, because we'd already shot for two days. He drove down to another movie set where I was working—it was not uncommon for actors to be shooting multiple movies at a time in the Hindi film business—and strode toward my trailer in what was clearly an agitated state. I was upset, too. I'd known there would be consequences to my leaving, but I didn't want to be in the center of a big drama, especially given that I was still a relative newcomer. My co-actor Salman Khan, who was and is a huge star in India, understood the situation immediately and intervened on my behalf. He waited outside my trailer, and when the producer arrived, he had a conversation with him that defused the situation. I'm not sure exactly what he said, but the producer was in a much calmer state when he spoke to me. I never told the producer the real reason why I'd left. I was a newcomer in a patriarchal industry and I'd learned that it was better not to poke the bear. *Keep your head down and keep smiling* was the rule for the girls, and I was already pushing boundaries. So rather than explaining what had actually happened, I told him that I'd misunderstood the character and wasn't comfortable playing her, and that I'd send them a check to reimburse them for the two days they'd have to reshoot with someone else. Which I did. The money that I returned for the cost of reshooting two days amounted to almost as much as I would have been paid for my twelve to thirteen weeks of work on the movie had I stayed.

With each new role, on each new set, and with each new director, I was learning more and more about what it took physically, mentally, and emotionally to be an actor, and what I needed in order to do my best work. A big part of all that was how I wanted to be treated. Early on, when a producer offered me less than 10 percent of what my male co-actor would be receiving for basically the same amount of work on a blockbuster film, I stood up for myself and suggested that I should be paid a little more. His response was, "You can ask for more money and make your point, sure, but you know that in these roles in these kinds of films, girls are interchangeable. If you don't take this opportunity as it is, some other girl will come along and grab it and be very happy about it."

It seems that the director on the set of the seduction song thought that girls were interchangeable, too. I wanted to be respected for what I brought to the table, not merely regarded as one object for titillation that could be readily swapped out for another. Quitting that movie at such an early stage in my career was extremely hard, because word travels fast in the entertainment industry no matter where in the world you are, and I didn't want to get a reputation as someone who caused trouble or couldn't be relied upon to behave professionally. But it needed to be done. Even if I couldn't articulate it at the time, I knew that maintaining my self-respect was more important than saving a big role.

The steepness of my learning curve continued. I understood more and more clearly that to build and maintain a career, I would need to do some serious networking. The early awards that I'd won were helpful, but they weren't enough to ensure that I would continue to work, because nobody knew me, and Bollywood was ruled by people who'd grown up in it together.

Writing a memoir jogs your memory, bringing to light things that have been pushed below the level of awareness, things that we might rather forget. One such memory—or in my case, a series of memories—relates to the nature of the favoritism that existed in the Hindi film industry when I was coming up. I faced it at many points in my career. Think of it as related to the kind of bullying that often takes place during the teenage years in a school setting: it's so much a part of the culture that rather than push back, you just accept it.

The Bollywood system was known at the time for having "insiders"—people with generational ties to the business—and "outsiders." If you didn't have an "insider's" familiarity with the powerful people, or the lifelong social bonds to fall back on, it was a struggle. You would have to work much harder to prove your talent and to earn the kinds of roles you wanted. As a nineteen-year-old newcomer to the entertainment world, it felt like a big boys' club that I'd never be able to break into. Over and over again I had to prove to the studios, which were mostly family-owned, that I deserved a seat at their table—which was not so easy when I over-heard comments at parties like "I got her cast in this movie and I can take it away from her as well" (eventually and unfortunately, the woman who made the remark did just that) and "She'll never make it as an actress, too *kaali*." I find it so painfully ironic that in a country populated by people who are all shades of brown, the standard of beauty is white. Hearing comments that dismissed me in such a matter-of-fact way was distressing, but I could steel myself against them and try to ignore them. The most difficult times for me, the moments when I felt the most hopeless, were when I was let go from projects because a co-actor, director, or producer who had grown up at the table wanted to gift a role to someone else. That always crushed me.

Relatively early in my career, the lead actor of a movie I was about to start shooting came to visit me on the set of a film I was then working on. "Listen, Priyanka," he said casually, "you may not be able to do this movie because I've promised the role to someone else." (The "someone else," I soon found out, was his girlfriend.) Stunned, I said that I'd already signed the contract and was counting on starting in just a few days. He shrugged. "We'll find something else for you to do." His tone was almost benevolent. It was the first time this had happened to me—it happened again a few years later—but, as I had been discovering, it was not all that unusual for things to unfold this way. As I look back now, the episode makes me shudder, not with disbelief at its occurrence or at how many others may have faced nearly identical situations, but because I did not raise my voice at that time.

As I have said, though, this favoritism was so normalized in that place and time that it simply never occurred to me to push back in any significant way. I had to work within the system, and so I worked within the system. But I can tell you that it was an isolating experience, one that slowly chipped away at my self-confidence. I felt like I was being bullied. And because I had been bullied before, I had some mechanisms to deal with it. After my high school experience, I was hell-bent on not succumbing or pandering just because it was expected that I do so. As a fifteen-year-old in Massachusetts, I had tried to soldier through the bullying but I hadn't had the internal resources. This time, I decided to stick it out no matter what. I put my head down, did my work, and blocked out as much as I could.

Fortunately, in the film industry as in life, the actions of a few don't always reflect the behavior of the whole. There were plenty of people in the Hindi film industry who focused on the talent of the actors they approached and on their ability to connect to an audience. There were others who had worked their way up before me, and there are those who will continue to do so after me. I was able to get—and keep—enough roles to build a solid career. Initially this fueled me. It also encouraged me to think beyond conventional opportunities and sink my teeth into characters and roles that I quite possibly would not have explored otherwise. It forced me to delve into areas that were outside my comfort zone. At the end of the day, the audience accepted me, and I forged a career I'm proud of.

The thing about favoritism and patriarchy is that they make it an unfairly steep climb for a large number of talented, deserving people—whatever the field. Having experienced that long, hard climb myself made me want to be part of the community that's working to make it easier for those who follow. We can't choose the family we were born into but we can choose our actions. We all want to take care of the people we are closest to, those sitting at our table. But is there a world in which those who are blessed with more might build a larger table rather than building a higher fence?

BY THE TIME I'd been working for a few years, I'd fallen in love with the work and with the industry. It no longer mattered much if I had to wait around for hours for my male co-actors to make it onto set; it didn't matter if I was wearing a flimsy chiffon sari in the snow, or a fur jacket in the heat of Mehboob Studio in Mumbai; it didn't matter if a hundred people watched me while I danced in the streets. I was in love with the movies. I often chose not to return to my trailer between shots, preferring instead to stay on set. I delighted in the hustle and bustle of movies being made.

So much of filmmaking, I realized, was about feeling confident, and I also realized that knowledge is a key to confidence. If you have the knowledge of something, you can walk into almost any room and hold your own. I relished honing my skills, learning and improving and growing. I loved taking lines of dialogue and transforming them into a multidimensional person with a past and a future and a unique take on the world. I developed a hunger for seeing how many personalities I could create, and how different they could be. Wondering what kind of person I'll be breathing life into next is one of the many things that keep me excited about this job of mine.

One of the ways I developed my skills was through studying my co-actors and my directors. I'd watch the directors and try to figure out why they made certain requests or decisions, even on the technical side of filmmaking—why would the director of photography choose a certain lens or want a change in lighting, for instance, or why would he suddenly go from a wide shot to a close-up—and that started giving me a larger lens through which to look at the way stories are told in this medium.

The more I studied my co-actors, the more I became convinced that the actors who made the most lasting impressions were the ones who did two things. First, they truly listened in every one of their scenes rather than just waiting to say their lines. Acting is primarily *reacting* truthfully in the moment, and that is dictated organically by what your co-actors do. Second, they found ways to communicate multiple thoughts and feelings simultaneously. In my experience, only children have isolated emotions. If a little child is angry, he's angry. If she's excited, she's excited. But as we evolve into adults, our emotional and intellectual capacities broaden and deepen, and expressing this complexity is one of the jobs of the actor. Think about it. Say you're having a terrible argument with your sister because you've discovered that she's been telling your parents hurtful lies about you. You might be furious at her, and you also might be feeling deeply betrayed. And of course you still love her. You've discovered her lies just as you were about to leave for an important appointment and now you're worried that you're going to be late. Then there's the physical piece—maybe it's a sweltering day and the air-conditioning isn't working, or it's a frigid day and the heat isn't up high enough. All of these things could be going on more or less simultaneously.

If I were playing a scene with a character in these circumstances, I would map out what my character is feeling at any given moment in the scene and what she's thinking but not saying. I'd figure out which emotion of the several that she's feeling is the one that has to dominate because of the story arc. I'd think about where she's coming from and where she's going, and how she responds physically, emotionally, and intellectually to the world and the challenges she encounters in it. A writer writes a film, and a director has a vision for it. As I see it, my job as an actor is to translate the words on the page into the compelling journey of my character between "Action!" and "Cut!" And this is why I love creating characters.

I had the chance to dive into a really meaty character journey early in my career when, in 2003, the successful brother team of Abbas-Mustan offered me a role in their dramatic thriller *Aitraaz*. I'd been hoping to work with them ever since 2000, when they offered me a role in their romantic thriller *Humraaz* after my Miss India win. It was the first role I'd ever been offered and I desperately wanted to accept it, and in fact had been advised by many to sign on. But the Miss World pageant was approaching and I didn't want to create any conflicts in the crazy eventuality that I came home with the crown—I *did* want the crown, no matter how minuscule the chances were that I'd get it—so I declined the role. When the opportunity to do *Aitraaz* came along, I grabbed it.

Aitraaz gave me the chance to play a really bold character—power- and money-hungry, sexually voracious, and willing to stop at nothing to get what she wants. Better yet, it showed me that I could create and inhabit a complicated character that many would find distasteful, and I could do it credibly and compellingly. The movie swept audiences up in its tale of love and betrayal and was a huge success, winning a number of awards. I garnered several, including my second Filmfare Award, this one for Best Actor in a Negative Role. I was only the second female actor to win the award since its inception in 1992—Kajol won it in 1998 for her role in *Gupt*—and so the honor was especially meaningful to me. (The award was discontinued after 2007, and Kajol and I remain the only two female actors to have received it.) More thrilling than even the awards, though, was the critical acclaim. It was my first taste of such rave reviews, and I began to see that there could be a big payoff to taking risks, that maybe pushing the limits was a way to blaze my own trail instead of doing what was expected of me. In Hindi movies at that time, it was the norm for female leads to play characters who were sympathetic and pure; my character in *Aitraaz* was anything but, and people warned me that future directors might typecast me into this kind of role, limiting my opportunities. Since childhood I'd always liked to be the first to do or discover things, and creating my own path was a way of staying ahead of the curve. This is not to say that there hadn't been female actors before me who had played bold parts. There had. But I figured that taking the road less traveled would help me stand out, because, as I was seeing again and again, being different was my superpower. And the possibility that it might expand the playing field for other female actors, too, allowing us all more freedom to play a larger range of roles, made the appeal, and the payoff, even stronger.

LIKE MOST ACTORS, I eventually hit a rough patch in my career. About five years after I started working, a run of six movies I made flopped back to back. That shook me up profoundly. I had invested myself in my chosen profession with everything I had, dropping out of school and working more or less nonstop. Mom and Dad had given up their hospital in Bareilly and moved to Mumbai to help manage my career. Sid was now back from the States and living with us. I had a Plan B—academics—but that meant accepting failure in my chosen field. I'd tasted the sweetness of success and I was hungry for more. I didn't want to revert to Plan B because I'd failed at Plan A. I needed to turn the tide. I was driven to turn it.

Time to sink or swim, I told myself. So I leapt into the deep end to try something few female actors were doing at that time in India: a female-led movie. I was warned that female actors usually only did that kind of film as a swan song because it was so risky. Why risky? Because just about all of the resounding box-office successes in the Hindi film industry were male-led. By that point, in professional free fall, perhaps, but at age twenty-five and nowhere near ready for a swan song, I thought a female-led movie would be worth the risk.

And there was another reason I was ready to take a gamble. After getting thrown off two films because the lead actor wanted the role for his girlfriend, and struggling to get cast in the kinds of big commercial blockbusters I'd imagined I'd work in, I decided to do a partial pivot and focus on unusual, challenging roles that I could win, and keep, based on merit.

I signed on to do *Fashion,* a drama helmed by the award-winning director Madhur Bhandarkar, in 2007. The movie follows the rise and fall of Meghna Mathur, a young woman from a small town who moves to Mumbai with the dream of becoming a supermodel. She succeeds, but at an impossibly high price. Meghna drives the story, and she's surrounded by a slew of other complex and compellingly written female characters. A few of the actors and directors I'd previously worked with suggested that this might not be the best move for me, starring as an extremely flawed character in a film where the action doesn't revolve around a male. I welcomed the challenge, though, wanting the responsibility of carrying a film. I was already all in with my career. Why not swim a little farther out from shore?

The movie was grueling both physically and emotionally. I had to gain a lot of weight for the beginning scenes and then lose more than I'd gained to pull off the supermodel look at the end of the movie. Madhur Bhandarkar was a wonderful collaborator and we worked together to create a graph of Meghna Mathur's evolution, from her ascension to fame and fortune through her ignominious downfall and ultimate resurrection. As a result of trusting my intuition and working with a filmmaker known for directing complex female roles, I followed a road less traveled and won my first National Film Award for Best Actress. Kangana Ranaut won Best Supporting Actress, and Madhur Bhandarkar was nominated for Best Director. The almost bigger achievement, though, was that the film opened strong and did well at the box office, proving that female-led movies were commercially viable. After that, I continued to take on a lot more films that were female-led, and it was largely my experience with *Fashion* that reaffirmed to me that I was on the right path when I was moving out of the safety zone and into the unexpected.

And in part, it was my experience with *Aitraaz* that gave me the courage to sign on to *Fashion*. Both films feature leading characters whose behavior ranges from unpleasant to edgy to morally offensive to illegal. If I hadn't had such success with Sonia, my character in *Aitraaz,* it would have been a lot harder for me to accept the challenge of bringing Meghna Mathur to life in *Fashion.*

Almost simultaneously, on the heels of *Fashion*'s success, came my next commercial blockbuster, *Dostana.* The feel-good romantic comedy opened two weeks after the much darker tale of Meghna

Mathur, and audiences loved this story of two guys who pretend to be gay in order to secure an apartment in Miami, only to both fall madly in love with their roommate/landlady, played by me. Starring John Abraham and Abhishek Bachchan, directed by Tarun Mansukhani—still one of my closest friends today—and produced by Dharma Productions, an A-list production house, the movie became a runaway success. It featured the catchy hit song "Desi Girl" with music by Vishal-Shekhar and lyrics by Kumaar. Suddenly I had a public nickname: Desi Girl. Even now I'm referred to as Desi Girl—Indian girl—especially in India. Nick performed the song the night before our wedding at our *sangeet* celebration, winning the hearts of everyone from my home country who was present and understood the reference.

Ironic, isn't it, that after deciding to focus on smaller movies and more unusual, demanding roles, *Dostana* became the kind of big mainstream success I'd been dreaming of for so many years.

AS MY CAREER started to move in the right direction, I was determined to build on it and take it as far as I could. I continued to develop my skills, make bold choices, and work almost nonstop. In India, the success of an actor is measured not only in terms of awards and box office but also by the major brand endorsements that they sign, so this was an important aspect of my quest to cement my growing position as a leading actor in the film industry. Early in my career I had declined many brand opportunities that came my way, because I really wanted to focus on aligning with the right kinds of brands. I wanted to take on partnerships with brands that were leaders in their categories and had products I could see myself using as a consumer.

As my popularity grew, the brands came calling. From Nikon to

Nokia to Samsung, and Pepsi to Sunsilk to TAG Heuer, I was proud of the roster of brands that I endorsed. But one important category remained unfilled: beauty and skin care.

It's important to note that at the time in Asia, it was as de rigueur for skin care brands to promote whiter skin as it was for hair care brands to promote dark, lustrous hair. Given India's history, the idea that a fairer skin tone is something to aspire to has been drilled into Indian culture for centuries, maybe longer. This destructive social norm isn't limited to India, of course. Skin altering is a huge problem throughout all of Asia. In India, part of the fallout is that many bestselling products from major skin care brands for women promote themselves as "fairness creams." While skin-whitening is a multibillion-dollar business throughout Asia, fair-skinned people in Europe, America, and elsewhere spend millions of dollars in tanning salons to darken their skin. The grass is always greener on the other side, I guess.

Given that brand deals are critical to the trajectory of an actor's career in India, and that beauty and skin care brands are the most coveted for women, when these offers came my way, it felt like a great opportunity. These were well-respected global companies, and this combined with the fact that they wanted to sign me as the face of their brands signaled to me that I had scaled the mountain of measurable success and arrived at the top.

The creative directions of these commercials were different but the communication was very similar . . . beauty equated to fair and light skin. In the ads, the lightening of my skin seemed to be a primary point, while other attributes of the product were minimally showcased.

In spite of the cultural acceptance of this norm, I vividly remember a conversation I had with the brand team about evolving the messaging around this noxious narrative. To be fair, they did make an attempt but the market research they conducted always came back to the original messaging being the strongest. All I could think of was how I'd felt as a teenage girl using store-bought and homemade fairness concoctions because I believed my skin color made me unattractive. I thought about how pained I'd felt when I was called *kaali* as a child. I was now promoting the destructive messages that had so eaten away at my sense of self-worth when I was growing up, and I knew the only person I could blame was myself.

At this point in my life, I had evolved enough on my own inner journey to reevaluate both the implicit and the explicit cultural messages I'd absorbed over my lifetime. My aversion to all forms of discrimination toward girls and women—color being a fundamental one—had become more pronounced, and I knew that I didn't want to be part of any campaign that perpetuated any feelings of insecurity or diminishment in our sex. So, I chose to take a definitive stance and distance myself from this archaic cultural norm. I haven't done a skin care campaign in India since that time, almost a decade ago.

Unfortunately, this standard of beauty is so deeply entrenched in Indian culture that the major skin care brands still focus on skin lightening. While some brands are now taking steps to rebrand and reword their messaging—using euphemisms like skin "brightening," for instance—the ads featuring popular faces still keep coming. I'm hopeful, however, that the more open discussion that's happening around the world will lead to a time in the near future when girls and women will no longer feel the pressure to alter their skin tones.

Looking back, this was one of the biggest missteps of my career and is one of my most profound regrets. I can't go back and change what I did, but I can apologize, and I do so sincerely. To all the people who saw the harmful messaging that I contributed to, to all the people who still have to see commercials like these in every medium—I am deeply sorry.

SHORTLY AFTER *Fashion* and *Dostana,* I signed on for the role of Sweety in *Kaminey.* People wondered why I would be interested in taking on a minor part after my triumphs in leading roles in those successful films. Two reasons: First, I no longer trusted that a film's success and positive critical reaction for my role in it were enough to help me build a career. Second and even more important, perhaps, was the fact that I really wanted to work with the director, Vishal Bhardwaj, and I remembered that at the beginning of my career, Amitabh Bachchan quoted Stanislavski to me: *There are no small parts, only small actors.* I took on the role, prepping for it as if it were a starring part, and I won a lot of acclaim for it even though I was in just a handful of scenes. It was positive reinforcement for following my instincts in order to work with Vishal Sir, whom I was to collaborate with again—this time in a leading role—not too far into the future.

I continued to work in a mix of genres featuring a plethora of wildly different characters. In *7 Khoon Maaf,* a noir comedy, I played a woman who kept killing her husbands—all seven of them. In *Barfi!,* I played a nineteen-year-old autistic woman in love with a deaf and mute man. I played the title role in *Mary Kom,* a biopic about the Olympic medal winner and the six-time world champion amateur boxer. In *Bajirao Mastani,* my role was that of a Marathi queen living in the 1600s. I played an aspiring actress, a kindergarten teacher, a fashion magazine editor, and an assortment of wives and girlfriends.

And so my Hindi movie career evolved. With each film, I added more acting tools to my toolbox; I gained more knowledge about the technical side of moviemaking; I understood better and better how to breathe life into the words on the page. With each film, I came to know myself a little more intimately as an actor, to recognize what came easily to me and what skills I needed to develop further, what excited me and what didn't. Because I was and am ambitious, and because I'd had the experience of losing career-launching roles at the very start of my professional life, I decided I would never say no to a role I felt strongly about, even if it meant shooting two or three movies at a time, even if it meant I rarely had a full day off for weeks and months on end. It's a decision that paid off well for me professionally, but the decision came with a price tag, and it's one I wouldn't understand for some years to come.

After throwing myself into my work for more than twelve years, just when it might have been time to reap the benefits of all the experience I'd gained and all the professional relationships I'd worked so incredibly hard to develop, just when I was at the top of my game in India, who knew my career would take another sharp left and I would, in essence, have to go back to walking into a room and introducing myself all over again?

As they say, "You want to tell God a joke? Tell her your plans."

7

TINSELTOWN

Mrs. Robinson, you are trying to seduce me. Aren't you?
DUSTIN HOFFMAN IN *THE GRADUATE*

THE OPPORTUNITY THAT initially uprooted me from the career I'd worked so hard for in India and took me halfway around the world to America wasn't acting. It was music.

In 2009, Anjula Acharia, a venture capitalist and tech investor, had an online platform called Desi Hits that was best known for taking artists like Lady Gaga and Britney Spears from America to India and producing music that was a cross-pollination of East and West. Legendary music producer Jimmy Iovine, co-founder of Interscope Records, who'd produced albums by Tupac Shakur, Eminem, 50 Cent, Stevie Nicks, and Tom Petty, among others, was an investor in the company. Jimmy had signed the *Slumdog Millionaire* soundtrack to Interscope and worked with Anjula on the "Jai Ho!" collaboration between the celebrated A. R. Rahman, the song's composer, and the girl band The Pussycat Dolls. It had become a huge international hit and now Anjula and Jimmy were searching for their next project. Which turned out to be me.

Rather than taking an American star to India, they wanted to bring an Indian star to the States. Anjula remembered seeing me in the rom-com *Bluffmaster!* on television years earlier while visiting her parents in England and thinking, *If any South Asian could break into America at all, it would be her.* It was the song "Right Here, Right Now"—a funky, sexy number—that had particularly impressed her. She forgot all about it, though, until her mother sent her a copy of the movie *Fashion* a couple of years later, saying, "It stars that actress that you like."

Right, thought Anjula. *I did like her.* She showed the clip of "Right Here, Right Now" to Jimmy, who said, "No-brainer." Because most of the musical numbers in Hindi films are lip-synced, though—the female part of this song was sung by Sunidhi Chauhan—he added, "Can she sing?"

Coincidentally, Anjula was working at the time with Salim-Sulaiman, an extremely popular and well-known music composer duo with whom I'd worked previously. It came up in conversation that they just happened to have a demo tape they'd done with me for fun a few years in the past, so the question of whether or not I could sing was easily answered.

I swear that was fate.

More than a whole year passed before things progressed. Anjula heard the demo and reached out to me, but I was finally working again with Vishal Bhardwaj, the director I'd wanted to work with so much in 2008 that I'd accepted a smaller part in *Kaminey* than I was then accustomed to taking, just for the chance to be directed by him. This time I was playing the lead character in *7 Khoon Maaf*—an intensely noir comedy based on the Ruskin Bond novella "Susanna's Seven Husbands"—and it was such an immersive experience for me that I wanted to keep myself completely focused on it. There were practical complications, too. We were filming in Coorg (now known as Kodagu), a hill station in the state of Karnataka in southern India. Our location was somewhat remote, and Internet and cell service were spotty. In order to speak to anyone, I had to go to the roof of the inn where we were staying and accept the call late at night after a full day of shooting.

One night I climbed to the rooftop to accept a call from Natasha Pal, who was my manager in India at the time and who now manages my digital strategy. She told me that she'd received several calls from Anjula and thought I should talk to her.

"I really don't have the bandwidth to think about this right now, Nats," I responded. "I don't want to be distracted."

"It will take ten minutes," Natasha said. "I think you should be working internationally, and what Anjula is proposing will give you an opportunity to do that." She let that sink in for a moment, then added, "I believe your career is global, Priyanka. At least talk to her."

I stood on the rooftop in the darkness and thought about it. And because it was Natasha saying it—one of my closest advisors and dearest friends—I agreed.

Sometime later I climbed to the rooftop again to accept a late-night call from this persistent woman whom I had yet to meet. She gave me a lot to chew on during our twenty-minute conversation, outlining the possibility she saw for me to be one of the first artists from India—as opposed to Indian artists who had grown up in America—to succeed in mainstream American pop culture. Natasha had put the germ of an international career in my head; Anjula was explaining how it could happen. She was a successful businessperson, had impressive music cred, and I could hear how strategic she was. This was undeniably a big opportunity, and I've always been drawn to trying new and risky things. How could I resist?

It was 2010 when Anjula flew to Mumbai with David Joseph,

who at that time was Universal Music's U.K. chairman and chief executive, and Andrew Kronfeld, the executive vice president of marketing for Universal Music Group International. She wanted me to take the opportunity seriously, I learned long afterward, so she talked to Jimmy, who advised taking David Joseph along; David suggested inviting Andrew Kronfeld, too. Power in numbers. It was a good strategy.

We had a great meeting in Salim-Sulaiman's studio, and the spark of curiosity about going international that had been planted in me was fanned into life. I didn't know if I would be able to make music that people would want to listen to, but it was a chance to do something I hadn't yet done professionally—music—on a huge stage I hadn't worked on before—international—and that was intimidating and exhilarating to me at the same time. Because my movie career was established and I had commitments into the future, I was going to have to work music around my movies, and I'd only have time for two films a year, say, instead of four. Which meant that both of those had better succeed. That added an element of risk to my current career, as well as the risk involved in diving into music. If you've read this much of my story, you know that I'm not afraid of risk, and also that I love a challenge. This was another chance for me to sink or swim, and so I dove in.

Together Anjula and Jimmy created a label called Desi Hits/Interscope, which signed me. Working in London made sense to everyone, as it was much easier to get back and forth to India from England than from the U.S., and I needed to work around my film commitments. But when I arrived in London with Natasha for my first week of recording, I became hyperaware of my inexperience. I was surrounded by incredible songwriters, producers, and sound engineers who were all being brought on board to help me succeed, but I hardly recognized the thin voice coming out of me as my own. I got to feeling so shy that I'd turn off the light in the sound booth so I'd be cloaked in darkness and nobody could watch me while I sang. Was this the same person who danced unself-consciously in front of hundreds of people with bright lights and cameras trained on her? Was it a foreshadowing of some sort?

Sometime not long after that I was in New York City and finally met Jimmy Iovine when he, Anjula, and I had a memorable dinner at the Monkey Bar in midtown Manhattan. It was one of those dinners when everything just clicks. I don't know what he was expecting, but as soon as Jimmy saw me, he turned to Anjula and said, "This is easy!" Right from the start he had a faith in my potential that I didn't necessarily have at the time. As someone who has launched so many careers, and with such deep experience in both business and entertainment—he also co-produced Eminem's critically acclaimed movie *8 Mile,* and co-founded Beats Electronics with Dr. Dre—he became an extremely important part of my music chapter in the U.S. Even now I see him as a mentor and a friend. His belief in me was the extra nudge I needed to quiet my doubts about succeeding in an entirely new creative endeavor in an entirely new environment. And by the end of the dinner, we'd made a decision to bring me to the States to record under the Desi Hits/Interscope U.S. label.

It turns out that Jimmy's "This is easy" assessment was overly optimistic. Given my lack of music credentials, we couldn't pretend that I had music relevance—I didn't, at all—and so it was crucial to establish myself as someone who was culturally relevant in the U.S. To do that, we would have to address the fact that even though I was at the top of my game in India, no one outside of the viewers of Bollywood movies knew who I was. So we focused on two major things: creating an awareness of me, and creating my sound.

The decision was made that it was important for me to spend more and more time in the U.S., flying in and out for important events, making sure that I met the Who's Who of the music and the media industries. This was far easier said than done. I had to go into the offices of magazines that I'd been on the covers of multiple times in India and introduce myself as an absolute unknown, saying "Hey, I've been on your cover in India and I'm coming to America. Here's who I am and this is my body of work." Not everyone was open to meeting such a complete unknown, no matter what her credentials elsewhere were, much less writing about her in their magazine. This was at a time when I was having huge successes like *Don 2* and *Gunday* and *Krrish 3* and *Mary Kom* in India. I swallowed my pride and reminded myself constantly that just because I'd received recognition in one part of the world was no reason that I should automatically receive it elsewhere. I'd seen what a sense of entitlement could do and I wanted no part of that.

I faced the same problem with parties and red-carpet events. I knew that we had to do everything we could think of to make my presence felt in the well-oiled machinery that was Hollywood. And if I wanted to make my presence properly felt, I had to demonstrate that I was a peer and not a complete newcomer to the entertainment business. I had to be seen as someone who was on the same playing field, not someone who was in the upper reaches of the stadium seating. That meant being at important events like the Grammys, the Oscars, the Met Gala, and significant premieres, among other things. But it took a long time for those invitations to come. Although I had a large body of work amassed over a decade on another continent, I was reminded daily that I'd barely made it to the starting line here.

Slowly, slowly, inroads were made. The first year I received an invitation to the Roc Nation pre-Grammys brunch, I was pumped. I arrived with Anjula, feeling psyched that progress was being made. Simultaneously, she and I realized that we were on one side of the gathering and all the A-listers were on the other side. There was an absolute separation between the well-known entertainers at the party and everyone else. Both of us gazed at this clique of strangers for a while, and then Anjula slowly turned to me and said, "I know who you are and I know what you've done, but you should walk in that direction and introduce yourself to those people." I looked at Anjula, understood what she meant, bent my head in humility, and walked into a sea of people who had no idea who I was.

I may have chatted with some of the people I met that afternoon, but it wasn't until a couple of years later that I made any kind of meaningful impact.

And of course there was the music piece of the puzzle, too. Every successful recording artist has their own identifiable sound. Because I'd been developing myself as an actor for years rather than as a singer, I didn't—yet. When I started recording in the U.S. in 2011, RedOne was brought in to produce the album I was now under contract for. A plan evolved to put me into a room with a variety of different songwriters and artists in order to help me find my own distinct sound and style. Between films in India, I'd fly to L.A. or New York to record, usually for a couple of weeks at a time, and there was always someone incredible for me to try out new things with: will.i.am, who worked with me on the song "In My City," an energetic, feel-good pop tune about my travels around the world and how a city can give you an identity; Pitbull, who worked with me on "Exotic"; The Chainsmokers, who worked with me on "Erase"; Matt Koma, who worked with me on various songs that still reside somewhere on both of our computers; and a number of others.

Some of the songs seemed to invite an infusion of my Indian identity, and when that was the case, it was really fun and satisfying to figure out the best way to make that happen. We added Indian instrumentation to "In My City" to give it a hint of South Asian flavor. After Pitbull sent in his lyrics for "Exotic," I suggested to RedOne that we add some Hindi lyrics to it, which I wrote when he agreed. We then incorporated Indian-inspired dance steps into the video for "Exotic" to carry the fusion through to the visual. All of the artists were talented and generous to me and I was energized by working with such masterful collaborators.

In September of 2012, "In My City" was my first single to be released, and a special video version of it was recorded for a weekly pregame promotion spot for the National Football League's *Thursday Night Football* on the NFL Network. It was a tremendous honor for me to be chosen by the network and the NFL, and I remember the thrill of turning on the television the first night it aired and seeing myself introducing the game in a prerecorded announcement, and then watching the upbeat "In My City" promo video along with the millions of others who were tuned in. From where I sat, there was no better way for me and my music to be introduced to mainstream America than through an NFL weekly spot. #GameOn!

My bubble was quickly burst. The excitement of having my first song debut in the United States on such a huge platform was completely destroyed by a storm of explicitly racist hate mail and tweets, including—among many, many examples to choose from—"What's a brown terrorist doing promoting an all-American game?" and "Go back to the Middle East and put your burka on" and—years later it's still hard to write this—"Go back to your country and get gang-raped." The song is all about joy and belonging, and yet the barrage of xenophobic messages coming in felt like an endless series of punches to the gut. The assault was shocking in its swiftness and brutality; I had not been prepared to be so publicly attacked on my very first artistic foray in America.

The NFL stood by me and the spot by using the song again for the 2013 game-opener. More than a year after the initial firestorm, in January of 2014, I gave an interview to *The Wall Street Journal* in which I said that the best way to deal with racism is to "shut down the detractors with your work. Just keep being an achiever and keep achieving, because there are so many people who support you." I do believe it's important to keep achieving in the face of your detractors, and I know that there are always supporters out there, too—many came to my defense on social media when the hate mail and racist tweets appeared. But as I look back on the experience now, I see that I was trying to put on a brave face publicly and not let people know how much the venom-filled speech affected me. Maybe I was too new to the business in America to feel that I could show any vulnerability or take any kind of stand, and so I overcompensated by trying to sound positive and strong. Or maybe I was scared. This was different from the Bollywood exclusionism that most "outsiders" in that system had to endure. The biting remarks and the casually cruel conversations that could affect a career in the Hindi film business usually happened in a rarified environment behind closed doors. Here the doors had been flung wide open on to an open-forum display of hostility directed at one person—me—for something I could not change: my ethnicity. If something like that happened today, I hope I'd talk about my belief that the art someone makes shouldn't be defined by where they were born or the color of their skin. That the virtual spewing of hatred toward those who are different is a lowly form of cowardice.

The release of "In My City" was followed by the release of "Erase" in late 2012 and "Exotic" in 2013. Then, in 2014, we recorded a cover of one of my all-time favorite Bonnie Raitt songs, "I Can't Make You Love Me," reimagined as EDM by the songwriter Ester Dean, with a music video co-starring Milo Ventimiglia from the hit television series *This Is Us*.

While "Exotic" went triple platinum in India within a month of its release in 2013, and made the dance and *Billboard* charts in the U.S., I feel like I never really cracked the code of combining East and West in a way that compelled English-language listeners like we wanted it to. As clear as that fusion of India and America is in me as a person, I couldn't seem to translate the fusion into sound; I worried that it sounded generic and contrived. Though I'd worked with so many incredibly talented people, my music fell short of my own artistic standards and expectations. After three years of trying my hardest to make my music career work, traveling tens of thousands of miles to record a couple of dozen songs in all styles and genres, I came to the difficult decision that it was time to move on. I'm so grateful to everyone who invested in that part of my journey, and I'm sorry I let you down. Maybe someday . . .

I OFTEN THINK about all the accidents of fate in my life that have felt like destiny, affecting who I became. I wanted to be an engineer, when suddenly the pictures Mom and Sid sent to Miss India changed my life forever and gave me a career in the Hindi film industry. Now, after I'd come to America to do music and felt like I'd slammed into a wall, another opportunity was about to present itself.

Between 2011 and 2014, I'd been traveling back and forth between India and America constantly. As soon as that period began, Anjula and I, in light of my busy film career at home, started to have conversations about my getting representation for acting here in the States, too. "Who knows?" Jimmy added. "At some point that might become part of your career here alongside your music." It was a moment when we were starting to see more much-needed female diversity on prime-time television. On ABC alone there was Sofia Vergara on *Modern Family,* Kerry Washington on *Scandal,* and Sandra Oh on *Grey's Anatomy,* so in that regard, the timing seemed good. In 2012, I signed with Creative Artists Agency; the headline in *The Hollywood Reporter* would later read: "CAA Signs Its First Bollywood Star." Given that my name wasn't in the headline,

I almost felt like I was representing the industry I'd come from more than myself.

The music and TV/film businesses are so connected that at every music party or event I attended I was bound to meet not only musicians and music producers but actors, casting directors, and film producers, too. It was no surprise, then, that in 2012 while I was working on my album, I happened to find myself at a small dinner party where Keli Lee, then vice president of casting for ABC, was a guest, too.

"America is going through a golden age of television," Keli told me as we sipped our adult beverages. "All of the great writing is on TV these days." We talked a little more about what ABC was doing as a network with its groundbreaking TV shows—and then she asked me what I thought about trying television in the States.

Episodic television series are long commitments compared to movies—if successful, a series commitment can last for years—so I had a conversation with Anjula and Natasha to discuss the pros and cons. One of the pros was that just as Keli had said, the quality of writing on American TV was terrific, and television had once again become a highly desirable medium to work in; chances were that if I took on a role in a series, I'd have a really meaty part to chew on. There didn't seem to be any cons, except in terms of long-term commitment.

"It's not like she's giving you a show that you have to commit to right now, Pri," Anjula reminded me. "She's talking about signing a talent deal, an opportunity to *possibly* do a show." I had a real concern that if I took a role in an American series I'd lose momentum in my Hindi film career because of the time commitment—but what could be the harm in just *exploring* an opportunity?

So Keli eventually flew to India, visited me in Mumbai on the set of the action thriller *Gunday,* and pitched me on doing a talent deal with ABC. The idea was that I would visit Los Angeles for two months during pilot season—traditionally the months between January and April when networks decide what new programming they're going to green-light for the upcoming season—and read through all the scripts ABC thought were right for me. Then I'd audition for the ones I was interested in, with no guarantee that I'd be cast. Keli convinced us of the power of American television to propel me straight into American pop culture if a good fit was found for me. The gamble was irresistible; my music had not borne the fruit that I wanted it to in the States, and this was another opportunity to consolidate my position in entertainment in a different country. And that's how I found myself on a flight to Tinseltown to explore doing episodic TV.

I spent two months in early 2015 reading a two-foot-high stack of scripts—twenty-six of them, to be exact—that the studio thought would be good for me. Keli recommended her three favorites, and it turned out that they were the exact same scripts I had chosen as my favorites, with *Quantico* at the top of both our lists.

Just because a studio is considering a script, though, doesn't mean it will necessarily be made into a pilot, which is a single episode intended to test the waters before the commitment to shoot a whole season is made. As it turns out, of the three scripts, only *Quantico* was chosen to be shot as a pilot; ultimately it was picked up for a full season—not all pilots are—and two additional seasons after that. Thank God we'd picked a viable script or I'd have been out of luck. It seemed like a Hollywood dream come true.

But this dream hadn't just fallen into my lap, it was the result of a ton of pavement pounding. By this time I'd been focusing on film and television in the U.S. for almost a year, and Anjula was managing me. Anjula had founded a successful online entertainment platform and was a venture capitalist, but she'd had no experience in managing someone's career. Dana Supnick-Guidoni had come on board as my publicist more than a year and a half earlier, while I was still trying to make a success of my music career, and while she had deep experience as a publicist for beauty brands, she had never represented an individual. Having done around fifty films in India, some of which received great critical acclaim, some of which were blowout successes, I was well known to the global community of Hindi film viewers, but as we've established, few people outside of that viewership knew me in the United States. So we had an unknown manager and an unknown publicist representing an unknown actor. We called ourselves the Three Blind Mice, because we were hustling and figuring things out on the fly, feeling our way through things.

Dana had been able to arrange the *Wall Street Journal* interview in 2014 and a few articles in *Variety,* but we didn't get much else. Once I signed *Quantico,* we thought it would be easier to get print coverage, but we were wrong. Having received so much of it in my home country, this was a lot to wrap my brain around. It was my new reality, though, so I put my head down and just kept working. Finally, *finally* after *Quantico* had established itself as a hit, I got my first magazine cover with *Elle* in February of 2016, and in time others followed.

I've gotten ahead of myself, though. Back in the late winter/ early spring of 2015, I'd picked *Quantico* as my first choice of the scripts that ABC showed me, but that didn't mean that the lead role of Alex Parrish, a young FBI recruit training to become a special agent, was mine. I still had to audition for it.

No big deal, right? After all, I'd done some fifty Hindi films by that point. But my audition for the role of Alex Parrish was the first real audition I'd had to do in over a decade. Because in India I'd gone from being Miss World to working in movies almost immediately, I didn't have that difficult period of auditioning repeatedly in order to find work. Once you're established there, like in the States, too, you often get straight offers. So now a simple audition

Natasha Pal's vision for me has always been expansive. She's been my trusted friend and advisor for more than seventeen years now, consistently nudging me toward possibilities I wasn't able to see for myself.

The filming of the dark noir *7 Khoon Maaf* required total concentration and focus, so I was reluctant to take a call about a possible opportunity in the West, even when Natasha encouraged me to. Working with the late Irrfan Khan on that film was a privilege.

The first time I met legendary music producer Jimmy Iovine was at the Monkey Bar in midtown Manhattan at a dinner with Anjula Acharia, a tech investor who would eventually become my manager.

One of my few live performances celebrated the release of my EDM cover of "I Can't Make You Love Me" in Mumbai, 2014.

Brampton, Ontario, in February 2013. While I was recording music in the U.S., I was also shooting films in India and promoting them around the world.

The cast of *Quantico*, season one. Left to right: Josh Hopkins, Aunjanue Ellis, me, Jake McLaughlin, Yasmine Al Massri, Tate Ellington, Graham Rogers (who knew he was a friend of Nick's?), and Johanna Braddy.

Feeling the love from Ellen Pompeo of *Grey's Anatomy* and Kerry Washington of *Scandal* at the ABC upfronts.

Larger than life: the Sunset Boulevard billboard. Driving by and seeing my name in huge letters in a country so far from home almost felt surreal; it reminded me of an earlier billboard moment in Mumbai that I'd celebrated with Tamanna, so I Face-Timed her and we celebrated this one over the phone.

In 2016 I became the first South Asian woman to win a People's Choice Award, which I received for Favorite Actress in a New TV Series. The following year I took home a second PCA, this one for Favorite Dramatic TV Actress.

I felt like the dancing girl emoji come to life when I was presenting at the 2016 Emmys. My joy at the acceptance I felt when *Quantico* became a global success had me floating on air all night.

The year 2016 was monumental for me. I attended the White House Correspondents' Dinner, where I was touched by the warmth and graciousness of the former first lady of the United States, Michelle Obama, and her husband, the former president, Barack Obama. It was also the year I made the cover of *Time* magazine's "*Time* 100" issue as one of the 100 most influential people in the world.

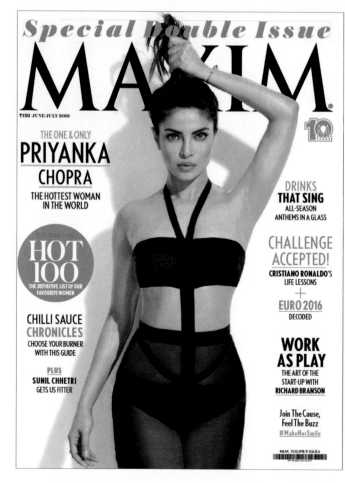

The cover that launched an uproar—ArmpitGate!

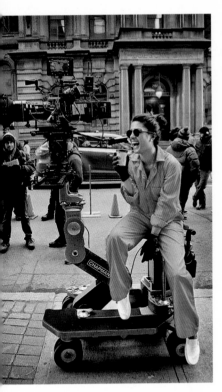

On the set of *Quantico* in New York City, season two. Coffee really kept me going during those long days of shooting.

One of my few fangirl moments: meeting Meryl Streep backstage at the Golden Globes in 2017.

One of the greatest honors of my life has been receiving the Padma Shri, India's fourth highest civilian award, from President Pranab Mukherjee in 2016. The recognition gave rise to a bittersweet moment, knowing how proud my military father would have been to see me being honored by our country.

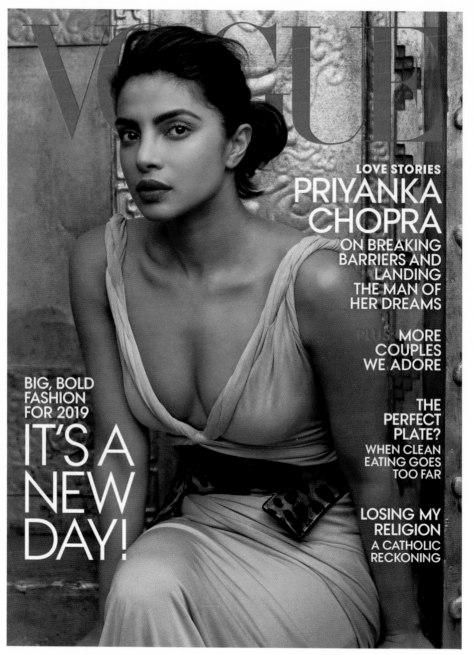

Though I had been on the cover of *Vogue* India many times, when I made the cover of American *Vogue* in January of 2019, I was the first Indian woman to appear solo on it in its 126-year history. Glad to have finally kicked down that door.

Left: I will never forget the kindness shown to me by my co-actor Hrithik Roshan on the set of the first *Krrish,* and by his father, Rakesh Sir, who directed the film. When my father suffered a life-threatening complication following his first surgery, Hrithik facilitated his immediate flight to Boston. *Right*: Getting my *Daddy's lil girl* . . . tattoo in honor of my father in Ibiza, where I was recording a song for my album in 2012 with RedOne. It was the tattoo artist's idea to have it be in Dad's handwriting.

At the TOIFA ceremony with Dad in April 2013. He died two months later.

Sid and I sleeping in the nurses' station outside of the ICU in the final weeks of our father's life.

Nick was good-natured about having to navigate around the twenty-five-foot-long train of my trench coat gown at the 2017 Met Gala.
It was his idea to stage an echo of the Gala shot at our wedding—where my veil was seventy-five-feet long! Good thing he'd had practice with the train.

Our first proper date alone. Nick could probably tell you who the Dodgers played that night but I only had eyes for him.

During Nick's first trip to India in June of 2018, we took a quick trip to Goa with my cousin Parineeti, Tamanna, and Sid.

On the magical island of Crete, July 19, 2018, just hours after our engagement.

At our *roka*,
August 2018.

Reviewing sketches and
embroidery samples with
Ralph Lauren and Andrea
Ciaraldi. For his unwitting
role in bringing us together
at the 2017 Met Gala, his
participation in our wed-
ding, and an assortment of
reasons in between, Ralph
Lauren will always be part
of our love story.

Our sisters-in-law, Danielle and Sophie,
really got into some of the Indian rituals,
especially the *haldi*.

My bridal *mehendi*.

After all of the musical performances at our *sangeet*, this exhausted but exhilarated collection of the most important people in our lives gathered to record the moment.

December 1, 2018. The long walk down the imposing staircase of the Taj Umaid Bhawan Palace to meet Nick at the altar. In the absence of my father, it was my mother who held my hand tightly, infusing love and confidence into me with every step we took.

December 2, 2018. Our Big Fat Chopra Jonas family. From left, Josh Miller (Nick's uncle), Kevin and Danielle Jonas, Cecilia Lucas (Nick's paternal grandmother), Paul Kevin Jonas, Sr., Frances Miller (Nick's maternal grandmother), Denise Jonas, Nick, me, Sid, my mom, Frankie Jonas, Sophie and Joe Jonas.

At the reception after the Indian wedding, I danced the night away with my forever Bollywood hero.

Three days later, wearing my wedding *chudas* and with my bridal *mehendi* still fresh, Whitney Wolfe Herd and I launched Bumble India.

Moving into our new house during quarantine was unusual, but we made the best of it, including a *Griha Pravesh* (house-warming) ceremony.

The growing Chopra Jonas family, with Diana, who chose me; Gino, a gift from me to Nick; and Panda, our latest addition.

I met Sunita when I was a National Ambassador for UNICEF India. The way she took charge of her own life, helping her family and community along the way, inspires me every day.

As a Global UNICEF Goodwill Ambassador, I showed off my Bollywood moves to children in Soweto, South Africa, as they showed off theirs to me.

Travels as a Goodwill Ambassador have also taken me to Jordan and Ethiopia, among other countries. The privilege of meeting strong, resilient children who make the best of impossible circumstances pushes me to be a better person.

Happy to be home. Feeling strong and free as I dance my way into the next chapter of my life.

scared the hell out of me. A dialect coach helped me prepare by working with me on getting my American accent right for the audition tape—and here I'd spent all that time working with Sabira Merchant getting rid of my "Yankee-sounding accent." Ha! Since Alex Parrish was an American girl, born and raised in Oakland, California, I wanted my speech to reflect that. Once I felt I was ready, Anjula, acting simultaneously as cameraperson and the off-camera scene partner reading opposite me, taped the audition.

The tape passed muster, which meant it was time for an in-person audition. I showed up at the studio to find two other contenders for the role running their lines in the hall as they waited; they looked poised, confident, and beautiful. It was the Ashoka Hotel and the London airport all over again, where I'd felt insecure in the face of competition that looked like it belonged, that looked like it had been in this situation before and knew exactly what to do. I slipped into the ladies' room and said a little prayer of thanks when I found it empty.

I took a breath, gripped the edges of the sink in front of me, and met my own eyes in the mirror. "Priyanka Chopra," I said, as if I were my mother trying to talk some sense into me, "what are you afraid of? You know exactly what you're doing. You can't even keep track of the number of movies you've starred in, that's how prepared and ready you are. Just go in there and do your work."

I'm happy to report that sometimes those pep talks we give ourselves actually do work. Or maybe it was hearing my mother being channeled through me. By the time I entered the audition room, I was relaxed again and confident in my preparation. I felt something when I walked into the room, a heightened quality of attention I couldn't really put my finger on. I did the scene, was happy with the way it went, and everyone was really nice. Two days later I got a phone call that I'd gotten the job. Sometime after that, Josh Safran, the show's creator, said in an interview, "When Priyanka walked into the audition, the molecules shifted . . . and we all sat up straighter in our chairs."

Maybe that's what I'd felt, the molecules shifting, people sitting up straighter in their chairs. Whatever it was, I sensed that everyone in the room was alert and paying close attention. Which was a great atmosphere in which to just go ahead and act the hell out of the scene.

Alex Parrish hadn't been written as having a particular ethnicity, but once I got the part, the writers decided to alter her background to make it authentic to me. They added in the fact that she was biracial—her mother was Indian and her father a white American—and decided that while Alex would be a thoroughly American young woman, born and raised here, she'd also be in touch with her Indian roots. I did a couple of scenes where I spoke some Hindi, and there were references to me having backpacked through India. Maybe most meaningful to me was the fact that I wore a bracelet with the "om" symbol on it, and the first shot of me in Episode 1, Season 1, is a close-up not of my face but of that om bracelet encircling my wrist. When I'd suggested the bracelet to Sami Rattner, the show's stylist, I had no idea it would mean so much to me, but that clear, simple reflection of my culture felt so personal at the time that even now I get goosebumps whenever I see the shot. The bracelet remained around Alex's wrist for all three seasons, reminding Alex and viewers of her heritage in a subtle yet concrete way. I know it's a small thing, but it felt like a big win to me.

My strategy for entering the American TV and film world was to initially play roles where my ethnicity did not define the character or drive the action; unfortunately, at the time, it seemed to me that once South Asian characters played ethnicity-defined roles, they often got stereotyped into a box, and I didn't want to fall prey to that Hollywood standard. I wanted to be able to play not only parts that required me to be Indian but also those that came from a larger pool of options where my origins didn't define my character or the story.

It felt like a big deal then, a huge deal, that I'd been cast as Alex Parrish. As the first South Asian ever to play the lead character on a network show (Kerry Washington became the first African American woman to lead a network drama in forty years with *Scandal* in 2012, which was a giant step in the right direction), I felt such a sense of achievement, and gratitude, too. But I also felt a lot of pressure. I was proud that I'd been cast in the role, but I worried that if the show didn't do well, it would be a step back for South Asian actors in general, and the weight of that burden—self-imposed, I know—felt enormous.

Fortunately, the weight was alleviated somewhat because the show was a success. I absolutely loved Alex Parrish. She was bold, brazen, and unapologetically flawed. Alex never felt the need to explain her behavior, which was a trait we shared. One of my favorite scenes, which kept the Internet busy for a few days, was in the first episode, where Alex has sex with a stranger in the backseat of a car at the airport. When they meet again, he pretends he doesn't know her, and she won't have it. "We had sex in your car six hours ago," she says to him in front of a group of new recruits, calling him out in front of everyone. That, to me, was the power of Alex. No one scared her. Her freedom and audacity made me itch to get my hands on the scripts for every episode.

I had played many audacious characters before. There had been Sonia in *Aitraaz,* Meghna Mathur in *Fashion,* and Susanna in *7 Khoon Maaf.* Nobody who had watched those films at the time complained about the behavior of those sexually active, blackmailing, murderous women; although some people may have been surprised that I'd taken on roles like that, I ended up winning awards for them. But that scene in the car in Episode 1 provoked a frenetic conversation on the Internet about how I had crossed a line and become too bold now that I was working in the U.S. I will admit that the criticism bothered me even as I thought it was ridiculous. The Walt Disney Company, which owns ABC, had clear mandates about acceptable levels of sexual explicitness and violence. Sexual activity, for instance, could be suggested to a degree, but not shown. I was a master of this, having worked in the Hindi film industry for so long, where you could show things but not *show* things. Disney felt the same way: the sounds of that sex scene in the car, for instance, were dubbed after the scene was filmed, and I was nowhere near my co-actor Jake McLaughlin when I recorded them. Ah, the magic of the movies.

The pressure of the work itself was intense. The first season, I was in almost every scene of every episode. We worked five or six days a week, fifteen or sixteen or eighteen hours a day. I'd usually be picked up at five in the morning and I sometimes wouldn't finish until eleven at night. On most weekends I'd fly into New York from Montreal, where we filmed, to do interviews, photo shoots, and television appearances to promote the show. All this on top of figuring out a new environment with new norms.

When I'd started in the Hindi film industry, I'd had no idea what I was doing when I first walked onto a set, and so I'd had to learn everything on the job. Now I knew my craft, but I had to get reacquainted with the culture. I'd last lived in the U.S. in 1998 as a teenager. America and I had both evolved since then, and when we met again we were strangers. Getting to know each other took a little time, not only outside the studio but in it, as well.

Again, I watched and observed, questioned, and soaked up as much knowledge as I could. The first couple of months I heard repeatedly from directors suggestions like "Maybe not with the hands so much" and "Just throw it away this time" and "How about we try a little less?" It took me a while to understand that large gestures were my natural way of expression, having lived almost all of my life in India. The acting in Hindi films is bold and forthright and energetic, reflecting the generally animated gestures of so many Indians. No surprise, then, that when I came to Hollywood my animation had to be contained. Tremendously! Once I realized that I had to recalibrate my brain to play things smaller, it all got a lot easier. Now, after all these years, I can finally do both styles, large and small, switching back and forth automatically as needed.

I also had to re-attune my ear to American speech and speech patterns. While my American accent had worked well enough in the audition, I decided I needed a dialect coach on set to help me avoid the occasional slips that happened, especially when a scene was really emotional and I slipped into my Global Confused Accent. Sometimes I felt like I needed a translator as much as a dialect coach. When directors would say things like "Let's not die on this hill" or "I don't have a dog in this fight," I didn't want to look as clueless as I felt, so I just walked around wondering what they meant. It was almost the high school cafeteria all over again: *Buffalo wings? Buffaloes don't have wings.*

Even film terminology sometimes perplexed me. On most films or television series around the world, at the end of each day of shooting, a schedule, known as a call sheet, is distributed to the cast and crew specifying what time each individual has to be on set or in hair and makeup the next day. In America and a few other countries, the first actor listed is the lead actor—"#1." This is not a term I was used to hearing in India—leads were never ranked by number, we just knew who they were—so the first time I heard "Let's get number one. Where's number one?" I had no idea it was me being referred to. And I have to admit that for the first few weeks of shooting, after I figured that out, it gave me a little thrill every time I saw "*#1 Priyanka Chopra*" at the top of the call sheet.

All these years later I'm happy to say that now I'm fully trilingual: I speak Hindi, English, and American, all of them fluently.

EVERYTHING SEEMED TO have happened so fast. Just a few months earlier, I'd been reading a pile of scripts poolside at my L.A. hotel. Now I was the lead in my first television show ever, in my first acting job in this country. Along with the unrelenting shooting schedule and the on-the-job learning was the need to promote the show. In May, I learned about one more piece of the promotion puzzle.

Every spring the major television networks preview their upcoming fall and midseason series for advertisers, the press, and the other industry people in a weeklong event in New York known as the upfronts. I was a bundle of nerves when I arrived at the red carpet for ABC's upfront presentation, but then I saw Kerry Washington and she waved me toward her, making me feel welcome and comfortable instantly. Later, in the greenroom with about seventy-five cast members from ABC's other shows, Kerry and Ellen Pompeo from *Grey's Anatomy* were both incredibly kind to me. As the lead actresses in their hugely successful respective network shows, maybe they saw how petrified I was and understood the rigor of my life that first year: ten months of shooting (most of which was yet to come), an endless succession of long days, and the weight of being "#1" on the call sheet. Having two of the biggest female stars in American television at that time sit me down, give me the 411, and take time for a pep talk helped ease my anxiety, and for that I'll always be grateful. I felt like they entered my train compartment and calmed the course of my journey. They probably don't even realize the importance of what they did for me, but I, for one, will never forget how they so generously took me under their wings that night.

ABC put a tremendous amount of support behind *Quantico,* especially when it came to marketing. My face was on buses, posters, and billboards across America. I remember gazing up at the huge billboard of my face on Sunset Boulevard in Los Angeles and thinking, *Holy shit!* It had been so difficult to get any kind of media attention here, and now there was a building-sized image of me in handcuffs, gazing over my shoulder at all who passed by below on the Sunset Strip in West Hollywood. It reminded me of a humid night in Mumbai in 2003 before my first movie came out. It was late, and Tamanna and I were sitting on Juhu Beach at a bend in the road where there were six billboards. I'd looked up at them and told her I wanted my face on all of them. At a moment some years later, that had actually happened and we'd celebrated together. And now, years after that and thousands of miles away on another continent, I was FaceTiming her about another billboard moment and we were celebrating again.

When the show launched on September 27, 2015, it worked. *Quantico* eventually aired in more than sixty countries in its first season to become a global success. The validation and relief were great, vindication from all the skeptics who just couldn't resist their sniping—those on the Internet who suggested I'd bought my own billboards, for example, or who wondered why I'd "faked" an American accent. What made me the happiest was that I felt with *Quantico* I'd made major inroads in breaking the classic stereotype of Indian actors in Hollywood: I knew that it wasn't very common for audiences to see actors of South Asian descent in mainstream leading roles or in roles much beyond the predictable sidekick, tech nerd, or exotic love interest. Mindy Kaling and Aziz Ansari, along with a few other actors of South Asian descent, had played extremely popular characters on network television. Then, going a step further, Mindy and Aziz had taken matters into their own hands by writing starring roles for themselves in their own über-successful shows. *The Mindy Project* and *Master of None* showed their leads as wonderfully flawed, human, relatable characters, opening up more room for actors of South Asian descent and other minority actors to be cast in a full range of roles that reflects our shared humanity.

When I was living in America during high school, years before Mindy and Aziz had their own shows, the only mainstream Indian character I saw on television was Apu on *The Simpsons*—who was played by Hank Azaria, a white American, I discovered years later when he was called out for it (and in turn announced that he has stopped providing the voice for the character). All the characters on *The Simpsons* are caricatures, so it's not like Apu's treatment as a stereotype singled out Indians or Indian Americans for poor treatment. But having people ask me on the regular why I didn't talk or act like Apu didn't do a lot for my sense of belonging. I became a huge fan of *Buffy the Vampire Slayer* because the protagonist, played by Sarah Michelle Gellar, was a powerful teenage girl who battled evil forces. She was an awesome teenage role model, but I wonder now if my fifteen-year-old self walking the halls of Newton North would have felt a little less awkward in the world, a little more of a sense of belonging, if I had seen someone who looked like me playing the lead in a TV show or a movie. With *Quantico*, I hoped that young girls of South Asian descent and anyone else who felt underrepresented would be able to look up and recognize themselves and feel seen, and I'm proud and gratified to be a part of this shifting narrative.

I ALWAYS KNEW that my career would never be just one thing—not just films, not just music, not just television—and that I would follow a multitude of paths to make sure that all of my creative interests and endeavors would be fed. That meant straddling two careers in two continents. During *Quantico*'s first hiatus—the break between seasons—I added American film work to the mix, shooting

Baywatch in 2016. Even before the hiatus began, I was finishing up *Bajirao Mastani,* in which I played an eighteenth-century Marathi queen. So on some weekends I would fly to India to shoot for one day, then come back and shoot *Quantico*. Translation: I flew out of Montreal to Dubai on Friday night, continued on to Mumbai, and took a helicopter to reach Wai, which is about 140 miles southeast of Mumbai, by Sunday morning. I'd film all day Sunday and leave as the sun was setting on that gorgeous, temple-filled riverside city, reversing my flight path. By Monday afternoon I was back in Montreal, ready to start shooting the next episode of *Quantico*. Airplanes became like flying bedrooms to me, and I swear I got to know some of the immigration personnel at the Montreal airport by name.

"What's up, Émile? How're you doing this afternoon?"

"Hey, you're back! Worked all weekend again, eh, Priyanka?"

That schedule was probably the hardest one I've ever maintained and my body took a beating for it, but traveling back and forth like that was the only way to have it all, and I wanted to have it all.

I'd been working crazy hours for six or seven days a week for my entire film career in India, so honestly, it didn't seem all that strange to me to be putting in this kind of time. There's not really a concept of "weekend" in India the same way there is in America. The school week is five and a half days, for instance, as it is for some businesses, too. Film schedules are made based on location, not week, so you may shoot for ten consecutive days in one location and then have five days off. When I got to the States, it was culture shock for me to be *required* to take two consecutive days off simply because everyone else did.

Quantico had a five-day shooting schedule that theoretically allowed for weekend breaks, but the show was so ambitious, with so many shots scheduled per day, that we often went over into a sixth day. Hence the extra-long workweek. When that happened, I couldn't understand why people grumbled about having to work on a weekend, especially since the union made sure we were fairly compensated for it. At that point in my life, a two-day weekend break seemed like a forced holiday to me. Not anymore! Show the thirsty camel some water. . . . Now I take weekends off in India, too.

Having had the success of playing a character who wasn't defined by her ethnicity in *Quantico* and later *Baywatch,* more recently I've ventured into playing characters who were written specifically as Indian or Indian American, like the character of Pinky Madam in *The White Tiger,* the adaptation of the 2008 Man Booker Prize–winning novel by Aravind Adiga. I read the book more than ten years ago, and its unblinking gaze at the harshness of the lives of India's impoverished affected me tremendously. When I heard that a movie was in the works, I called my agents immediately and said I wanted to be a part of it. I was so keen to be involved—both because of the book's impact on me and because I was eager to work with the award-winning director, Ramin Bahrani—that the size of the role didn't matter. I made my agents call the producers multiple times. I met with Ramin multiple times, too, because this story of my homeland is such an important one to me that I was determined to be a part of it. I lobbied to executive-produce it as well as to appear in it, and I'm grateful that Netflix and Lava Media agreed, so I get to play that role, too. As of this writing, *The White Tiger* is in postproduction and I hope audiences will soon see it roar to life.

In the same way that I pursued involvement with that movie, I decided that I wanted to collaborate with actors and writers of South Asian descent here in America to create more and more opportunities for myself and others like me. Mindy Kaling is one of those writer/actors whom I deeply admire. When she wanted to explore being a leading lady, she didn't wait for someone to invite her to the party; she wrote her own damn show, which then ran successfully for five years. She and I are now working on a buddy comedy for Universal Pictures that mines the humor in the differences between Indians raised in America and Indians from India. Plenty of room for humor there, trust me.

With films like this and *The White Tiger,* and my first-look deal with Amazon, there are a lot more projects in development. I'm creating more and more of my own opportunities, going after projects that I believe in and people I want to work with. I've been inspired in my efforts by many actors who, like Mindy and Aziz Ansari, have taken matters into their own hands, especially female actors like Kerry Washington, Eva Longoria, Anushka Sharma, Salma Hayek, Reese Witherspoon, Deepika Padukone, Nicole Kidman, Queen Latifah, and so many others who are now producing projects for themselves and in the process of opening up opportunities for others. I find their examples powerfully inspiring. Although I've been bold in many of my career choices, only now, after twenty years in this business, do I feel I have the courage and the credibility to move confidently in the direction of originating my own projects. And I've got to say, it feels good.

FORGING MY OWN way hasn't always felt so good, though. At some point after *Quantico* took off, at a nascent stage in my American career, I seemed to have become a social media sensation—in a very good way and a very bad way. For example, in 2017 when I was promoting *Baywatch* in Berlin, India's prime minister Shri Narendra Modi was also in Berlin, to meet with German Chancellor Angela Merkel. The prime minister and I happened to be staying in the same hotel, and I contacted his office to request an audience with him. We got permission, and Sid, Dana, and I sat with him for a few minutes. We took pictures together, which we then posted online. Because I was promoting *Baywatch* that day, I was in a dress, not a sari. It was knee-length, high-necked, and long-sleeved. When we posted the photos to social media, there was a furor around the fact that I was meeting with the prime minister with my legs exposed. On top of that, people commented that because my legs were crossed in some of the photos, my posture seemed arrogant and therefore inappropriate for a meeting with a head of state. It was one of the first times I became global news, and I swear that was not the way I wanted to make global news. I was angry and confused. My response to the anger was to take a picture of my mom and me out at dinner that night in our short skirts and with our legs crossed, and to post it online with the caption "It runs in the family." But all joking aside, I felt that I had presented myself respectfully. I had worn skirts and dresses all my life in India, at school and elsewhere, and I didn't understand why it was now considered so unacceptable. The whole uproar baffled and saddened me.

The year before, in 2016, I'd made the *Maxim India* "Hot 100" cover. The photo of me on the front of the magazine had one of my arms above my head with my armpit exposed—which gave rise to a massive controversy because *Maxim India* was accused of photoshopping my armpit! Specifically, smoothing and whitening it. My armpit actually trended on social media with various hashtags, including #ArmpitGate. I was at Paris Fashion Week while this was all happening, and my team and I were mortified, appalled, and hysterically laughing all at the same time because we couldn't get over how ridiculous and surreal it was to have my armpit go viral. Did this mean I'd finally made it? To commemorate the moment, I took a quick pic of my pits and posted it with the hashtag #WillTheRealArmpitPleaseStandUp.

Unfortunately, the controversies I've experienced haven't always been laughable. During the third season of *Quantico,* an episode aired that was about Hindu extremist terrorists trying to blow up Manhattan with the twist of blaming the attack on Pakistan. There was a huge outcry about it in India, attacking ABC for what people felt was an offensive plotline, and attacking me for agreeing to be in it. I got worldwide backlash for being part of a plotline that involved Hindus as terrorists, but I wasn't a writer or a producer, and I didn't have any control or input into the storyline. Not to mention the fact that we'd had villains of *every* ethnicity trying to blow up New York over the course of the show. The uproar lasted for a very long time. There were online threats warning me not to return to India, and effigies were being burned outside my home there. When I did go back, local police needed to provide security for me. It became so out of control that ABC had to apologize and make a statement: "ABC Studios and the executive producers of *Quantico* would like to extend an apology to our audience who were offended by the most recent episode, 'The Blood of Romeo'. . . . The episode has stirred a lot of emotion, much of which is unfairly aimed at Priyanka Chopra, who didn't create the show, nor does she write or direct it. She has no involvement in the casting of the show, or the storylines depicted in the series. . . . *Quantico* is a work of fiction. The show has featured antagonists of many different ethnicities and backgrounds, but in this case we inadvertently and regrettably stepped into a complex political issue. It was certainly not our intention to offend anyone." For a while I refused to comment or explain. Eventually, though, I too made a short statement on Twitter to try to calm the storm: "I'm extremely saddened and sorry that some sentiments have been hurt by a recent episode of *Quantico.* That was not and would never be my intention. I sincerely apologize. I'm a proud Indian and that will never change." The moment I made the statement, another wave of condemnation came flooding in, this one led by people who called my apology a form of pandering. Damned if you do, damned if you don't. The whole situation was deeply disturbing.

Over time my relationship to the Internet changed. When the World Wide Web came into being, I saw it as a thrilling opportunity to connect with people everywhere. I got onto social media early on—I was one of the first actors in India on Twitter—and I loved the direct access to fans and well-wishers without anyone in the middle. I had a great time doing interactive sessions and talking to fans regularly. After negativity and attacks came my way for multiple years, though, a relationship that had once been enjoyable and positive eventually transformed into one of mistrust and fear. I'm not alone in feeling this way, I know. We read about the very dire consequences of hate and negativity expressed directly over social media all the time. Once I felt that it was unsafe to show myself in all my vulnerable humanity, I pulled back. It was instinctive.

This evolution of my relationship with social media has been sad for me. Cancel culture and social media shaming have in many ways stopped me from having the meaningful conversations I used to have, and still want to have, with followers. For now, what seems to work best for me is to engage with online negativity or controversy as little as possible. If I feel that I've done something out of ignorance that could have been avoided, I will apologize. If I feel that I was wrong—for whatever reason—I will apologize. On those occasions when I've made a mistake that I can fix, I will try to fix it. But when rage spews without any form of fact-checking, it just seems futile to engage. I've come to see that there are times when you should speak up, and times when it's better not to. So I've started picking my battles.

I take seriously the responsibility of having a career in two polar-opposite countries and cultures. They both matter to me; I'm an amalgamation and a product of both. I wish there were an infallible guidebook for how to keep different cultures and peoples calm and open and willing to look for common ground simultaneously, not just in India and the U.S., of course, but all around the world—and all over the World Wide Web, too. Like all of us, though, I've yet to find that guidebook, so I'll continue my quest for it, as I genuinely hope all of us will. I'm concerned that we have all become so afraid of our differences that we step back every time we encounter them. If only we could strive to take small steps toward ideas and people that are different in order to understand them. When I say "we," I'm including myself: I've just acknowledged, after all, that I've taken a step back from the Internet. My hope is that we can all work to find ways to be curious and kind, which would be a step toward bringing us together in spite of our differences, rather than letting our fears and insecurities become shackles that keep us apart.

I WAS ON a steep learning curve my first few years in the States, dancing as fast as I could to learn what I needed to as I traveled back and forth to India for work and personal reasons. Once I established myself in the U.S. with *Quantico,* the crazy pace continued. At that point, though, all of the long days may not have been solely about getting the work done. I was running as hard as I could toward a goal, but I didn't realize that I was running away from something just as hard.

8

GRIEF

Be patient toward all that is unsolved in your heart and try to love the questions themselves like locked rooms and like books that are written in a very foreign tongue.

RAINER MARIA RILKE, *LETTERS TO A YOUNG POET*

T O UNDERSTAND WHAT I was running from, we have to rewind a bit.

At the dawn of 2005 my career was finally starting to take off. *Bluffmaster!*, in which I played opposite Abhishek Bachchan, was soon to be released and I was shooting *Krrish*, with Hrithik Roshan, which was a sequel to *Koi . . . Mil Gaya*. That had been a very successful movie, and consequently *Krrish* was seen as one of my biggest movies so far. Both of my parents were working as part of my team, even as my father continued the job of medical administrator at a Mumbai hospital, which he'd accepted shortly after moving there. Sid was in high school, and we were all living together in Mumbai. At twenty-two, I felt a glorious sense of optimism and excitement; I was ready for anything!

Except what came next.

My mother and father had their annual checkups that year in February, as they always did, and when the radiologist spotted something on the scan of my father's liver that he identified as a fat-sparing area, he said, "It's nothing. Tiny. A half a centimeter." Dad knew it wasn't nothing, and went on to have further imaging that showed he was right. The correct diagnosis was cholangiocarcinoma, a rare and aggressive form of cancer. Within a week he and my mother had arranged for what turned out to be a nine-hour surgery to remove 80 percent of the right lobe of his liver. Mom was in the operating theater the whole time observing, and she reported that the surgery went beautifully. But when the surgeon stepped out to talk to our family, Dad's intestine was nicked with some rubber tubing as the incision was being closed. It didn't look bad at the time, but within a week my father had developed peritonitis, which was initially diagnosed as pancreatitis. Dad remained in the hospital for about six weeks, deteriorating faster and faster, until he had to be put on a ventilator.

"Get him out of that hospital," my mother's brother Vimal Mamu said. My mom had been keeping Mamu, by then an anesthesiologist at Beth Israel Deaconess Medical Center in Boston, closely informed, and he'd been keeping his friend Dr. Mark Callery, the chief of general surgery and a specialist in pancreatic and hepatobiliary surgery there, closely informed. It was decided that if my father could be transported safely, he would be moved to Beth Israel. But how could we get Dad halfway around the world safely? The challenge felt impossible given his dire condition, but we had to try.

Every day I'd been going from the set of *Krrish* straight to the hospital, so my co-star, Hrithik Roshan, was aware of what was happening with my family. Incredibly, Hrithik, who is hugely successful in the Hindi film industry, got on the phone and used his connections at Air India to arrange for my father's immediate flight to London. My mother had to sign numerous waivers and disclaimers and arrange for Dad to be accompanied by another doctor (in addition to my physician mother) and twenty small cylinders of oxygen. The final obstacle was the difficulty in acquiring the surgeon's sign-off on permission to fly. We couldn't let that stop us, and so I showed up at his office at 6 A.M., before I went to the set. My memory of the encounter is clear: I told him that I would go public if my father died on his watch unless he gave us permission to fly. After a frustrating few minutes, the doctor signed the orders.

But it was done. We had permission, we had a seat, we had a doctor and oxygen and a handful of frightening waivers that basically said we understood that my father could die en route and we wouldn't hold Air India or anyone else responsible. The ten hours of that flight to London, with Sid and me on the ground in India, and Mom and Dad in the air with no way to be in touch, were the longest, most excruciating hours of my life.

They made it to London, where he was immediately transferred by a waiting ambulance onto a flight to New York, complete with a fresh supply of oxygen. From New York he was whisked onto a medical helicopter so efficiently, my mother says, that the chopper was able to take off with him within a minute of the flight door opening on the runway in New York. By the time my mother arrived in Boston—dear Vimla Mami, the Pied Piper of children when I was a teenager living with her and Mamu in Newton, drove the three-plus hours to meet my mother and then turned around and drove Mom the three-plus hours back to the hospital in Boston—my father was out of surgery.

If we hadn't had people around us who were so kind and so

willing to act on our behalf—Hrithik and his father, Rakesh Sir, who was the director of the film; our family in Boston—I doubt that my father would have made it. There's no way I can ever express my gratitude adequately to them, but it is deep and it is enduring.

My energetic father, the eternal life of the party who'd always been strong and fit and active, had wasted into skin and bones. He remained in the ICU in Boston for six weeks and in the hospital for six months, and the nurses and staff there were better than angels. It would be the first of many close calls before Dad went into remission.

Having been so close to death, Dad, once he regained his health and his strength, jumped back into life with all the gusto that he'd always had. He and Mom started socializing again. He invited musicians into our home so they could jam. Dad had an incredible voice but he'd never played an instrument—except the table. Not the *tabla,* but the *table,* as in any desk- or tabletop, which he would slap and pound and drum on with his hands like a percussion instrument. "Dr. Chopra plays a *mean* tabletop," all of his musician friends would say. And he did.

He resumed his pro bono work. He started sketching again, something he hadn't done in years. He and Mom traveled to Europe to visit Sid, who by then was in a hospitality school in Switzerland called Les Roches. And Dad gave up the job in medical administration that he'd taken upon moving to Mumbai, putting down the paperwork to pick up the scalpel again. In early 2009, after traveling to Italy, Israel, and Colombia for training, he and my mother opened Studio Aesthetic, a cosmetic clinic in Juhu where he performed liposculpture and she performed all the nonsurgical procedures. My dad was a man in love with life.

I'd thrown myself back into work again, shooting several movies a year, including *Fashion, Drona, Kaminey, 7 Khoon Maaf,* and *Don 2.*

I'd also signed my agreement with Desi Hits to record an album and was flying back and forth between the U.S. and India regularly. When they weren't working at their clinic or traveling elsewhere, both of my parents came to visit me in the U.S. when I was recording, and Dad was in heaven visiting sets and studios where he found himself surrounded by so many talented musicians.

But in 2011, Dad started to feel weak. He'd been having regular scans and was advised that there was nothing to worry about at the time. When Dad's sister-in-law, Badimama, a radiologist in Delhi, finally discovered the six-centimeter mass buried deep in his liver, there was plenty to worry about. By then the tumor had grown and spread and was now stage 4.

For the last two years of his life, my father fought incredibly hard against a disease that was unrelenting. Mom and Dad came up with a game plan, which included traveling back and forth to Beth Israel in Boston, and also to Rochester, New York, in the northwestern part of the state, where they explored the possibility of a liver transplant but ultimately opted for stereotactic radiation followed by surgery. The team in Rochester at Strong Memorial Hospital was magnificent—caring, compassionate, and highly skilled, and my parents were fortunate to be hosted in that city by Dr. Randeep Kashyap, who performed the surgery, and his beautiful wife, Dr. Rupa Kashyap. Thanks to the friendship and graciousness shown to them by the Kashyaps; Dr. Ashwani Chhibber, a friend of my father's from medical school; and Dr. Vikram Dogra, his radiologist, the emotionally draining time my parents spent in that city was made as comfortable as it could possibly be. In my years of travel around the world, I've noticed that South Asians so often come together for their own, whether they know one another or not. There is something powerful about belonging to this community, and my parents' experience in Rochester, thousands of miles from their home, was a beautiful demonstration of that.

Both my parents had spent their lives wanting my brother and me not to see any of their perceived weaknesses, and it was no different with this illness of Dad's. When they were in India, if I arrived for a visit with Dad in his hospital room and he had been expecting me, he'd be sitting up with his hair combed and wearing cologne, somehow always managing to look fresh. If I stopped by without warning, he immediately pulled himself together, sat up, and put on a strong front. He knew how much I'd always looked up to him, and he was determined not to let his illness get in the way of that.

He was also determined not to let his illness get in the way of my career. Throughout most of my father's hospitalizations—and there were many during the two years that followed his remission—my mother always said to me, "Just go to work. He'll be fine. He wants you to work." And I knew that was true. If I visited him in the middle of the day, he would say to me, "Why are you here? Why aren't you on set?"

Time passed with few bright spots in my father's situation. Early in 2013, I was nominated for a TOIFA—*Times of India* Film Award—for Best Actress for the role of Jhilmil in *Barfi!* The awards ceremony was to be held in Vancouver, in British Columbia, Canada, that year on April 6, and while I hadn't won any other awards for my role as an autistic young woman in that movie, I thought I had a reasonably good chance of winning this one. More than anything, I wanted my father to be there to share in the recognition. He had been my biggest cheerleader my entire life, voicing his encouragement loudly—sometimes embarrassingly loudly—every time I won even the smallest award from the age of two on. And he had earned this celebratory moment, if indeed I were to win, with all the help and support he'd given me along the way, and all the sacrifices he and my mother had made on my behalf. I knew he couldn't travel easily—he was weak and in pain, and had to wear bile duct drainage bags inside his shirts—but I also knew that he had to make a trip to North America anyway, for treatment in Rochester. And I thought the awards ceremony might be a bright spot for him. So at dinner one night I casually mentioned the idea of combining the trips to Vancouver and Rochester.

Immediately, Dad was hell-bent on going. "Yes! I'll come for the TOIFA ceremony, and then I'll go to Rochester for my treatment, and then I'll take a break and come home!" As if it were all very casual, this trip between continents, when of course it wasn't casual at all. It would be grueling for him. When the time came, he and my mom left days ahead of time from India so that they could build in breaks on the long trip west across Europe and the Atlantic Ocean, and then all the way across the North American continent to British Columbia. Then Dad rested for three days in the Vancouver hotel before the actual event.

When I walked into his hotel room for the first time after I'd landed in Canada, I took one look at him and said, "You don't have to do this, Dad."

Seeing him lying exhausted on the bed, with all his tubes and bags, it was impossible to imagine him having the strength to get dressed, much less make it to an awards ceremony. Mom waited for the right moment, then took me aside and said she agreed with me.

"I've come all this way for exactly this and I'm going to be there to watch her win this award," he called from his bed, knowing exactly what we were talking about even if he couldn't actually hear us. Mom tried to argue with him but he would have none of it.

He made it there. He wore a suit and tucked his drainage bags under his shirt and tie. We used a wheelchair to get him through the hotel and then the theater, where he sat next to me in the front row. When the Best Actress category came up near the end of the ceremony and my name was called, he radiated joy. I could literally feel it emanating from him. I had thought I might ask him to come up with me if I won, but I hadn't said anything to him, not knowing if he would be able. Now it seemed only right to accept the award with him at my side. "Will you come onstage with me?" I asked. And he did. It took what felt like an eternity for him to walk to the stage, but he made it. In my acceptance speech I thanked all the people I'd worked with on the film—including, of course, my director, Anurag Basu, and my co-actors Ranbir Kapoor and Ileana D'Cruz—and with my father standing next to me, I thanked him, too, "for teaching me to take chances and to stand up for what I believe in: for truth."

And then my beautiful father gathered his strength and spoke to the audience: "I thank you a lot from my heart for your love and blessings. You have truly recognized a true actor; I am so very grateful." My father was alluding to the fact that while I had received great critical acclaim for my unusual, unglamorous role in *Barfi!* I hadn't received major award recognition. That was Dad, standing up for me one last time.

My father got a standing ovation, at which point he started to cry. I'd been blinking my own tears away, acutely aware that it could be the last time we would ever celebrate an achievement like this together. Holding each other and with the help of the hosts of the evening, we slowly made our way off the stage.

Dad lasted through the whole three hours of the program, a feat that almost defies belief given that he was so weak, but he did it. That's who he was. When we got back to my parents' hotel room later, he collapsed on the bed, unable to do so much as lift his arm to unbutton his shirt.

When I look back at pictures and videos from that night, they crush me. Dad had always been like Superman to me. All my life, he had been able to do anything, including save countless people's lives over the course of his medical career. He had been six foot one, energetic and robust, an absolute mountain of a man. To see how the disease ravaged him, how thin he was, how laborious his speech and movements were—anyone who has seen a loved one go through this kind of disease knows that there is nothing worse. It was the last time my father appeared in public. Two months later, he was gone.

WHILE HE WAS alive, my family never spoke about where Dad's illness was inevitably leading, what we were all thinking and feeling. I'm not sure if that's the right way to go through this kind of experience, but every family is different and that was our way. By the time he was at the end, I admit that I was prepared to let him go. It was terrible watching him become a shadow of himself. He was depressed and suffering. My big, strong father was reduced to a shell of himself, lacking the energy to express his anguish with anything more than a silent tear.

When I think back on the final year of his life, I often regret not taking more time off to be with him. But that's not what he wanted. He wanted me to work, to focus on the career he'd helped me build. Neither he nor my mom wanted my life to be interrupted or halted by his illness. Now I wonder why I listened to them. Why hadn't we had those important conversations that families have when someone is dying? Why hadn't my father and I talked about things we'd never talked about before? Why hadn't I reminisced more with him about our family travels, and about the music he loved to play? And about one of his favorite subjects—my childhood? Recollections of mischievous young me never failed to bring a smile to his face. I think somewhere inside I just didn't believe he would go. He'd been on the ventilator twice, in the ICU eight times, and he'd always survived. Why wouldn't he continue to survive?

My father died on June 10, 2013, two months before his sixty-third birthday. My initial reaction was a kind of irrational rage. *How could you leave me?* I wanted to yell at him. *Why did you go?* Of course I knew that he'd held on for eight years because of my mom, my brother, and me; I knew he wanted to make sure that Sid was settled in his life and I was moving ahead in my career and Mom was doing well in their new business. And of course I wanted him to be in a place of peace rather than to continue on in suffering. But still I was gutted by the loss.

I didn't want to feel my overpowering grief, so I walled myself off emotionally. In the weeks before and after my father's death, our home was full of family and friends. Mom was hosting our whole family—my parents' brothers and sisters, and all their husbands and wives and children—all of whom had come in his final days to say goodbye to him. And while Mom was hosting and making sure everyone had a place to stay, while she dealt with the details of the rituals that would happen in the days after Dad's death, I sat numbly on the couch, unable to talk, unable to move.

Dad died at around noon on the tenth, and the cremation was held at 4 P.M. To my astonishment, it seemed like the entire Hindi film industry showed up—actors, directors, producers, camera people, lighting people, hair and makeup and set designers and their assistants. I had no idea how everyone knew, but they did, and the support they showed me and my family temporarily pierced the walls I'd erected in an effort to protect myself from my grief. The walls were pierced again at the *chautha,* four days after his death. Over the course of four hours that day, it felt like a thousand people came to show their love and respect for my father. All of his life, his warmth, inclusivity, and joy had drawn people to him, and now, in addition to family, there were people from all of the parts of his life—doctors, patients, army friends and fellow officers, musicians. And the film industry was there again in a massive demonstration of support. Many of my colleagues knew him and had been touched by him in some way, and I'd like to believe that a good number of them were there not just for me, but because they genuinely grieved my father's passing. Although I desperately wanted not to feel any-thing, it was hard not to look around and be moved by all the people who felt compelled to honor my father's memory.

The hole my father's absence left in our family, in my heart and in the hearts of my mother and my brother, was almost unbearable. I was accustomed to always moving forward, always going on to the next thing rather than facing my feelings. From my perspective today, I see that it had been my method for coping with pain and grief ever since my boarding school days, and now, more than twenty years later, I was still doing the same thing. I had no tools, no internal mechanism, no experience that could help me deal with such devastation. Until then, my mother had never really be-lieved in therapy, but after she went to a grief counselor, she advo-cated that I try it as well. Although I tried a few therapists, I never found one who was right for me, and for reasons I still don't en-tirely understand and cannot explain, I did not pursue getting help from a therapist or grief counselor beyond those short-lived efforts encouraged by my mother—though I would have immediately ad-vised any friend in a similar circumstance to do so. Instead, I turned to what I knew and felt I did best: my work.

During the final months of Dad's life, I was training to play the title role in the movie *Mary Kom,* a biopic about the gritty, self-made Indian Olympic boxer. In order to play her credibly, I not only had to learn who she was, I also had to thoroughly learn the sport and develop a boxer's body. I trained for two to three hours every morning, practicing footwork, working with a punching bag, and sparring. In the afternoons I'd have another two-hour gym session to build my muscles and my endurance. In a certain way, the extreme physicality of playing an athlete was its own kind of release, helping me deal with all the fears and worries that go along with watching a loved one fade away in front of you. Five days after Dad died, the day following my father's *chautha*, *Mary Kom* was scheduled to begin shooting, and although the film's producer, Sanjay Leela Bhansali, offered to postpone the start date, the sense of duty and discipline I'd inherited from my father and his twenty-seven years in the military wouldn't allow me to accept his offer. I was concerned that Sanjay Sir would take a hit on this small-budget movie, and I honestly felt it was my moral duty to show up.

As always, work was my therapy. I put all of my grief and a piece of my soul into that character and that film. It's what drove me and it's what allowed me to continue functioning. I'd show up on the set each day prepared and focused on the work at hand, just as I always had been, but I was also slightly dazed and certainly numb. In a way, it was just the right movie for me at that time. It was so intensely physical that my numbness might have actually served me well.

I was still living in the same apartment complex that my parents had lived in, and that my mother now lived alone in. We had separate units on the same floor so that we could all have freedom and privacy while still feeling connected as a family, and it was an arrangement that had worked well. During the weeks following my father's death, when I came home exhausted, bruised, and aching after shooting the grueling boxing scenes, Mom would knock on my door and remind me to soak in a warm bath with Epsom salts to ease the muscle pain. And every night I would cry in the tub and think, *I can't do this*. But in the morning I'd wake up and remember my father and how he'd willed himself onto that stage at TOIFA, how he'd willed himself to hang on during those final, difficult years. And I'd think, *I will do this. For him, I have to do this*. Stiff and sore, I'd rise from bed to begin another day of work.

My mother, Sid, and I all grieved in our separate silos. We didn't cry in front of one another; we tried to be strong for one another. Mom went through a really difficult time, so difficult that sometimes I wondered if she would ever come out of it. My parents had been partners and sweethearts for thirty-two years, a true story of love at first sight that had endured through pain and loss and challenge as well as all the joy they'd shared. At the end, my mother was Dad's wife, his friend, and his consulting physician even as she protected my brother and me from seeing the worst of his decline. I know it was traumatic for her, and I know it was lonely. Six months after Dad died, in December of 2013, Mom, Sid, and I took a family trip to Turks and Caicos. The time together, out of our normal environment, allowed us an opportunity to begin to talk about Dad's death and our grief more openly than we had been doing. It was a small step but it was a step in the right direction, and I believe it allowed us all to feel just a little less alone.

Beyond those few conversations with my family, though, I never really examined or dealt with my grief. Instead, I tried to power through. I was doing my best to be resilient, but the fact is that I was burying my grief rather than coming to terms with it. I moved from one extreme to another, like a pendulum, always in motion, always swinging. Either I was working long hours, moving fast, traveling, not giving myself time to think, or I was completely inside myself, shut down, uninterested in seeing friends or seeking company. Over time, I came to realize that my grief, rather than diminishing, had simply become an ever-present companion. Once I realized that it wasn't going anywhere, instead of trying to distance myself from it, I allowed it to move in with me, as if I were a host, perhaps, and we were in a symbiotic relationship. I accepted that I would take it with me wherever I went, like I took my cellphone and my keys. Or perhaps like I took my determination and my loyalty, which are simply parts of me, as grief was, too, now. You might think this would be an impediment, but somehow the comfort of knowing that this grief, so personal to me, was like a priority item in the tuck box of my life allowed me to move forward. I knew it would always be there. It might change, evolve, become larger or smaller, but it would always be there. And this acceptance, it seems, helped me move forward.

About a year before my father died, I got a tattoo on my right wrist while I was in Ibiza, Spain, recording part of my album there. Late one afternoon after we'd wrapped and had a few glasses of rosé, my manager and friend Natasha, hair stylist and friend Priyanka Borkar, and I decided that we would get tattoos together to commemorate our trip. I knew that I wanted something related to my father, which is how I came up with *Daddy's lil girl*. . . . That's what he always called me, and how he addressed the cards he sent to me. It was the tattoo artist's brilliant idea to have the words inked in my father's own handwriting, so I called Dad and told him that I needed him to write those words out for me. I didn't tell him it was for a tattoo; after seeing how he and my mother reacted to the belly button piercing I'd gotten when I was twenty-two, there was no question of what his response to a tattoo would be. So I lied and said that I needed it for artwork for my album cover. Dad was sick enough by then for it to be really hard for him to hold a pen—my coordinated, adept father, who had been such a skillful surgeon— but as always when I asked him for something, he made it happen. Mom told me that he practiced writing those words over and over again until he was satisfied. When I received the best of his efforts from Mom, it was perfect.

Later when I showed the tattoo to him, I smiled sweetly and said, "Do you forgive me?"

He laughed, delighted. "You tricked me! And of course I forgive you." He is now on my wrist forever.

ALMOST THREE YEARS after my father died, in the spring of 2016, I moved from Montreal to New York to shoot the second season of *Quantico*. I imagined I might leave behind the sadness I was still feeling when I left Canada. Instead, I fell into a depression. While I thought I had powered through my grief, I was still carrying it with me, apparently keeping up my end of the deal to hold it close wherever I went.

From what I understand, clinical depression is usually considered something separate from, or unrelated to, the sadness you feel when a loved one dies, so I don't think I was clinically depressed. And I was fortunate to be able to continue working, which was my salvation. Still, the time felt like a never-ending slump, a long sigh of sadness, a sort of pause in my life that lasted almost two years.

By the following year, 2017, I was deep into a period full of endings and loss. I was still living in New York; still grieving my father; still nursing a broken heart from a previous relationship; and shooting what would be the final season of *Quantico*. When I wasn't actually on set or on location, I was mostly alone. I would eat by myself, watch TV by myself, and stay up well into the early-morning hours even though that meant I got little sleep. That was okay, given that the little sleep I got never seemed restful anyway. I put on almost twenty pounds. On social media, people made unkind comments about my weight; in texts, friends took me to task for backing out of the few plans for drinks or dinner that I had forced myself to make. Finally they just stopped inviting me. I couldn't blame them, but I couldn't seem to help myself, either. I had always been curious, optimistic, and full of energy. Now I went through most of my days and nights like a zombie, so much so that I don't remember a lot about that time except that I felt numb for most of it. When I wasn't feeling numb, I felt lonely, sad, and isolated. No one understood what was going on inside me, because I didn't tell anyone.

I'm not saying there weren't a few bright spots, times when I delighted in the world around me. Mercifully, there were, and meeting Nick that year—however briefly—was one of them.

Mostly, though, my days and nights felt gray. I tried not to share my struggles with my mom; I didn't feel comfortable leaning on her when she was struggling, too. Instead, I hid my difficulties from her, which was relatively easy to do, since she was in India and I was mostly in America; we weren't in the kind of close physical prox- imity where you can readily sense the shifts of mood and emotion in those you love. But I'm sure she probably had a mother's instinct that something wasn't quite right, no matter how much I tried to act as if all was well. I could sense it in her, after all.

I was also dealing with the pressure of having to establish myself professionally all over again. I'd worked so hard to build one career in the Hindi film industry, then another in the music industry, and then a third in Hollywood. I was exhausted. I had never before felt so sad or weighed down that I couldn't do anything beyond what was absolutely required, but that's what I felt like for long portions of 2017. My asthma, which I'd had since childhood, got worse and my immune system weakened. I slept less and less. I was sick a lot.

When Dad died in 2013, I had made half-hearted efforts to find a therapist to help me with my grief. This time, in a more paralyzed state, I didn't even try. I should have. I didn't consider medication. I should have. All I wanted was to spend time alone, until finally, *finally,* I was tired of being sad. It would be so simple if I could point to one specific catalyst for this change, but that's not the way it hap- pened. It took almost two years, but eventually I realized that some small inclination toward life inside me was tired of sitting on the sidelines. I tried to remind myself of who I used to be when I'd had a spark. After a long time, I realized that I missed that person. I wanted to be her again.

Ultimately, I understood I was at another turning point in my life, another juncture where I had a critical choice to make: Was I going to remain in my despair and lose the career I loved and had worked so hard for, or was I going to bring back the spirit that I used to have each morning when I walked out the door thinking, *This will be a great day.* It had been *fun* to be that person. I liked her. My work hadn't been affected yet—I was thriving in my career— but I was tanking emotionally and I knew it was only a matter of time before that caught up to me professionally. I was not going to let all the good things in my life slip away from me because I was emotionally devastated. I was not going to give in to the darkness. I decided I had to choose myself, and I had to do it immediately. I knew it's what my father would have wanted, and I realized with a jolt that I wanted it, too.

Maybe it sounds simplistic, but I decided to focus on the bless- ings that I'd been given instead of focusing on what I was missing. I started to treat myself with kindness. I told myself not to blame myself for feeling alternately bereft and numb, for having indulged in such a long, quiet period of sadness. That's what my body had needed, I realized; that's what my spirit had needed—to mourn and mourn fully. To feel the sadness I hadn't wanted to feel. I didn't know exactly how to move from a world of gray back into a world of vibrant color, but one day I figured out one simple thing I could do: I could stop hiding and reengage with life. And that would re- quire me to step out of my apartment.

I spent New Year's Eve of 2017 as I usually did those years, with my best friend, Tamanna, and the man she had by then married, Sudeep Dutt. After our conversation that night, the next day—the first day of 2018—I made a conscious decision to start doing small things to help me reengage with the world. When I returned to New York, I made an effort to reconnect with people—just a few at first—breaking my nightly pattern of coming straight home from work, for instance, and instead meeting a friend for dinner, or inviting someone over to hang. I found that I felt a great comfort in simply being in the company of friends, even when I didn't talk about my problems; I felt less alone, less sad, less isolated. Once I started talking about what I was going through with people who cared, I started learning how to process my feelings.

Physically changing the routine I'd fallen into within my apartment helped, too. I stopped automatically sinking into the lovely safe spot on the couch that beckoned me to watch television there after a long day of work. Oh, how that comfy couch called to me. But rather than automatically go to it, I changed things up by going into the kitchen and sitting there for a while, or gazing out my large picture windows at the street below or the skyline beyond. Or maybe I'd just watch TV from my bedroom instead of the living room. Or I'd take my dog Diana for a walk. I found that simply changing my location sometimes changed my perspective, allowed the anchor that was holding me in place to shift a bit, to lose some of its paralyzing weight. It sounds small, I know. But changing my pattern was the beginning of real change for me. Gradually my soul started to feel less heavy.

But wait. I need to back up for a moment to tell you about Diana. In November of 2016, I did an interview with BuzzFeed in which they decided it would be fun to unleash a few wiggling puppies on me as I sat on the floor for the interview. I am eternally grateful that they did. When Diana, as I soon named her, started chewing on my Burberry shoes in the interview, I immediately understood that she had excellent taste. And then at some point she started snuggling under my arm. I was smitten. Brando, my dear cocker spaniel companion of twelve years who was being cared for by my mother and brother in Mumbai, was too old to travel. There was no way he could have moved to the States. But here was this sweet and loving bundle of intuition in whose presence I felt comforted, and so the next day I officially adopted her.

I am 100 percent certain that Diana chose me. She came into my life for a reason, helping me reengage with life before I even recognized that I might want to do so. When I arrived on set at 5 A.M. on my bleakest days, she accompanied me. When I couldn't sleep at night, she was happy to walk with me on lonely city streets or snuggle with me in my bed. She was one of my portals back to life and she is still with me today, loving me unconditionally.

During my solitary time, I came to understand myself better. As is no doubt clear by now, I have always been a person who wants and expects to work hard, who takes pride in the fact that I work hard. This period of being alone showed me that I needed the space to do nothing, too, to just be. It turns out that every single thing that my friends had ever told me about taking time for myself, and that I'd read in self-help books, and that I'd heard from Oprah, was true. If I'd listened better or paid more attention to what I'd heard and read, maybe I could have saved myself a lot of time and pain. Or maybe not. I think part of the human journey is figuring things out for yourself, and apparently, that's what I had to do.

Now I make sure to build free time into my day. After I wrap from work, I give myself three or four hours to do what I want before I have to be in bed, and after I finish whatever work I'm doing, I put my phone away. It might not surprise other people but it certainly surprised me when I realized that having that time to unwind and rest actually made me more productive.

I would never presume to speak to the pain of real clinical depression, or to compare my own period of depression with that condition. I'm only sharing what helped me return from a very dark period in my life, a period of deep grief that I didn't deal with when it first settled in with me. Gradually, the heavy sense that I woke up with every morning and went to sleep with every night, the sense that life was just too daunting, dissipated. I saw that I liked laughing again. I liked people. I liked life.

For me, one of the hardest things to accept in life is that control is an illusion. I hate that I can't control what happens in my life, but I can't. Loss happens. Failure happens. Sorrow happens. I can't always control where I'm headed, either. Sometimes sadness is the destination, whether or not it's where I want to go. During my time there I had to learn to trust that I was visiting for a reason, but that it would not be my permanent place of residence, my forever state of being. That, like water, I would flow past it eventually and end up where I was meant to be.

9

WHEN YOU KNOW, YOU KNOW

The most important relationship in life
is the one you have with yourself.
DIANE VON FURSTENBERG

GROWING UP, I'D seen my parents' marriage as rock solid, em-
bodying the security that comes from knowing you have a
true partner in this world. I wanted that, too. Since my professional
life at times felt transitory and ephemeral, as my childhood had in
certain ways—always moving, always changing—I longed for con-
sistency and stability in relationships. Once I got involved with
someone, I would give everything I had to keep our bond intact.
Often to a fault.

Throughout most of my twenties and into my early thirties, my
romantic pattern went something like this: I'd get involved with a
wonderful man and we'd have a lovely time, usually for a period of
years. By the end of the relationship, though, I'd have lost myself

somehow. I'd be exhausted, discouraged, and disappointed, and I didn't know how I'd gotten to such an unhappy place.

As almost all of my days were spent working on location and on set, most of my adult romantic relationships were with public people. I respect the privacy of those people and I respect my own, too—most of us are married now, and some of us have children—so I don't see the need to name names. And this conversation is not about them. It's about me. It's about my emotional evolution. It's about the growth it took to get where I am today in terms of understanding that true partnership is a two-way street.

Looking back on that time in my life, I see that I was working way too hard both professionally and personally. I made four films a year for almost a decade. In order to do that, I worked fifteen- or eighteen-hour days, including weekends. That's simply the investment that was required if I wanted to reach the highest echelons of the film industry in India. But it left me almost no time outside of work, and as I reflect on that period now, I wonder if that's how the problem started.

I know that I felt guilty about having so little time to spend with whomever I was dating during those years and so I'd end up overcompensating. I would prioritize my partners' schedules over mine, canceling work commitments or what little time I had with friends and family in order to accommodate the needs of my partner at the time. I never missed a shoot, but I might go late to set or I would keep set waiting because I was on a phone call in my trailer. The professionalism with which I normally conducted myself seemed to disappear when I was romantically involved with someone. It would be years before I figured out why I fell into this pattern.

Eventually most of my relationships would reach a point where a breakup was inevitable because this out-of-balance situation went on for so long that there was no way to move forward. We'd get mad at each other for no obvious reason, or for a ridiculous reason, and end up arguing. Eventually that led to resentment on both sides. I'd start to feel terrible about myself, invisible and undervalued, and almost every time it happened, I believed the problem mostly lay in my partner. I never considered that maybe the problem, or at least part of the problem, lay in me.

What's strange is that my mom did not model this behavior for me in her own marriage, not even remotely. All the women I was raised by—my aunts, my grandmothers, my mother—had extremely solid individuality in their relationships, so why didn't I? Why was I so afraid that I might let someone down? Why did I feel so guilty at that thought? Had I taken the romanticized messages of self-sacrifice that girls and women hear all the time—that it's our responsibility to accommodate men; that we are natural caregivers and it's our job to care for others first, ourselves if there's time—too much to heart? It's not a new thought that we women are socialized that way; it's the water we swim in from a very young age. And working at my career as hard as I did, maybe I'd never given myself enough time to drag myself out of that pool, or even see that I was swimming in it.

Whenever my mom or my friends pointed my romantic pattern out to me, I'd shrug it off. Now I think I was just avoiding taking a deeper look at myself and the pattern I was locked into. And let's be clear: I'm the one who created that pattern. I was the eraser and the erased. Before I could move forward and change the pattern, I had to own the part I played in creating so much pain for myself. I'm not unique in this; we all have our own painful patterns. Somehow I finally figured out that the only way to break the cycle was to accept my truth and continue from there. Which meant walking through a fire of sorts.

In 2016, after my last big breakup, I consciously decided that it was time to take a dating hiatus. I was finally realizing that whatever I was doing in relationships wasn't working, and I knew I needed to focus on myself in order to understand why. Equally important, maybe more so, was the fact that my father had died more than two years earlier and I was still struggling with that grief. I had initially tried to block out my emotional devastation by throwing myself even harder into work, if that's possible. But my grief, my confusion, and my exhaustion were all catching up with me and I was coming to understand that I needed time alone, time without a relationship. So after being in back-to-back relationships for more than a decade, I hit the pause button hard.

At first, it felt impossible. I missed having someone to call first thing in the morning, someone to wish me luck on the day's filming, someone whom I could encourage and support in return. I missed having someone to talk to at night who was interested in how my day had unfolded. But slowly, with no one else's behavior or needs or feelings to prioritize over mine, I began to consider my own more deeply. I began to have more of a relationship with myself.

Part of what I realized was that while I was bold and fierce in my professional life, in my personal life, where I spent way too much time looking after the needs—or what I perceived as the needs—of the men I dated, I was the exact opposite. My mother and my friends had long seen that, and now, with a little perspective, I did, too. But while my behavior in my professional life and my private life seemed polar opposite in some ways, maybe there were also some connections between those arenas. When I walk onto a set, I take my responsibility extremely seriously. I am always prepared, in part because preparation leads to confidence, and in part because there are so many people involved every day in every production that it would be irresponsible to waste people's time by not being completely ready. In other words, at the end of each day, I want to know that I've done the absolute best job I possibly could.

Had my professional do-my-best attitude somehow bled into my private behavior? Was my reluctance to end a relationship I hadn't been happy in for some time related to a fear that I hadn't done my best to make it work? That I hadn't done absolutely everything in my power, in fact? I have always been a solution finder professionally and don't hesitate to take control when a problem needs fixing. If something doesn't feel right on a set, I find a way to address it; if what I'm doing in a scene isn't working, I find another way to approach it. Was I taking too much responsibility for solving the problems in my relationships by trying to control as many aspects of them as I could?

I finally realized the futility of this—and the craziness of it. I can't possibly control a relationship, because I can't control how other people think or feel about me. The only thing that I can control is myself. If I'm solid in myself, happy in myself, confident in myself, well, that's what I can bring to the table in a relationship. And I was beginning to understand that that's the first step in having a healthy relationship, a relationship of partners who give and take equally, who think about how things affect each party and make decisions accordingly.

At the end of 2017, I had turned a corner in my grief; I felt ready to spend more time with friends and less time on my own. As usual, I spent New Year's Eve with Tamanna and Sudeep. I'd been single for well over a year at that point, and they joked that they were a little tired of our get-togethers being the two of them with me as a third wheel. "When are we going to go out as couples?" Sudeep teased. Then he asked me to write down the five things that were most important to me in the person I wanted to be with, five qualities that were absolute and that I would not compromise on. I started this exercise to humor my good friends, but I ended up with a frank and truthful list.

The first nonnegotiable quality of My Future Person was honesty, because there were times in some of my previous relationships when I'd been hurt by dishonesty. The second was that he had to appreciate the value of family—because a house full of kids and relatives visiting from all over the world is what I love and what I'm used to. Third: he had to take his profession very seriously, because I take mine very seriously. Fourth: I wanted someone who was creative and had the imagination to dream big with me. And fifth: I wanted someone who had drive and ambition, like I did, someone who wanted to continue to grow and evolve in all his endeavors.

I wrote the list down and saved it in my wallet. It reminded me of the clarity I'd achieved in my period of romantic solitude. I wasn't looking for a new relationship, but I knew that when one eventually came along I wanted to enter it as my own complete person, someone who was bringing her own happiness and self-confidence to the table. Then I got to work shooting the final season of *Quantico*, traveling for UNICEF, and immersing myself in film projects I was developing.

Sometimes when you're not looking for love, it appears right in front of you.

Okay, before I get into this part of my story, I want to say that not much surprises me as much as Nick Jonas did. And in a weird way, I feel like my mom manifested him. A year or two earlier, after my last disastrous relationship, she had said to me: "My wish for you is that someone would just come in and sweep you off your feet." She and my father had married only ten days after their first date, after all.

And that's just what Nick did. He swept me off my feet. Once we started dating, I felt like I was being carried by a giant unstoppable wave. At times I had no idea where the wave was taking me, but I rode it anyway. Have I mentioned that I love control? So you may understand how disorienting this was. But it was also thrilling.

Nick entered my life in a serious way a mere five months after I wrote my list of nonnegotiable qualities—qualities that pretty perfectly describe him, by the way. But that wasn't the first time I'd encountered him. In the fall of 2015, I'd received a direct message from him on Twitter:

"Several people have told me we should meet."

Several people? Really? Who were these several people? Not too long ago, Nick and I were trying to unravel how our first communication actually came about. He remembered that he was seeing my *Quantico* billboards—the series was just premiering—and that his older brother Kevin, who'd watched the show, thought the two of us should meet. Then Nick scrolled back through a few years' worth of texts to his friend and my *Quantico* co-star Graham Rogers and found his first text to Graham about me: *Priyanka. Is. Wow.* (That was fun to read.) Nick heard back from Graham right away that Graham thought the two of us would really hit it off. No introduction followed, though, so Nick took matters into his own hands and DM'd me on Twitter.

When I received the message, I stared at it for a few moments. *Nick Jonas.* I knew who he was, of course, but I didn't know who he *was*.

So naturally I did what any self-respecting girl would do. I consulted Dr. Google and got an in-depth tutorial. When I watched the music video for "Close," which is still one of my favorite Nick songs, I was like, *Okay, I have to at least go on a date with this man.* Famous last words.

Curious, I DM'd him back, and somehow we managed to get past the first awkward hurdles of meeting over social media and made a start at getting to know each other.

Cut to fifteen months later. We'd been texting back and forth from time to time when Nick called unexpectedly to ask if I would be his date to President Obama's farewell party at the White House in January of 2017. If there were a Best First Date *Ever* competition, that would be the hands-down winner. Alas, that is not a part of this story. *Quantico* ended up filming and I couldn't leave the set. *Huge* disappointment.

But Fate made it up to me. In February of 2017, I attended the

Oscars for the second time, and then the after-party hosted by *Vanity Fair*. On my way out, this guy grabbed my hand as I walked past the bar. He turned me around and lo and behold it was Nick, who then proceeded to get down on one knee and say, "You're real. Where have you been all my life?" I had a car waiting and a flight back to India to catch, but Nick convinced me that five minutes was enough time for a drink. One super-quick drink later, I climbed into the waiting car and sped off to the airport, a big, dopey grin on my face. And that was the first time we met IRL.

SOMETIME THAT SPRING, the Ralph Lauren atelier invited me to my first Met Gala. The gala is an extravagant star-studded fundraiser for the Metropolitan Museum of Art's Costume Institute, hosted by *Vogue*'s editor-in-chief, Anna Wintour. Held each year on the first Monday of May, it is the Super Bowl of fashion. I was beyond thrilled to receive my first invitation to it. The gala's theme that year—every year has one—was "Rei Kawakubo/Comme des Garçons: Art of the In-Between," which to me meant a kind of androgynous look, a combination of male and female. I ended up wearing a dramatic Ralph Lauren trench-coat gown with a twenty-five-foot train—definitely a statement. I absolutely loved it.

Not long after the initial invitation came, the atelier approached both Nick and me separately to invite us to walk the carpet together at the event since we would both be wearing Ralph Lauren. It sounded like fun, so independently, we agreed.

About five days before the gala, Nick and I met for a drink at the Carlyle, an elegant hotel full of old-world charm located on New York City's Upper East Side. The neighborhood is largely a mix of upscale residential brownstones and high-rises, the designer shops of Madison Avenue, and Fifth Avenue's stately museums. I was forty-five minutes late because I came straight from shooting *Quantico* and the day had run long. He had recently been to the Masters golf tournament, and early on the conversation veered into two topics that threw me for a bit of a loop: cigars and golf. Cigars and golf? What twenty-four-year-olds talk about cigars and golf? (A lot, as I now know.) Much later, we would laugh at our initial misunderstandings—he'd thought I'd been playing a game by making him wait; I'd thought he was trying to assure me that he wasn't too young for me given our ten-year age difference.

We enjoyed the conversation enough for me to invite him back to my apartment nearby after the Carlyle closed, around midnight. It was also a place where Nick, prohibited from smoking at the hotel bar, could enjoy a cigar. In the car on the way there, I'm certain that I told him that my mother would be there, but Nick doesn't remember that. All he remembers is walking into my rented duplex expecting a private romantic setting, and seeing my mother curled up on the L-shaped couch in the living room in her nightgown, watching TV—she was getting her nightly murder fix with an episode of *Law & Order: SVU.* Our favorite show.

"Oh shit," she said, in an embarrassed whisper. I'd failed to alert her that I was bringing someone home. Oops.

So I took Nick downstairs. I put on some music and we sat on the back patio to talk. It was raining a little, and unseasonably chilly for a night in late April, and while there were sparks of real intrigue and interest between us, it was clear that nothing was going to happen that night. When Nick left at around 1:30 A.M., he gave me a nice little platonic hug and a pat on the back. *A pat on the back???*

The night of the gala, we both had rooms at the Carlyle. Nick's older brother Joe and Joe's then girlfriend (now his wife) Sophie Turner, whom I knew from Montreal—I had filmed Season 1 of *Quantico* there while she was filming *X-Men: Apocalypse* there— were also staying in the hotel, and they suggested that Nick go to my suite to see how I was doing. "We're not a couple," he responded, and instead went to the lobby to wait for me downstairs.

Which is where Dana, my publicist, found him. In classic Dana style, she urgently whispered, "We need you right now. We gotta go." Idling outside the hotel was a fifteen-passenger minibus, and when Nick climbed aboard, there I was, standing at the front and taking up the entire vehicle with my trench-coat dress, the very long train of which had been carefully draped over the seats from front to back in a sea of lustrous, khaki-colored silk. Nick was undaunted by the spectacle. "I don't need much space," he said with a hint of a smile, maneuvering around the train to make his way into a corner. My heart may have fluttered just a little.

When we got to the Met, we ended up taking some pictures together on the carpet and some separate photos, too. There are a few where it's just me with Nick photobombing at the edge of the shot, having to work hard not to step on my train. But as tricky as the dress was to maneuver in, I felt great in it.

Not long after we'd entered the grand marble foyer of the museum, Nick went off to say hello to some people. While I knew this wasn't an actual date and I didn't really know this man, I was acutely aware of his absence. Suddenly there wasn't a person I knew in sight. I felt adrift in that moment, which was strange because I'd done so many big events in my career and I was accustomed to navigating them on my own. But at that particular moment, in a room full of strangers I'd mostly seen on TV, the world seemed to freeze, and I felt utterly alone. That's when Nick turned around, took one look at me, and immediately brought me over to include me in the conversation. After that, we didn't leave each other's side.

The night flew by in a haze of flirtation and champagne. As we got into a car to leave the after-party, we held hands for the first time. I was flying out, almost straight from the event, for a UNICEF trip to Zimbabwe—my first trip as a global ambassador for the organization, though I'd been involved with UNICEF India for a decade—and I think we both felt a sense that there was now something between us. Again, there was no kiss—and this time not even a pat on the back. But there was a lingering hug. I'd had so much fun that evening, and I was now deeply curious about this man.

While we tried to connect in the weeks and months after the Met Gala, it never worked out. Nick had been quite clear about wanting to take me out the next time I was in L.A., but to be honest, I may have been a little reluctant to move things forward. As intriguing as I found him, I knew that when I was ready to be with someone again, I wanted to be with someone who wanted a family. He was twenty-five and I was thirty-five, and I assumed he didn't, at least not anytime soon. (*Note to self: Remember that lesson you thought you'd already learned? When you assume, you make an ass out of u and me.*)

IT WOULD BE a whole year before we'd meet again. We continued to be in touch randomly during that time—a funny text here, a flirtatious one there. Then, a few weeks before the 2018 Met Gala, I texted to ask Nick if he would be there. He said he would.

That year's theme was "Heavenly Bodies: Fashion and the Catholic Imagination," and I again wore Ralph Lauren, a long, dark red velvet dress with an intricately bejeweled gold hood that had been embroidered in India. I arrived at the gala, joined the line for my entrance onto the carpet, and bowed my head to adjust the gold mesh of the hood. When I looked up again, the man in line in front of me turned around: Nick. We looked at each other with expressions that said *This is unbelievable.* Because the timing actually *was* unbelievable. But we didn't talk much in line; I, for one, was trying to play it cool. Or coy. I couldn't decide. We walked the carpet separately, did our own photos, and hardly saw each other once we entered the museum.

A couple of weeks after the 2018 gala, I posted some photos on social media from a UNICEF trip I was on in Bangladesh. Nick responded, saying that he found the pictures moving, and that the good I wanted to bring into the world inspired him. I was touched by his thoughtfulness and we exchanged a few more texts. It was late May and we had no idea that in less than two months we'd be engaged.

WHEN I GOT back to L.A. from Bangladesh, Nick texted to say that he'd gotten tickets to see *Beauty and the Beast* at the Hollywood Bowl. He was going with his brother Kevin and his friends Greg and Paris Garbowsky, and he invited me to come and bring a friend if I wanted. No pressure. Have I mentioned that he's a smart guy? My friend Rebel Wilson, with whom I was filming the movie *Isn't It Romantic,* was playing LeFou in *Beauty and the Beast* and I really wanted to see it. So I called Mubina Rattonsey, a longtime friend from Mumbai who now lives in L.A., and she and I joined Nick's party.

We all met up beforehand for drinks at the Chateau Marmont, and Kevin—who had been married for eight years at the time and was the father of two young daughters, and therefore didn't get out as much as his single younger brothers did—was essentially playing Nick's wingman. Every time there was an opportunity in the conversation to hype Nick—"Nick's the best baseball player! Nick could have gone pro!" "He's the best housecleaner! He could go pro at that, too!"—he took it. It was totally hilarious and charming and I loved seeing that relationship between the brothers; I'd seen the closeness between Nick and Joe, too, when I'd watched them together at the 2017 Met Gala. I know now it's that closeness that infuses everything the brothers do together.

After we got engaged, Nick told me that the minute I walked into the bar at the Chateau Marmont that night, he'd said to himself, *That's my wife.* And that the following morning he'd called his mother and told her he was going to marry me. And that shortly thereafter he'd flown to Australia to meet up with his brothers and told them, too, that he was going to propose. But of course I knew none of that at the time.

We spent every day of the week following *Beauty and the Beast* together. We went to a Dodgers game, we went out to dinner, we hung out at his place or mine just getting to know each other. One day he invited me to the studio to watch a fifteen-member gospel choir record a song from a musical he'd written. As I observed him conduct these incredibly gifted musicians and understood what total control of his craft he had, my knees literally went weak.

The week tumbled into Memorial Day weekend, and Nick had rented a boat that Saturday to hang out with a small group of his family and friends—and Mubina, whom I was now dragging everywhere with me. I'd been swept away by this magical day of eating and drinking and laughing, but now it had to end because I needed to get to a meeting that night with my Indian management team and my American management team, who are hardly ever in the same place at the same time. Nick's friends had other ideas.

"Don't work!" they cajoled. "It's Saturday night of a holiday weekend!"

The water rocked the boat. The gulls screeched overhead. "Well," I said, "if I had a reason to stay, I would, but clearly there's no reason to because *no one* is telling me to stay." I may have sounded just a bit like my six-year-old self wheedling to get my father's attention. I said it once. I said it twice. I may have even said it a third time. Finally Nick took me aside.

"I'm not going to ask you to stay," he told me. "Not because I don't want you to, but because if you *could* cancel, you'd have done it already." Then he took my hands. "I'll never be that guy, Pri. You've worked so hard for so many years to be where you are, and you know what's best for your career. And I will never stand in your way." A small smile played at the corners of his mouth. "But I know you're feeling some FOMO here, so I'm going to take all our friends out for dinner while you're at your meeting, and we'll wait for you to come back."

That may have been the moment I started to suspect he was the one for me.

The whirlwind romance continued in June when I flew to Atlantic City, New Jersey, for the wedding of Rachel Tamburelli, a longtime friend of Nick's who, like the rest of her clan, was more like family. There I met Denise and Kevin Sr., his parents; his younger brother, Frankie—the only brother I hadn't met—his best friend, Cavanaugh James; and aunts, uncles, and cousins. It was perfect timing because I was eager to meet everyone who was important to him. The entire month was spent exploring what his life was like, what my life was like, who his people were, who my people were.

In the first few weeks of our getting to know each other, Nick had told me that he had type 1 diabetes. I remembered seeing a mention of that when I googled him after he'd first reached out to me in 2015, but I hadn't thought too much about it. Once I understood what a serious condition it was, I found myself worrying about him almost constantly. Fortunately, that didn't last long. As we spent more and more time together, I saw how extremely disciplined he was about checking his blood sugar multiple times daily and monitoring his food and making sure that he was 100 percent on top of his health. He'd been managing his illness since he was diagnosed with it at the age of thirteen while touring with his brothers, and I came to understand that he is never reckless with his health. Instead of letting the disease control him, he's controlled it so well that he leads an almost completely normal life. I observed what he did to keep himself well and I observed how fully he embraced life, and my love for him only grew.

There was a lot of attention on us by then—the tabloids had picked up on the fact that we were together—and paparazzi were following us constantly. In our business, there are some people who can handle the relentless public scrutiny and then there are others who prefer to safeguard their privacy ferociously. Previously, I'd been part of the latter group as far as relationships were concerned. With Nick, it felt like nothing mattered but us. If we wanted to go out for dinner, we'd go out for dinner. If we wanted to go to a movie, we'd go to a movie. It was unfamiliar territory for me, but also liberating. I felt protected whenever I was with him, and slowly, all the walls I'd built up over the years crumbled away.

MUMBAI, THE MAXIMUM CITY: maximum people, maximum traffic, maximum noise, maximum energy. The city I now call home in India is a whirlwind of chaos that somehow works beautifully. I had a trip scheduled there later in June, and Nick wanted to come with me. "I want to see your country, your home, where you come from, meet your friends," he said. And then he added, "And I want to see your mom."

Really? Had meeting my mom that night when she was watching *Law & Order* on the couch in her nightgown left that much of an impression?

As much as I really, really liked him, I was nervous to have Nick come home with me. It was a huge trip for a new boyfriend to make, and we'd be there for a good ten days. I was going for work, for a friend's pre-engagement party, and to see family and friends in general. Other than visiting people, what would we do in Mumbai all that time? And what would he do by himself when I was working? I can be a bit of a worrywart, but Nick being Nick, he calmed my overactive nerves and took the stress out of the situation. "Don't worry, babe. Just do your thing and I'll take care of myself." And so I agreed.

As usual we were greeted by media when our Emirates flight landed at Chhatrapati Shivaji Maharaj International, but we found our way to the car and made it out of the airport. The first thing I did was to roll down my window and take in the heavy, humid air; I never feel like I'm entirely home until I'm breathing it in. With the people everywhere—in cars, on bikes, in the streets, on the sidewalks—and the noise of car horns and vendors hawking their wares, Nick remarked, "It feels like a concert has just let out at every single moment." I laughed because it was so true, and because it was such an observant, Nick thing to say.

My first work commitment was a few days after we arrived, and of course I started to worry again about how Nick would spend his time. "I got this," he assured me. "Go do what you have to do. I'm going to take your mom out for lunch."

Some people might think, *Oh, how sweet.* Not me. I zipped right into worrying mode. Why did he want to take my mother out to lunch alone? What would they talk about? Would either of them accidentally say anything that would embarrass me? That afternoon I sat in a meeting surrounded by twenty people and couldn't stop wondering what Nick and my mom were doing *at that very moment.* Unable to take the suspense any longer, I sent a member of my security team out to take pictures of them at the restaurant they'd gone to—okay, to spy on them—so I could study their body language using my *Quantico* skills. #NotProud.

As it turned out, Nick had taken Mom to lunch that day to ask her permission to marry me. NBD. Afterward, when I asked, they both omitted that small detail. Much later Nick reported that my mom had told him he didn't need her permission. "Well, I'm not asking for your permission, necessarily," he'd replied carefully. "But I do want you to be happy with this, so I'm asking for your blessing." Nick sensed that what Mom was feeling but not saying was that she didn't think it was her role to approve of our union; that such a thing would have been Dad's role. It must have been a bittersweet moment for her. And yet it was already clear to her that Nick was the one for me, so she put aside her concerns about roles and gave her wholehearted and unequivocal blessing.

EVERYTHING BETWEEN NICK and me felt right. But because the relationship was happening so fast, I was having a hard time processing it all. I tried not to overthink things, to let myself just ride the glorious wave that was carrying me forward and bringing me so much joy. Usually I succeeded, but other times I simply could not believe that Nick was real, and that our relationship was as happy and healthy as it seemed.

Despite my disbelief, Nick was sure. He had been sure from date two or three. Once we were engaged, he even played me a version of a song that he'd written after we'd spent only a few days together, a song about our future that would later become the song "I Believe."

Call me crazy
People saying that we move too fast
But I've been waiting, for a reason
Ain't no turning back
'Cause you show me something I can't live without
I believe, I believe, I believe.

Less than two months after Nick wrote those lyrics, he proposed to me in Greece, on the enchanted island of Crete. We'd gone there to celebrate my birthday, and he held off until the day after my birthday because—*wait for it*—he didn't want to take the attention away from My Day; he wanted us, in the future, to always be able to celebrate those occasions separately. It was just after midnight on July 19, 2018, when he got down on one knee and said, "You checked all my boxes. Now will you check one more?" He held out a Tiffany box just the right size for a ring. "Will you make me the happiest man in the world and marry me?" According to him, I waited a full forty-five seconds before I answered with an emphatic "Yes!" I don't remember the lapse, but if there was such a pause, please chalk it up to my being in shock.

I remember telling Nick that night about the list I'd made on New Year's Eve with Tamanna and Sudeep. He smiled and said he had a similar one. In the days following our engagement, he told me that weeks earlier in London he'd taken his brothers along with him to Tiffany to pick out the magnificent ring I was now wearing on my hand—Tiffany had closed the store to give the brothers privacy—and the closeness of their relationship, the fact that they would do this together, made me want to laugh and weep for joy at the same time.

Once I'd said yes, we stayed up until eight-thirty in the morning FaceTiming our families and friends. Then the wedding planning essentially began. At first, we thought about getting married the following year, sometime in 2019, but in August when Nick was visiting India again, he said he didn't want to wait. Neither did I. We knew we were ready, and our families knew we were ready. Why wait? we thought. Let's just do it.

When you know, you know. And so we did.

10

SHAADI

Give your hearts, but not into each other's keeping.
For only the hand of Life can contain your hearts.
And stand together yet not too near together:
For the pillars of the temple stand apart,
And the oak tree and the cypress grow not in each other's shadow.

KAHLIL GIBRAN, *THE PROPHET*

FOUR WEEKS LATER, Nick and I were in India for our *roka* ceremony, the formal North Indian ritual that marks both families' approval of the union and recognizes the beginning of a new
relationship for not just the couple but the families as well. Nick's
parents, Denise and Kevin Sr., were there with us, as well as a group
of about thirty of my family and closest friends. Four *pandits,* or
priests knowledgeable in Vedic scripture, chanted for our peaceful
union on a sun-drenched afternoon at my home in Mumbai. When
it was our turn to chant, we repeated the Sanskrit prayers phrase by
phrase after them. Maybe because he's so musical, Nick was able to

pull off the tricky pronunciations and intonations, sometimes even better than I was. My friends and family were so impressed with their "National Jiju"; shortly after we made our engagement public, the affectionate nickname had been given to Nick by print and social media in my country, and now it seemed that we were hearing and seeing the term—*Jiju* translates as "sister's husband" or "brother-in-law"—everywhere.

The *roka* is the first of the pre-wedding rituals in Hindu tradition, so naturally we had been looking forward to it. What I couldn't have imagined was how meaningful it would be to me. At this ritual, which is all about the joining of the families, I watched our two families start to braid themselves together. After the Sanskrit Vedas had been chanted, my mother asked Kevin Sr., a former pastor, to lead us in prayer. He and Nick and Denise—who wore her sari as if she had been born to it—had just participated in a ritual full of meaning for us, and now my family and friends had the chance to participate in a ritual full of meaning for them. It was the first step in creating one family out of what had been two.

Nick and I had started thinking about the kind of wedding we wanted to have almost as soon as we decided to get married. As an actress, I'd played a bride many times, and just like in real life, playing a bride in the movies is a big production; it would take at least four hours in hair and makeup alone to get me ready to shoot. After I'd played my thirty-fifth bride or so, I was just so over it. I decided that whenever I actually got married, I wanted to be able to be dressed and ready in an hour. It would be quick. It would be simple. No big deal.

Ha!

As it turned out, our wedding was a huge, insanely joyous celebration, and the planning for the whole thing took place in just two months. Because we were having two weddings—both Hindu and Christian ceremonies—and because there are many Hindu pre-wedding ceremonies, our events would be spread out over three days. That feels really long to most Westerners, whose weddings usually last a few hours, but it's pretty normal when it comes to the Indian scenario; our weddings routinely last a few days, even without the Christian service added to the proceedings. To make things even more interesting, many Hindu weddings are at night because of the recommendations of astrologers, who must be consulted to determine an auspicious time for the ceremony. After comparing Nick's and my birth charts, it was determined that on December 2, 2018, the date of our Indian ceremony, our auspicious time would be 10:30 P.M.

When Nick and I were initially contemplating where to get married, I'd thought about somewhere that wasn't America or India, somewhere that would be completely private with just family and very close friends. But one night during one of Nick's many trips to India in August and September—there were at least six of them—we were talking with Tamanna and Sudeep, who were practically giddy with excitement about my new relationship status and the new configuration of our get-togethers. "At last we've upgraded from a three-wheeler to four-wheel drive!" Sudeep crowed. When they described to Nick their own wedding a few years earlier in Rajasthan, Nick said, "Why don't we do it in India? Don't you think I should take my bride from her home with all of her family and friends surrounding her?" Nick had learned what a big deal it is in India for the groom to travel to the bride and take her from her home in order to start their new life together, and his desire to honor that tradition made my heart melt all over again. We decided if it was logistically possible, India it would be.

I told Nick about the Taj Umaid Bhawan Palace in Jodhpur, where I'd shot a commercial for Lux soap in 2009. I'd been enchanted by the sweeping grandeur of the royal residence, by the elegant grounds and the regal interior. Nick said we should find out right then if it was available. This was at 11 P.M. We called our travel agent, Aparna, and she called the Taj the next morning, and unbelievably they had total availability for our exact dates. For two hundred people. Right from the start, it felt like the universe conspired to make the many moving parts of our wedding fall into place.

Nick and I always understood that this wedding would be a cultural and religious education for both of our families: the Western wedding would be an education for the Indian side, and the Indian wedding would be an education for the Western side. That's why we prepared funny, informative booklets for all our guests: *Indian Weddings for Dummies* and *Western Weddings for Dummies*. That way everyone would be prepared for each of the rituals and ceremonies as they happened, and we could explain which elements were traditional and which were our own personal variations. We also set up a bazaar in the hotel that featured clothing and jewelry created by local designers I'd worked with or knew of; I knew that family and friends coming from the States might want to partake in their offerings. All of the most important people in our lives were going to be there with us, and we wanted to create a cross-cultural event they'd both understand and never forget.

The morning of November 30 dawned bright and clear in Jodhpur, as do most mornings at that time of year. We'd had a welcome dinner for all of the guests the night before, and this was the day of the first of the pre-ceremonies since the *roka*: the *mehendi,* the henna ceremony, and the musical *sangeet* celebration. I was so excited to introduce Nick's family and all our Western friends to these functions, as we Indians refer to them, that I may have literally danced my way to the shower that morning. It was in the palatial bathroom that my dance moves came to an abrupt end as I stepped down hard on a sharp two-inch piece of wood sticking up out of the beautiful old plank floor. This was no splinter or sliver; it was a small spike that drove straight into my heel and more or less buried itself there. Alone in the giant bathroom and unable to make it to the door, I sank to the floor and squeezed my foot to stop the bleeding, then shouted to my longtime assistant, Chanchal Dsouza, who I knew was just outside in the next room. When she entered the bathroom and saw me sitting in a puddle of blood, she shrieked. I told her to get Nick, who was in the shower in his own bathroom. He arrived moments later, and it would have been a comic scene if it hadn't been so painful: Chanchal screaming, Nick in a T-shirt with a towel wrapped around his waist, a hulking member of our security team who'd heard all the commotion and was checking to make sure we were safe, and me on the floor with blood seeping out of my foot.

A doctor was on the way, but I was impatient to start getting dressed for this day I'd been looking forward to so much. So Nick quickly pulled on shorts and held my foot steady while I doused it in the only antiseptic I could think of—perfume (alcohol)—and then pulled the bloody spear out with a pair of tweezers. After years of enduring blistered feet through never-ending dance rehearsals and earning scars in complicated stunt sequences, I had developed a high threshold for pain, thank goodness, and I was pretty stoic about the whole thing. That's probably why when the slightly messy medical intervention was complete, Nick deadpanned, "This is my future wife. I'm scared." By making a joke about how tough I was and what that boded for him, he defused the tension, made us all laugh, and reminded me that all would be well because (a) I *am* tough, and (b) I was marrying the man of my dreams.

A few hours later I limped to the *mehendi,* where I had henna applied to my hands and legs in beautiful, intricate designs, and so did the women in my family and any other female guests who wanted to adorn themselves in this distinctive traditional way. And that night I danced at my *sangeet* wearing heels, because nothing—

not even a wooden spike in my foot—was going to stop this from being the best damn party of my life.

The *sangeet*—which translates as "song" or "music"—is basically like the rehearsal dinner the night before Western weddings combined with music and dance performances by the families of the bride and the groom. Because we are who we are—the Chopras and the Jonases—our *sangeet* looked like Coachella, complete with a stage, lighting, costumes, and sound system. There's a certain element of competition in any *sangeet;* each family wants to outdo the other. Nick and I had boosted the level of competition by offering a champions' trophy at the end for the winning family, so for an hour and ten minutes we had a fully rehearsed extravaganza of a show. My family went first, and then Nick's. We had the home court advantage, naturally, since everyone on my side knew what a *sangeet* looked like and had participated in one or more before. My clan, with the help of Ganesh Hegde and his team, with whom I had done multiple stage shows, came up with a script that was hilarious and musical numbers that had everyone laughing, stomping their feet, and clapping. My mom and I even showed off some of our dance moves together. It was just like a big Bollywood movie.

But it was Nick's friends and family who blew me away. Unbeknownst to me, they'd hired an Indian choreographer and had rehearsed synchronized dance routines complete with Bollywood moves *long-distance by video* (since some of them live far apart) back in the States long before arriving in India. They pulled it off gloriously. Most of the groom's side was onstage and had a part to play. My heart was so full to see Nick's loved ones go all in for him, wanting to do him proud and to demonstrate to their Indian counterparts their appreciation for our tradition. Their commitment to it amped up the joy for me of an occasion I'd thought was already at a 10. We both conceded defeat. The trophy was shared.

All this, and we hadn't even had the weddings yet! The first would be the Christian service the next afternoon. It was to be officiated by Kevin Sr., which lent an air of intimacy to our joyous extravaganza. We had decided to have the Christian wedding first because it's simpler than an Indian wedding and we thought it would be a good idea to pace ourselves.

After the *sangeet* and the post-*sangeet* partying came to an end, Nick and I headed to our rooms with our groomsmen and bridesmaids, respectively. We'd decided to spend our final night as single people surrounded by our closest friends but apart from each other. When I opened the heavy door, Nick managed to take my breath away without even being there. Lit candles flickered throughout the darkened room and roses were strewn everywhere. And then I noticed the gifts that my husband-to-be had left to surprise me, and the notes giving voice to his respect, faithfulness, and love. My bridesmaids and I were speechless. But while I couldn't use my voice to form words, I was somehow able to formulate them in my head. *I really must have done something right,* I remember thinking. How else was it possible that I had found someone who appreciated me and loved me so dearly? And who knew me so well. Who knew exactly what I needed to be reminded of the night before our wedding.

THE NEXT AFTERNOON, I was standing in a ground-floor room of the palace, waiting to take the long walk across the lawn and out to Nick at the altar. It was a gorgeous, sunny day, and Nick was flanked by his groomsmen, including his brothers and his closest friends; Kevin Sr. was standing behind the altar ready to conduct the service. I was wearing Ralph Lauren again. It was only the fourth wedding dress Ralph had ever made and the first for someone outside his family. The dress had not only been designed for me but further personalized: into the scads of the gown's hand-embroidered lace had been stitched names and words that were meaningful to me and to us:

Nicholas Jerry Jonas   Love   1st December 2018   Compassion
Family   Hope
Madhu and Ashok   Om Namah Shivay

Ralph Lauren and his atelier, initially with their role in bringing Nick and me together at my first Met Gala, and later with this exquisite gown, will always be a part of our love story.

To complement the gown, I wore a seventy-five-foot veil that had to be stitched into my hair by Priyanka Borkar so that it wouldn't be dragged off by its own weight. The very long veil—almost exactly the length of a tennis court—was the brainstorm of Andrea Ciaraldi, the creative director of the Ralph Lauren Women's Collection. Because it was such a lengthy walk from the palace to where Nick would be waiting for me at the altar, Andrea thought the dramatic visual impact would serve us well while I covered the vast distance. And if I was going to have an extremely long veil, I wanted it to be the longest in the world. As fate would have it, I lost that competition; just three months earlier a bride in Cyprus wore a veil that was 22,843.9 feet long, the length of sixty-three and a half football fields! But seventy-five feet was plenty long for me. Thank goodness the twenty-five-foot trench-coat dress train had given me practice. (It had given Nick practice, too, and we staged some funny wedding pictures that referred back to the 2017 Gala of the Infinite Train.) And now I will always have a special place in my heart for gowns with dramatic swaths of material trailing behind.

As a final special touch, Aydin Ahmed, my nephew and the ring bearer, would be carrying the ring on a pillow that incorporated the lace of Denise's wedding veil. And the next day, at my Indian ceremony, my *lehenga* would include a portion of the border of my mother's beautiful wedding sari stitched inside. I wanted both of my mothers close to me as Nick and I made our promises to each other—the mother who had traveled with me in my train compartment since birth and the mother who had just, to my delight and gratitude, so gracefully stepped into it.

With Yumi Mori putting final touches on my makeup and Priyanka finally getting my veil secure, the bridesmaids started their own lengthy processional. And as I waited for the moment when I, too, would step out of the door, a wave of anxiety washed over me. Behind the curtain that separated me from the grounds of the palace and everyone I loved in this world, I closed my eyes and took a moment to talk to the one person I knew could calm me. "I wish you were here, Dad," I said. "I hope I'm doing the right thing." And then the curtain opened and I saw Nick's face. I saw his eyes. My doubts lifted and I knew, absolutely, that in walking toward Nick I was walking toward the man I wanted to create my future with.

Mom met me as I approached the altar and she walked me down the aisle, even though when we'd first discussed it she'd said she couldn't. "I'm a woman. I'm not allowed," she'd said. *Not allowed? My strong, independent mother?* "It's 2018," I'd replied. "Whatever we want is allowed at our wedding."

The afternoon was perfect. And yet, I couldn't help missing Dad's presence. He would have been in his element that afternoon. Actually, he would have been in his element for the entire three-day celebration. He would have sat and jammed with Nick and been the life of the party, the consummate host. It was one of his life's dreams to see me happy like that, to see me with someone who understood, respected, and treasured me, someone who grounded me and made me laugh. The fact that Nick was a musician would have been the icing on the wedding cake. I can imagine Dad taking his new son-in-law by the shoulders and saying, "All right, come on, let's sing a song!" and Nick, being his own understated self, nodding and smiling a little smile and just going with it. I would have loved to have seen that.

We had decided on a mother-daughter dance at the reception following the service instead of the traditional father-daughter dance of Western weddings, and Nick suggested the soulful ballad "Unforgettable" in honor of my father. A beautiful idea, Mom and I agreed. When it came time for the dance, we took the floor and the first expressive strains of the music came up. Dad's absence, which we had felt all day, became acutely visceral in a way we could never have been prepared for. All we could do was hold tight to each other and cry our way through it.

And yet, I had no doubt that my father was there. There had been a number of minor miracles throughout the planning of the wedding, including the Taj Umaid Bhawan Palace's availability for such a large party on such short notice, for starters, and the fact that almost every one of our closest friends and family was available to attend—a miracle if there ever was one, considering the schedules of so many people and the distances that needed to be traveled—and I knew beyond the shadow of a doubt that Dad had had a hand in helping us pull everything off. So he was there watching over me and us, of that I was certain. I just wish he had been *there* there.

THE FOLLOWING DAY, December 2, was our *shaadi*—our Indian wedding. Most Indian weddings have little games intertwined with a lot of the rituals. The idea, as I understand it, is to keep the bride and groom apart for as long as possible so that he really has to work hard to get her. The first ritual of the day was the *haldi* ceremony, in which the bride and the groom get covered with turmeric paste by the family. The purpose of the ceremony is to cleanse and purify the body, mind, and soul of the bride and groom to prepare them for their next phase of life. The women are the ones to apply the *haldi* paste, so imagine the fun they had when it came time to put it on Nick's face and chest. There may have been the ripping off of a shirt involved.

At the end of our *haldi,* we played a game where milk is poured into a large bowl of water, clouding the liquid so you can't see into it. Then the wedding rings are tossed in and the bride and the groom have to fish around in the bowl with their hands to find them. According to tradition, whoever finds a ring first will be the more dominant one in the marriage. Nick won. He won twice, actually. I wanted a do-over after the first try—I can't remember the excuse I came up with—but it didn't matter. My guy fished out the ring both times fair and square.

The last pre-ceremony before the wedding itself is the *baraat,* in which the groom makes a grand entrance to the wedding site riding a horse and accompanied by his friends and his family on foot. Nick's *baraat* was a colorful and joyous procession. He and his horse were bedecked in finery, and everyone was dancing and playing music and enjoying the excitement leading up to the wedding. While a *baraat* is primarily a celebration of the groom, it's also a make-the-bride-and-her-family-wait game. So Nick and his *baraat* party took their time while my family awaited their arrival. Some say that it's good luck if the bride catches a glimpse of the groom during his *baraat* before he sees her at the *mandap,* so I knew I had to find a secluded place from which I could watch Nick's grand entrance. I wanted that moment of good luck.

The room where I was getting ready was quite far from where Nick would be arriving on horseback, but that didn't stop me from putting my stealth-observation plan into action. In all my paraphernalia—with my elaborate *nath* hanging on my nose, *maang tikka* flapping on my forehead, multiple bridal necklaces, and arms full of jingling *chudas*—I lifted my heavy *lehenga* and ran up a flight of very steep stairs to a balcony that overlooks the entrance of the palace. My bridesmaids got left behind because they couldn't run in all their finery, but they didn't have the motivation that I did. When I arrived at my hidden viewing spot, I saw Nick riding in astride his horse, wearing his gold and white *saafa* and looking every inch a prince with that wedding turban on his head. Down below, my family welcomed his family in the *milni* ritual: the uncle meets the uncle, the auntie meets the auntie, the cousin meets the cousin, the brother meets the brother, and so on. His friends danced. The band played. I felt as though all my childhood dreams and fantasies had just come true.

I returned to my room and sat down for a minute to collect myself before making my own entrance. I was late, of course, because of my crazy run up to the balcony and back. All the same, I took a moment to appreciate the unbelievable good fortune that had brought me to this time, this place. Unlike many Western girls, who dream of getting married in a beautiful white gown, Indian girls dream of getting married in red wedding finery—red for love, prosperity, and fertility. And now here I was in my beautiful red Sabyasachi *lehenga* and veil, about to marry a man whom I loved with all my heart, and who loved me with all his heart right back. I couldn't stop smiling.

An Indian marriage is basically a promise, not a contract, and the couple takes a vow that they're going to be married for seven lifetimes. A temporary canopy-like structure called a *mandap,* or "wedding altar," is constructed, and for much of the ceremony the couple sits under it. In a ritual called a *mangal fera,* the couple walks around a fire seven times, promising to find each other in every lifetime. When it was time for me to make my entrance, Sid and my cousin-brothers walked me out in a procession to meet Nick. Now it was time for the *kanyadaan,* the giving away of the bride. Normally this would be a joyous responsibility for the father of the bride. My mother honored her brother, Vimal Mamu, by asking him to step in, and so my uncle—who had helped raise me in the United States, facilitated medical treatment for my father during his illness, and been there for our family always—placed my right hand in Nick's right hand. We looked into each other's eyes and vowed to find each other in this lifetime and every other one.

But again, even around taking a sacramental vow, there is an element of fun built into the ceremony, one that my side of the family wasn't going to let slip through their fingers. When Nick first approached the *mandap,* he, like everyone else, had to remove his shoes because it's a sacred space. While most of our guests were focused on the prayers and rituals of the hours-long ceremony, my female cousins and friends snuck off to steal Nick's shoes. When the ceremony was over and Nick walked out of the *mandap,* the girls came out in a mob and demanded payment to get them back. *Joota churi* is a common game at North Indian Hindu weddings, though I must admit my friends and cousins took it to a new level by stealing not only Nick's shoes, but a handful of other men's shoes, too, including his brothers'. Luckily for Nick, I'd prepped him on what he might expect (minus the surprise theft of his friends' and family's shoes). He had little diamond rings for all of my cousins and friends, impressing them enough to get his shoes back right away, and everyone else's, too. Which meant that we could all go dance, celebrating our union and our great good fortune once more.

SHORTLY BEFORE OUR wedding, a friend of mine observed to me that a marriage is different from a wedding. What I understood her to mean was that this one amazing day in our lives was just the beginning of something that we would work on every single day of our lives. It was the formal beginning of supporting each other's dreams, of understanding each other's needs in a balanced way, of being able to talk about those things openly and honestly. A wedding is a lot of fun. A marriage is a lot of fun, too, but it's also work.

Three days after our *shaadi,* it was time to embark on the voyage—and the work—of our marriage. That was the day, December 5, 2018, that Bumble India launched. It was a labor of love that had been a year in the making.

Bumble is the dating app where women make the first move, and when I first met the company's founder, Whitney Wolfe Herd, in 2017, I immediately asked her if she'd ever thought about going international.

"Oh, we're thinking about that now," she responded.

Sparks ignited in my head; I may have actually started to tingle. In a country like my own, where women are finding their voices and pushing back the patriarchy, giving them the tools they need to make the first move would be game-changing. "India would be totally *amazing* for Bumble," I told her.

And so a partnership was born. I invested in Bumble—my first tech investment—and partnered with the company to bring the app to India. And now, just days after my *shaadi,* all of our work was coming to fruition.

The atmosphere at the launch was one of great celebration and possibility. I'd worked hard to help make this happen, and the sense of gratification I felt was huge. The jubilation of the evening was amplified by the fact that it was the first time I was appearing in public at a work event with my new husband by my side. All evening long Nick was such a supportive partner, so full of pride for my role in this newer methodology for the empowerment of Indian women. During my speech, during my conversations about how excited I was about Bumble India and the opportunities it offered, I'd look at Nick's face and what I saw written there was, *This is my wife and I'm so proud.* And that's how I felt, too: *This is my husband and I'm so proud.*

Just days earlier we'd been in the midst of our fairy-tale wedding celebration, and now, with the *mehendi* still fresh on my hands and feet, here we were turning that celebration into a marriage, into the reality of a life lived together. And I hope that the joy, and the work, of our shared life will always be something I look forward to every day into the limitless future.

11

HOME

I am large, I contain multitudes.
WALT WHITMAN, "SONG OF MYSELF"

"T HERE?" I POINT, pausing to visualize the option. Then I turn to point across the living room. "Or there?"

Nick smiles that wry, just-north-of-mischievous smile of his and says, "Wherever you want, babe."

I make a face at him; we both know he's better at these kinds of decisions than I am. I'm just not that good at—or if I'm really honest, not that into—picking couches and wall colors and accent pillows. Doesn't mean I'm not house-proud, though. I am. I love having an uncluttered, beautiful space to live in and welcome friends and family into, so I'm lucky that Nick enjoys the settling-in process, and I trust his aesthetic completely. I don't know anyone with finer taste than Nick, so it seems kind of pointless for me to get too involved. Just as he did during the final phase of planning our wedding when I was shooting *The Sky Is Pink,* he took the lead on getting our home ready for us.

The house we've just moved into after a year and a half of marriage is the first home I've owned since I moved out of my apartment in Mumbai not long after my father's death. In the seven years between then and now, all of the places I lived in were rentals or hotels. I seemed to be returning to my old nomadic ways, or maybe I just hadn't been ready to plant myself in one spot and watch myself establish roots. But here, now, roots seem like a good thing, and so does stability. *Who is the person writing this?* a part of me asks as I watch those words take form. *Roots? Stability? Really?* Yes, really, I answer. And now, with this light-filled, airy home where Nick and I and our families and friends can gather and grow, a home where we can celebrate Diwali and Christmas with everyone we love around us, I feel like I have them.

Our house is planted on a hillside with a view of Los Angeles below. We are solidly on the ground here, and yet with the expansiveness of the outlook, I sometimes feel that I could almost take flight. I love this new vantage point: feet planted firmly on the ground, eyes gazing up to the heavens. It allows me to consider what I have in my life—who and where I come from, what I've learned, the work I've done and will continue to do—and my dreams for the future. Our house has room for all of those things, both who I am and who I will become. We haven't moved all the way in yet, so my new home is a work in progress. Like me, it is unfinished.

As I consider the potential of this house and these rooms that I now inhabit, I feel myself wanting to explore another, less literal set of rooms. Looking forward into the inner landscape of my future, if my life were a home, what kind of rooms would it need?

I plan to be in the world of entertainment for as long as I can, stretching myself by learning new skills and venturing into new kinds of roles for as long as audiences will have me. So in my inner house there's a large room for the actor in me, a room big enough to fit all of the writers, directors, co-producers, and co-actors I'll be collaborating with in the future; big enough to contain the piled-high stacks of scripts that I still love reading in a physical format; big enough for me to stride or tiptoe or pace around in as I find the feet of whatever character I'm preparing to inhabit. It's a space that inspires creativity and risk-taking, so plenty of bold strokes and touches of edginess belong in this room; as much as I'm enjoying my sense of groundedness right now, I've always been one to push boundaries, and that's not going to change anytime soon. #cantstopwontstop.

There needs to be a room for business endeavors, too, because in addition to being an actor, I've been a film producer for more than five years now, and I see myself doing more of this in the future that I'm envisioning. Shortly after I stepped into my thirties, my mother said, "You know that female actors in Bollywood have a shelf life. As soon as you hit the ripe old age of thirty-five, no one will be interested in you as a love interest anymore, even if the man you're starring with is in his fifties. Or older. If you're going to be financially independent"—this was a theme of my mother's and her mother's before her, too: financial independence—"you need other options."

The ripe old age of thirty-five is no longer an assured expiration date for leading-lady roles, thanks to the growing number of women of all generations who are working hard to push the envelope— although there's plenty of room for continued improvement. That was not the case when my forward-thinking mother set up Purple Pebble Pictures in 2015. When I asked my mother how she came up with the name, she responded, "Purple stands for royalty, and you're a queen." Then, laughing at her own joke, she added, "And you're moving all the time, like a rolling stone, but you're not big enough to be a stone yet. You're still a little pebble." And so the name stuck.

My thought was that I would not star in the films that Purple Pebble Pictures produced, at least not at the start. I wanted to be able to take myself out of the equation so that the business could stand on its own feet. While I handled the creative aspects of the films, from poster design to postproduction, my mom handled the business side of things. Mom has a natural business sense and is savvy with money; she always made the investments and financial decisions in our family—whatever salary my father received he put directly into her hands—and so she was eminently qualified to handle the finances of our production company. Any business acumen that I have, I've learned from her.

We decided that rather than producing Hindi films, we would start with regional ones. There are twenty-eight states and eight union territories in India, and many of them have their own language and their own film industries, though they are smaller relative to the Hindi film industry. My father was from Punjab, my mom grew up in Bihar, and her mother was raised in Kerala, at the southern tip of India next to Tamil Nadu. Having myself grown up in so many different places, I'm an accumulation of many different parts of India, but I didn't see a lot of stories that were reflective of all of those places being brought to a mainstream audience. My nani used to tell us about her school days in Kerala, where she lived on a rice paddy farm in a hut on a river, and how in order to go to school, she and her siblings had to travel by boat. I was fascinated by that world and eventually I visited her old home with her, but not before I'd fully imagined the landscape and made up my own stories about all the details of her young life.

I believe that good stories are universal, and that they come from everywhere. The idea of our production company was to shine a light on storytellers who didn't get the platform that Bollywood movies provide. I'm a big believer in creating opportunity where I don't see much happening, and so I wanted to put my might behind those filmmakers. Now a lot of Hindi movie producers are going regional, too, which is good news, but when I started doing it I was one of only a handful. We also back a lot of first-time filmmakers. Someone's got to take a chance on newcomers, after all. When I started working, it was extremely hard being a newcomer in an industry where success can depend on personal connections and whose favor you find yourself in at any given moment, or not in, as the case may be. I want to create opportunities based on merit in my company. I want to give back to artists what the arts have given to me: a livelihood and a purpose.

We've done nine regional films so far, in five languages: four in Marathi, two in Bhojpuri, one in Assamese, one in Sikkimese/Nepali, and one in Punjabi. Within our first few years in business, two of our films won a total of four national awards—*Ventilator* received three and *Paani* received one—which was both gratifying and mind-blowing in equal parts. We co-produced our first Hindi-language film—our tenth movie—the 2019 release *The Sky Is Pink,* because the based-on-real-life story was too moving to pass up. Once I decided to start originating more of my own projects, it made sense to slowly spread the wings of the company and bring it to the U.S., and so Purple Pebble Pictures is involved with Netflix's *The White Tiger* and my joint venture with Mindy Kaling at Universal Pictures, as well. I'm also developing multiple projects for Amazon in my first-look deal with them, focusing on creating global content in multiple languages for me to produce or star in, and actively exploring collaborations with other partners in both India and the U.S.

The taste of business I'd gotten with Purple Pebble Pictures whetted my appetite for more. I knew I wanted to invest in tech.

Bumble India's success since its launch at the end of 2018 consolidated that desire and I see myself doing a lot more tech investing in the coming years. I don't know where my future will take me, but I know being an entrepreneur will be a part of it.

This room for my business endeavors needs to reflect all of the different influences in my life, and so I envision it as a mix of East and West, old and new, traditional and modern. There will be books galore, in scads of languages, bursting with stories that want and need to be told, and there will be a monitor on a neatly organized desk for all my video calls. A wide-screen TV with comfy chairs and couches nearby will allow us to watch the fruits of our labors when they air. And of course there will be a purple accent or two in the room—or maybe just a royal reference.

The next room in my inner house will be the most enticing of all. Anyone looking in or passing by should feel an immediate desire to step inside and learn more. Or better yet, to be inspired to action. This room is one that's especially close to my heart.

One day in 2006, a few years into my career, I finished shooting early and went home unexpectedly in the middle of the day. Actually, I stopped by my parents' apartment, which was on the same floor as mine. I'd just grabbed a snack from their refrigerator—my own kitchen being a storage facility for all my suitcases—and had plopped down on their couch to watch television when I noticed my parents' housekeeper's ten-year-old daughter sitting quietly on a chair and reading.

"Hey, what's up, *choti*?" I asked. I didn't think it was a school holiday, but sometimes I lost track of things like that. "Why aren't you in school?"

"I don't go to school anymore."

I blinked. "Why not?"

"Because my brothers have to." It was offered as a simple fact.

No longer hungry, I put my cold *pakora* down and went to

find my mother so we could get to the bottom of whatever was going on.

Even though in India education is mandatory until age fourteen, our housekeeper and her husband couldn't afford to send all four of their children to school anymore, because even in government schools, the most inexpensive education option in India, there are expenses—books and fees of various sorts. And those small fees add up when you are living close to the bone. Given the choice of educating sons or educating daughters, the sons—and there were three of them in our housekeeper's family—were almost always going to win out, even if they were less suited to academics than their sisters.

"She's going to be married and so she can learn to cook and clean and do the things that she's going to have to do when she gets married," our housekeeper explained. "School is not as important for her."

I had seen the undervaluing of a female's life and future play out years earlier in terms of health when I assisted at one of the free medical clinics my parents offered periodically in rural underserved areas, and girls in need of medical attention hadn't always received it. I had seen it play out when the tiny newborn girl had been left under my mother's car when I was seven, and I'd grappled with making sense of a world in which this could happen. I'd seen it play out during my travels as Miss World when I visited children in need around the world. And now, in my parents' own house, it was playing out again.

I couldn't sleep that night. I thought about the ways in which my parents had always, *always* encouraged me to do well academically and become financially independent, and how they had always, *always* supported my dreams and then told me to dream bigger. My heart actually hurt as I thought about the way I had been encouraged to create the life I wanted in contrast with the way so many girls in my country and around the world were given no choice in their lives. I had seen what that lack of choice led to: the likelihood of receiving little or no education; becoming a child bride and often a child mother; and not getting adequate health care, resulting in unnecessary affliction and disease.

When I got up early the next morning to go to work, I had an idea to propose to my parents: we would personally take on the financial responsibility for educating the children of any of our employees who desired assistance. Over the next few years, we slowly expanded to include others who reached out to us. Because I come from a medical family, our informal initiative eventually addressed health concerns as well, and in 2011, the Priyanka Chopra Foundation for Health and Education became an official nonprofit organization.

Our small, private, and self-funded organization has provided numerous children with higher educations to date, many of whom are girls, and we've provided much-needed medical services to people in need of emergency surgeries or treatment they couldn't afford. By starting small, with the children of people we knew, we made it an easy thing to do, but we quickly saw how just a little bit of effort on our parts could go a long way in the lives of each of these children.

The Miss World pageant has long included a focus on humanitarian work through its emphasis on "Beauty with a Purpose," and a good portion of my duties when I wore the crown involved making a difference in children's lives by raising awareness of their rights to food, clean water, safe places to live, and education. After I surrendered my crown at the end of 2001, I continued my efforts to contribute to those in need, but in a somewhat scattershot way. Eventually I realized that most of my efforts involved children, whether they were suffering from a lack of basic resources or ill with thalassemia or cancer. In 2007, I decided I could be more effective if I consolidated my efforts, and so I began volunteering for UNICEF—the United Nations Children's Fund—in India, initially doing isolated events in my home country so that the press would shine its light on the many causes that needed attention.

Natasha and I worked closely with UNICEF India for three years, until in 2010 I became their national ambassador for India and started doing fieldwork to support UNICEF's peer-to-peer awareness system, through which it goes into communities to educate people, often girls and women, inspiring them to reach out and educate others in their communities in turn. It's a brilliantly effective system because UNICEF India relies predominantly on local volunteers to understand what the major problems facing any given community are. They then empower local women and girls to go house-to-house with pamphlets that address the needs of that particular community. Having a neighbor knock on your door and then say, "Auntie, your young daughter should not be getting married yet," opens up conversation in a way an outsider could never do.

My role was to visit safe spaces that UNICEF India has created for girls and women in villages, towns, and cities throughout the country, houses and rooms where they can go to get information about hygiene, nutrition, female health issues, education, and other matters, and where they can speak openly to one another about their concerns and learn from one another's experiences. After meeting some of the girls who frequented these safe spaces, I'd visit one or two of them in their homes or neighborhoods to see how they'd used the tools they'd been given. Then came the real purpose of my involvement: showcasing their stories by bringing them to the media and my social platforms.

What I saw and heard in my travels around the country as a UNICEF national ambassador made me a permanent foot soldier for change. One of the first trips I made was into the slums of

Mumbai. I was following a young girl that day—let's call her Saira—who'd frequented a UNICEF safe space near the place she sheltered with her family. Child marriage is illegal in India, but she hadn't known that, and she'd learned that she had a right to say no to it, something that had never occurred to her. A child activist was born. The barely teenage girl was able to convince her parents not to force her to marry, and after changing their minds, she went on to become an advocate in her community, sharing what she'd learned with her peers so that they could convince their own parents not to rush them into marriage.

In Chandrapur, a village on the outskirts of Nagpur in Maharashtra, I visited the home of a teenager named Sunita, who lived in a mud and thatch hut with her father, a farmer, her mother, who did small clothing repairs for extra cash, and her two sisters. When her father fell ill, and later her mother, too, they said, "You can't attend school anymore. We need to get you married because we can't provide for you."

Sunita wanted an education and she knew that in order to get one, she'd have to change her parents' mindset. "I can help you," she replied, "but not by getting married." Her mother taught her to sew and Sunita became so good at it she was soon doing more business than her mom. She became so skilled, in fact, that she was able to save up money for a sewing machine. Then she started a business making new clothes rather than just repairing tattered, worn-out ones. Over time, she was able to pay for not only the sewing machine but her schooling, her sisters' schooling, and her parents' medical treatment. She now has three or four sewing machines, and employees.

I saw a lot of girls like Sunita and Saira all around India, girls who have been empowered to create new realities for themselves. Not all of the girls that I met knew of me, but many did. Having someone they'd seen in movies or on television, I was told, made the girls feel that the outside world cared about them, which gave them hope, something they sorely needed. Beyond that, publicizing stories like theirs through the press and social media both illuminates the problems that women and girls still face in our society and shows without a doubt that positive change can and does happen. This good news helps to increase support for the changes that we all want to see, since it's been shown time and time again that investing in girls and women brings stability to families and communities.

When UNICEF asked me to become a global ambassador in 2016, I was beyond honored. After almost six years of doing field trips throughout India, I began visiting rural villages and refugee camps around the world, starting in Africa and the Middle East, focusing much of my time and attention on the children in these communities. On my first trip, to Zimbabwe, I spent time in a UNICEF shelter for girls who have suffered sexual violence. I heard many devastating stories, the most heartbreaking from a fourteen-year-old who'd been married to an older man and subsequently had a baby. When the man became sick shortly before she gave birth, a local traditional healer told him that if he had sex with a virgin he would be cured. A day after his daughter was born, he tried to have intercourse with the newborn and she died. (This is, of course, an extreme example, and I subsequently learned that the man was ultimately tried and sentenced in a victim-friendly court, part of a network of courts that address the needs of all victims deemed as vulnerable during criminal proceedings. These courts, too, are supported by UNICEF.)

And yet in spite of her trauma and loss, this fourteen-year-old, like almost all of the children I have met on my travels, was not hopeless. What I have seen no matter where I am is that even when they have seen horrors, even when they have had their homes and families destroyed, even when they are lacking basic necessities like food, clean water, and permanent shelter, children want an education. The children I met in Ethiopia and South Africa want an education, and so do those that I met in India, especially the girls. At the Jamtoli refugee camp in Bangladesh, I spoke to Rohingya children who were full of aspirations. One little girl wanted to be an actress, another one wanted to be a dentist. A six-year-old wanted to be a doctor, an eight-year-old hoped to be an engineer. One five-year-old, who for the first time in his life had access to basic reading, writing, and math instruction, told me he wanted to be a journalist. When I asked him what he would tell the world, he responded, "When countries fight, it's bad for everyone."

At the Zaatari refugee camp in Jordan, the world's largest refugee camp for Syrians, a woman told me her story: Her neighborhood was being bombed, so she grabbed her children and her Prada bag—which she used for their papers and other essentials—and left her large, comfortable four-story home, thinking she'd be back in a few days. It's been more than seven years, and she is still living under a tarp with her children in that sprawling, makeshift camp that is home to more than seventy-eight thousand of her fellow Syrians. Her children at least have a memory of another life. A whole new generation of Syrian children has been born in the camp and knows no other reality. These children, too, want an education, and in the face of enormous obstacles, Jordan is making big strides in its efforts to provide them with one.

I have to acknowledge that I find these trips heartbreaking. It's not easy to see the levels of poverty and disease and trauma that characterize the lives of the young people I meet through UNICEF. Looking at their bright faces shining up at me in any given location, I know that because of their lack of formal education, most of them are not going to be able to achieve the dreams they so eagerly share with me; most of the refugees I meet don't even have any papers or identification, essentially making them citizens of nowhere. But my job is not to show my sadness or my sympathy; I have to leave those things outside when I walk into the room.

At some point after I became a public person, I realized that having a platform where people would be willing to hear what I have to say could be one of my greatest strengths, and so I decided to use my voice to amplify the voices of people who weren't being heard. My job, then, is to be a means to an end, to get the attention of people and direct it to conditions or situations that cry out for change. For example, when I did a Facebook Live event from the Kutupalong refugee camp in Cox's Bazar, Bangladesh, it generated 10 million users, 4.4 million views, and nearly 500,000 engagements, making it the most successful Facebook Live event ever hosted by UNICEF. I believe that I have a duty and a responsibility to use my platform to amplify the voices of those forgotten, ignored, or abandoned by society, and as long as I can see that using my voice gets results, I'll keep doing it.

We as human beings have a tendency to look away from what's uncomfortable or painful. It's natural. But if we can turn our gaze to what is difficult, or open our eyes just a bit wider, we have the chance to do something life-affirming. Some people think being philanthropic means you have to empty your wallet. It doesn't. When you can look at someone in need and do something about it—whether it's offering a smile or a sandwich or a few dollars or, sure, a hospital wing if you can afford it—that's philanthropy. The simple gifts of time, energy, and compassion can be life-changing for those on the receiving end. Those gifts make our world a much kinder place. And that's the world I want to live in. A world of kindness and compassion in action.

The room I'm envisioning will have plenty of well-tended plants to remind us that with enough care and nourishment, all living things can flourish. It will have blossoming wildflowers, too, representing the unruly nature of life. It will have comfortable couches and pillows and chairs so that people can gather to laugh and cry, where we can all brainstorm and recharge together and then go back into the world to continue our work. And it will radiate hope, because in order to do the work that needs to be done, you have to believe we can heal.

You see why I dream of this space as an inviting one. No one person can do all that needs to be done alone. We need to act together for whatever positive change we want to bring into the world. Yes, there's much to be done, but let's not use that as an excuse not to get started. All the good intentions in the world cannot replace positive action. We need to act and we need to act now, for whatever change we are passionate about, in whatever way we can, small or large. There's space in this room for you. I'd be honored if you'd join me here.

We're coming to the end of our tour, but there are a couple of spaces we've not yet explored. The first is the one I envision for family, the large extended family that Nick's and my union has already created, and the more intimate one that we hope to create in the future. Having gotten a sense of the importance that both Nick and I place on family, you won't be surprised to learn that this, too, needs to be a spacious room, though perhaps it will have alcoves and nooks throughout, so that individual members can slip off for some occasional solitude while still being part of the larger whole. Again, there will be a glorious sense of all the influences that make us who we are: Eastern, Western, American, Indian. There is a Mandir next to a grand piano; business spreadsheets and a baseball glove; film and TV scripts, and two sets of golf clubs. Toys and books for young people abound, because children—nieces, nephews, and maybe our own brood someday—will always be a part of my family life. As much as I love having a neat and orderly home, this room will very likely look slightly mussed and lived in, and that's just fine with me. The life of a family, both interior and exterior, is not always orderly, and there's room for that in this inclusive space.

The final room in my inner house is for Nick and me. It's smaller than the other rooms and more intimate. It's where the two of us come to be alone—to share our hopes and dreams, or to simply sit together in silence. Whenever I want to reflect in solitude, to find a sense of stillness that may be eluding me, this is the room I come to. And while I've been open with you about my journey to date, this room is one that will remain relatively private. It's the 90/10 rule. While I may be open about 90 percent of my life, there's 10 percent that remains just for me.

The remaining space is not a room with four walls. It's the outer landscape that houses my inner landscape—the physical terrace and lawn outside our actual physical house. It, too, is unfinished and here's how I envision it in the future: Depending on the day, the sun may be beating down or a soft breeze may be delivering the scent of the honeysuckle or *mogra*. Brilliant fuchsia bougainvillea vines provide bright splashes of color. Flowers abound. Along with the loud excitement of Diana and Gino—the German shepherd puppy that joined our family in 2019—and Panda, our new Australian shepherd-husky mix rescue pup—the laughter of children fills the air.

I'll have planted a *gulmohar* tree, also known as a royal poinciana or flame-of-the-forest tree. With its magnificent orange-red flowers and its graceful fernlike foliage, it was my father's favorite tree. When we lived in Lucknow, there was a huge one that reached the second floor of our temporary accommodations. I had a few pet rabbits that I kept under its shade, and every evening it left us with a red carpet of fallen flowers. My family loved that tree.

Gulmohar trees are fast growing, which is good news for me because I look forward to the day when I can gaze out on its vibrant, life-affirming blossoms and be reminded of my father. We'll put a bench under it where I can sit one day with our children, nieces, and nephews and tell them about their amazing grandfather and how he helped make me who I am today. Then we'll all walk around to our front door and I'll tell them a story they've heard time and time again.

When I was in kindergarten, my parents and I moved from one army home to another. Outside every house in the new neighborhood was a nameplate so you knew who lived there. When ours was put up, I saw that it read *Major Ashok Chopra, MBBS, MS, Captain Madhu Chopra, MBBS DORL*. Surprised and hurt, I asked, "Why isn't my name on the nameplate, too? Don't I live in this house?"

Without missing a beat, my father answered, "So what would your name read?"

I took a few seconds to think. "Priyanka Mimi Chopra, Upper Kindergarten." Which was added to the nameplate as *Miss Priyanka Mimi Chopra, Upper KG.*

I tell this story because it's such a perfect example of how my parents raised me: with a sense of individuality and as a person who had rights, even at a very young age. When I questioned Dad further about it that day, he told me that I was correct to point out the omission. "You live in this house, too," he'd said. "Your name should be on it." Many parents wouldn't have taken a complaint like mine seriously, but he and my mother did. The lasting effect was that I was not shamed for my feelings, my wish to be included, my keen sense of what's fair and not fair. I was taught self-worth. I was given a voice.

It is through my voice, I believe, that I can be of most use in this world.

I believe that the purpose of every life is to make the journey the best one that we can for ourselves and for those around us— those people who sit by our sides in our train cars, sharing joint hopes and dreams; those who leave sooner than they should; those whom we encounter briefly at one station or another along the way; and those whom we may never meet personally but who are part of our larger world. When we act with care and kindness, we lift up ourselves and others. By working hard to create the circumstances that allow us to flourish, we help pave the way for those who travel alongside us and those who come after us, too. That is what I will tell my children each time I tell them the story of the nameplate.

Which is why I offer the story to you.

PHOTO CREDITS

PAGE 2:

Top: Photo from the author's personal collection; middle: Bob D'Amico/Amanda Hall/ Walt Disney Television via Getty Images; bottom: Photo from the author's personal collection

PAGE 3:

Top: Photo from the author's personal collection; bottom: © Kevork Djansezian/Getty Images Entertainment via Getty Images

PAGE 4:

Bottom: © Robyn Beck/AFP via Getty Images

PAGE 5:

Top: Photo from the author's personal collection; bottom: © Nick Saglimbeni

PAGE 6:

Top: Photo from the author's personal collection; middle: Photo from the author's personal collection; bottom: © *Hindustan Times/Hindustan Times* via Getty Images

PAGE 7:

© Annie Leibovitz

PAGE 8:

Top left and right: Photo from the author's personal collection; bottom right: Photo from the author's personal collection

PAGE 9:

Top: Neilson Barnard/Getty Images Entertainment via Getty Images; bottom: Photo from the author's personal collection © Purple Pebble America, LLC / Photography by Jose Villa and Joseph Radhik

PAGE 10:

All photos from the author's personal collection

PAGE 11:

Top: Photo from the author's personal collection; middle: Photo from the author's personal collection; bottom: Photo from the author's personal collection © Purple Pebble America, LLC / Photography by Jose Villa and Joseph Radhik

PAGE 12:

All photos from author's personal collection © Purple Pebble America, LLC / Photography by Jose Villa and Joseph Radhik

PAGE 13:

All photos from author's personal collection © Purple Pebble America, LLC / Photography by Jose Villa and Joseph Radhik

PAGE 14:

Top: © Saurabh Anjarlekar; middle: Photo from the author's personal collection © Purple Pebble America, LLC / Photography by Jose Villa and Joseph Radhik; bottom: Photo from the author's personal collection

PAGE 15:

All photos from the author's personal collection

PAGE 16:

Photo from the author's personal collection

ACKNOWLEDGMENTS

Many people made this book happen . . .

My collaborator Nan Satter, who patiently laughed at my jokes and meandering stories;

Pamela Cannon, my editor, who worked closely with me and had faith in me as an author from the beginning. Her knowledge, keen eye, and dedication truly helped bring this book to life, as did the thoughtful suggestions of Manasi Subramanian at Penguin Random House India and Daniel Bunyard at Penguin Random House UK.

My production team at Ballantine, especially Kelly Chian;

My former agents at WME, Nancy Josephson, Richard Weitz, Brad Slater, Esther Chang, and Mel Berger, who made my idea for a memoir a reality;

And Laura Zigman, thank you for your time and contribution.

My family . . . without whose support I would not even be a fraction of who I am.

My father and my biggest cheerleader, Lieutenant Colonel Dr. Ashok Chopra;

My mother and my greatest champion, Dr. Madhu Chopra;

My husband, Nick, thank you for always being in my corner. I love you.

And last, but definitely not least,

My brother, who kick-started this whole thing, Siddharth Chopra;

My nani, who raised me much of my life, and subsequently my cousins and my brother;

My dada and dadi, for showering their blessings;

My nana, for teaching me the ABCs;

Kiran Masi and Amitabh Mausa, Vimal Mamu and Vimla Mami, Neelam Masi and Manoj Mausa, thank you for graciously letting me live in your homes when I needed to explore new horizons, and for not even blinking an eye and raising me like your own child.

Munnu Masi, Leela Masi, Parwez Mausa—thank you for the love always.

Baby and Baboo Bua, for always being my dad's reflection on me;

Fufs, for being my father's best friend;

Krishna, Shireen, and Aydin . . . the next generation will take us forward;

Badepapa and Pawan Chacha, I will never forget the way you cared for my dad on his deathbed. I'm indebted.

To the IX-ers . . . my cousins, who are more like my siblings: Bhaiya, Divya, Chummu—us against the world.

Sana, Rohan, Parisa, Pooja . . . thank you for the constant love and support.

Nile, Bhaskar, Stacy, and Ashwin . . . you will always be my family.

Badimama, Reena Chachi, Titu Chacha, Sweety Chachi, and Raman Uncle. I don't see you enough to tell you how much you all have influenced my life, but you have.

Bhai (Sunny), thank you for always being there;

Teddy, Bunny, Bubbles, Tisha, Sahaj, Shivang, Ridhima, Radhika, Barbie, Mitali, Mrinal . . . you will always be my siblings. Thank you for showering your love and support on me always.

My new family . . .

Denise and Kevin Sr.; Kevin, Dani, Valentina, and Alena; Joe, Sophie, and Willa; Frankie, Nana, and Mama. Thank you for the love.

Friends . . .

Tamanna—there is so much we have shared and learned from each other, and now Thiaan will, too. Sudeep, thank you for being my brother;

Mubina—my troublemaking twin. I love you;

Shrishti (Nanu)—ups or downs, we always meet in the middle.

My team . . . that has stuck it out with me. You are my pride and joy.

Natasha Pal, for being around the longest. Thank you for everything you do.

Anjula Acharia, for dreaming big with me, and of course her mom, Shami Acharia;

Dana Supnick-Guidoni, for never letting me fall;

Robert, Sonya, and Ashni, for fighting the big fights;

Lou Taylor and Tristar, for being my armor;

Mrinal—love you;

Reshma, Vivek, Toral, and everyone at Matrix—we're going to do so much together.

Rohini Iyer and Raindrop Media, for being my shield;

Chanchal and Ruby—what would I do without you?

Aparna from East West Travels—you magic girl, you!

Anand and Shyamji—thank you for keeping an eye out for me.

Mary Rohlich—PPP is in good hands.

59th Parallel and Social Fleur, for your hard work;

James Gartshore Boulter—glad you're on board;

My agents at UTA—Jason Heyman, Chris Hart, Marissa Devins, Neil Bajaj, Keya Khayatian—you're the dream team.

And . . .

Pradeep Guha, for having vision!

Jimmy Iovine, for believing when no one did;

The Miss India and Miss World organizations that gave me my break;

My UNICEF family around the world, especially Geetanjali, Marissa, and Victor, for your continuing contributions to the betterment of children everywhere;

My PCF family—let's keep doing good together;

All the filmmakers that have shaped me;

Neil Jacobson and Jurgen Grebner, for showing faith in my music;

The dream wedding team: Sabyasachi and your amazing team; the incredible Ralph Lauren Atelier—Ralph Lauren, Kimball Hastings, Andrea Ciaraldi, Annarita Cavallini, and the entire team; Abu Sandeep and his wonderful team; Adi and the Motwane team; Ami Patel and Sanjay; Micky Contractor; Yumi Mori; Priyanka Borkar; Mimi Cuttrell and team; Jenya Flowers;

Chaandji, for being one of the good ones;

Teachers that shaped me;

All of the incredibly talented stylists, hair and makeup teams that have helped me feel and look my best;

Dancers I danced with, fighters and doubles I did stunts with;

Photographers and DPs that see me through a lens;

Directors that made me better, writers that gave a voice to the beloved characters I have played throughout my career;

Co-actors that were my best bounce boards;

North Shore Animal League and Hollywood Huskies for our beautiful rescues, Diana and Panda, and Kreative Kennels for Gino;

My dad's doctors, you do God's work and you're truly angels on earth.

Naysayers that have made me stronger and always pushed me to keep climbing and wanting to achieve even more;

And finally, all the fans and well-wishers. You have been the highlight of my life over the past twenty-plus years. You are the wind beneath my wings, and I would not be here without you. Thank you!